S0-BDO-115

The Star Raft

The Star Raft

China's Encounter with Africa

Philip Snow

Cornell University Press

Ithaca, New York

to Esrom Maryogo and Tang Tien-chung

Copyright © 1988 by Philip Snow.

All rights reserved. Except for brief quotations in a review, this book, or parts thereof, must not be reproduced in any form without permission in writing from the publisher. For information, address Cornell University Press, 124 Roberts Place, Ithaca, New York 14850.

Cornell Paperbacks edition first published 1989 by Cornell University Press.

The author and the publishers are grateful for permission to quote from the following: 'As I walked out one evening' by W.H.Auden, copyright © 1938 by W.H.Auden, reproduced by permission of Curtis Brown Ltd, London and New York; and Lenrie Peters, *Satellites* (African Writers Series, 1967), reproduced by permission of Heinemann Educational Books Ltd.

Printed in the United States of America

Library of Congress Cataloging-in-Publication Data

Snow, Philip.
 The star raft.

 Bibliography: p.
 Includes index.
 1. Africa—Relations—China. 2. China—Relations—Africa. I. Title.
[DT38.9.C5S56 1989]   303.4'8251'06   88-43399
ISBN 0-8014-9583-0 (alk. paper)

The paper in this book is acid-free and meets the guidelines for permanence and durability of the Committee on Production Guidelines for Book Longevity of the Council on Library Resources.

◇◇◇◇

Contents

◆◆◆◆

Illustrations

Portraits of Mao being distributed to Malians (Camera Press, London)
Chinese actors performing in *Battle-Drums on the Equator* (SOAS, London University; from *Evergreen*, Special Number, August 1965)
Mobutu receiving an award from H.K.Yang (Associated Press Ltd)
Mao greeting Mobutu in Peking (Camera Press, London)
Mao and friends (Camera Press, London)
Siad Barre addressing a rally, 1973 (photo by Tony Delano, Camera Press, London)
Chinese anti-aircraft gun captured in Ethiopia (Camera Press, London)
Desmond Tutu in Shanghai (Popperfoto)
Chinese engineers working on the Tan–Zam railway (photo courtesy of Adam Williams)
Chinese and Africans on the Tan–Zam railway (Camera Press, London)
Chinese and African labourers sharing their water (Camera Press, London)
Chinese-built bridge in Sierra Leone (Camera Press, London)
Tan–Zam railway terminus, Dar es Salaam (Camera Press, London)
Chinese clinic in Zanzibar (Camera Press, London)
Advertisement in Mali for Chinese Essential Balm (author's photo)
African students demonstrating in Peking, 1986 (photo © Janet Wishnetsky)
Chinese teacher in Africa (Associated Press Ltd)

Illustrations in the text

Maps

Acknowledgements

This book could not have been written without the help of a large number of institutions and individuals, in Africa, China and the West.

I am indebted, in particular, to two bodies which gave me generous and vital support. The Ford Foundation made it possible for me to spend the nine months in Africa in 1981–2 during which much of the basic research for the book was carried out. The British Academy enabled me to complete that basic research by spending two months in China under their exchange scheme with the Chinese Academy of Social Sciences.

A glance at the notes will indicate how much hospitality I received from a wide range of government departments in Mauritius, Tanzania, Kenya, Somalia, the Ivory Coast, Senegal, Mali, Zimbabwe and Madagascar, and from the Chinese embassies, news agencies and economic aid teams stationed in those countries. It will not, however, reveal the considerable help and advice I also received from a number of British high commissions and embassies, and from the staff of several British and French trading companies and of such Western aid organizations as USAID and the European Development Fund. The Chinese Academy of Social Sciences arranged for my travel and accommodation throughout my stay in their country, and several of the Academy's subordinate institutes held discussions with me. I appreciated especially the long hours spent in my company by the Institute of West Asian and African Studies. I learnt much from an afternoon session with the Ministry of Foreign Affairs in Peking, and from a series of interviews with representatives of the foreign aid bureaux of Fujian and Guangdong provinces.

Numerous individuals have helped me, over many years, in all kinds of ways. Many, again, are identified in the notes, but there are some not mentioned there whom I should like to single out. I remember with much gratitude Ken and Charlotte Campbell, in whose house the idea was conceived, and Professor Glen Dudbridge and Mr Michael Yahuda, who encouraged me to pursue it. Dr Tao Tao Liu and Mrs Anne Lonsdale of the Oriental Institute, Oxford, both gave me support in the early months when support was sorely needed. The first chapter was improved by some useful discussions with a number of archaeologists and historians, including the late Dr Neville Chittick, Dr Mark Horton, Mr James de Vere Allen and Mr Hamo Sassoon, and Professor Ogot and Dr Odhiambo of the University of Nairobi. I was helped to clarify some obscure points of German colonial history by Dr Wolfgang Moser and Dr Herms Bahl, who translated a manuscript for me, and my sister-in-law, Sophie Whitmore, who carried out some valuable long-distance research. Mr Basil Davidson helped me to get the Chinese contribution to the liberation movements in perspective. Various useful insights on contemporary matters were given me by Dr Simon Munzu of the University of Yaoundé and Dr Taisier Ali of the University of Khartoum, by the staff of *Africa Now* and its former managing editor, David Coetzee, and by Elizabeth Wright of the BBC External Services. Mr and Mrs Brian Smith, formerly of Mogadishu, Mr Iain Orr, currently of Shanghai, and Mr Eric Lanning, MBE took a lively interest in the project and steered me towards several pieces of data I could not otherwise have obtained.

Helpful books and articles were supplied to me by M. Jean Queval of Héricy, Mr Aidan Foster-Carter of Leeds University, Miss Natsuo Miyashita, Miss Chi Hsüeh-chen, and Mr Hu You'e of the Institute of West Asian and African Studies. Mr Adam Williams, formerly of the Sino-British Trade Council, and Mr David Tunnicliffe, formerly of the British embassy, Mogadishu, contributed two of the more striking photographs, and Mr Ken Wass of University College London uncomplainingly shouldered the task of drawing five complicated maps. Mr Stefan Polter read my most primitive synopsis, and Miss Chang Ning and Dr Robert Stone both read and commented on parts of the near-completed text. Mr Adotey Bing read the whole text, and also helped with a number of urgent late-night investigations.

I have saved to the last the most fundamental debts of all. Mrs Maria Ellis typed my entire manuscript, from the first chaotic drafts to the final version, with speed, wonderful accuracy and unfailing sweet nature. Mrs Kay Catchpole tidied my accumulating notebooks, and created an environment in which the work could proceed. My sister and brother-in-law, Lindsay and Eric Avebury, gave me hospitality and encouragement at the end of many an arduous day. My agent Andrew Best of Curtis Brown, my publisher Linden Lawson, her predecessor John Curtis, her former colleague Elizabeth Burke and her United States associate Mark Polizzotti all supported me with almost incredible patience during the years this book took to prepare. My friends Rose Heatley of the BBC and Nicolas Wolfers of the Midland Bank read the entire manuscript chapter by chapter as it was written, and gave me the benefit of their knowledge of China and Africa and their wise and sensitive advice. My friend Yvonne Tan listened to countless paragraphs recited over the telephone, and sustained me in the darkest hours with constant moral and material support. My wife Amanda appeared on the scene at a late stage, endured the incessant strains of the last few months, commented on the text with her usual acuteness and was largely responsible for the fact that I arrived, at long last, at the end.

Finally I have received all manner of help and guidance from my friend Mr Esrom Maryogo of Tanzania, and my friend and teacher Mr Tang Tien-chung. Any errors of fact that this book may contain are mine and not theirs, and they had no share in my deductions. But it seems only right that the book should be dedicated to them.

PHILIP SNOW, LONDON, DECEMBER 1987

Introduction

In the decades since the break-up of the old colonial empires, we in the West have shown a persisting interest in the encounter between our culture and those of the various peoples we once tried to control. We look back in fascination on the British *raj* in India and the Christian missions in China, on the feats of H.M. Stanley in breaking his way through Africa and of Commodore Perry in opening up Japan. It is understandable that we should do this. For five hundred years, since the West arrived in the Indian Ocean at the end of the fifteenth century in the person of Vasco da Gama, the story of mankind has been in very large measure the story of the response of Asia and Africa to the alien culture of Europe and, latterly, the United States. How China resisted it; how Japan, after an initial resistance, deftly co-opted it; how India and Africa, in part, succumbed. It is still the story today. Twenty years ago Iran appeared to accept Western cultural values while China rejected them. At present Iran rejects Western culture violently, while China opens its doors to Kentucky Fried Chicken and students on Chinese campuses agitate for Western-style freedoms. The action and reaction of Western and non-Western values is one of the major themes of the modern world, and is likely to remain so even as the Western tide recedes.

But even before the West arrived there were contacts between cultures. Asia and Africa dealt with each other through complex networks of diplomacy and trade. Arab and Persian merchants plied between the Gulf and the fringe of Kenya. Merchants from African cities like Mombasa and Kilwa ventured as far as Malaya in Indian trading fleets. And seventy-five years before Vasco da Gama and his ships sailed round the Cape of Good Hope to found a Portuguese empire in the Indian Ocean, great expeditions sent by the court of Ming dynasty China crossed the Indian Ocean from the other direction and called repeatedly at the ports of the East African coast. Now, as the Western tide recedes, those early contacts are being renewed and strengthened. This is another major phenomenon, and one of which most Westerners are almost unaware.

Insofar as they have noticed it their response has been one of unease. Any Asian interest in Africa, any African sympathy with Asia has been seen as constituting an implicit threat to the West's supremacy. This unease had its origins in colonial times. European settlers tended to think of Africa as their exclusive preserve. They looked with distaste on the immigrants who came to their African colonies from the crowded lands of the East, and worried at the possibility that a hostile Eastern power might one day intrude into their continent and dislodge them from their place in the sun. Some Europeans expressed concern in the 1930s that their grip on Africa might be threatened by the ambitions of imperial Japan. In 1942 the British actually occupied Madagascar to avert the imagined possibility that the Vichy French authorities on the island might allow the strategic northern port of Diégo-Suarez to fall into Japanese hands.

In the event the Japanese never made an appearance in Africa. But the Chinese did. As the different African countries began to attain their independence in the late 1950s, envoys of the new Chinese Communist state stepped coolly and confidently into their midst. Irked by a hundred years of humiliation at the hands of the European powers and America, China was setting itself up as a major challenger to the Western domination of world affairs. Africa was the obvious arena in which the Chinese challenge could be mounted. Large parts of its territory were still under European rule. Its new independent governments were weak, divided, permeated by Western influence but also, in many cases, deeply resentful of it. For fifteen years, right up to the mid-1970s, Peking pressed its challenge on the continent, by political, economic and sometimes military means, and ministries in London, Paris and Washington buzzed with speculation about Chinese designs. Serious observers predicted the arrival of Chinese warships in the ports of the western Indian Ocean and the East African coast.

The fears were exaggerated. The Chinese were able to play a significant part in delivering several African territories from European rule. But they possessed nothing like the strength required to detach the continent from the political and economic orbit of the West. And they had other preoccupations. As the years passed their activity in Africa was devoted more and more to the pursuit of a bitter campaign against a different adversary – the Soviet Union. By the mid-1970s, too, they had begun to feel an increasing urge to withdraw from foreign commitments and concentrate on meeting their own country's development needs. Today, in the late 1980s, it is difficult to remember that the alarm was once so great. China is quietly pressing ahead with its modernization programme, aided by a badly needed supply of capital and technology from the Western economies and Japan; and Europe and the United States have come to regard it as an amiable semi-ally in their confrontation with the Soviet camp. Africa has remained what Metternich called Italy – a 'geographical expression'. It has not found strength or unity, and it has not been able to free itself from Western influence. Most of its states continue to be economically feeble and sustained by constant transfusions of European and American aid. Some of its most anti-Western governments have felt obliged to drop their rhetoric and follow the prescriptions of the International Monetary Fund. Neither China nor Africa seems likely, in the near future, to disturb the West's repose.

But the quiet may be misleading. The purge of 'liberal' officials and academics which took place in Peking and other cities in the first weeks of 1987 was a reminder to anyone who might have begun to doubt it that China is no satellite of the West. It is still deeply ambivalent in its response to Western values, and determined to steer its own course. And the process of modernization in which it is engaged will enable it, in the end, to assert its will far more effectively in distant parts of the planet than it was able to do in the crusading days of Chairman Mao. Africa may not always be weak. The continent may look a very different place, for example, when the *apartheid* regime in South Africa finally collapses and is replaced by a black-ruled state, rich, powerful and equipped with the nuclear arsenal which the defeated white minority will probably leave behind. And as African countries slowly become more stable and more prosperous, their leaders can be expected to grow increasingly impatient with the continent's unhappy state of disunity and dependence on Western funds and advice.

The Chinese have lately kept a lower profile in Africa, but they have not disappeared from the scene. They continue to nudge the continent gently out from the Western shadow. And they continue to urge upon Africans the need for developing countries to join forces in the battle to win a better economic deal from the industrialized world. Their business activity on the continent has grown as their political manoeuvres have subsided. And whatever role they may choose to play for the rest of this century, their reappearance in Africa in the last generation must be considered an important chapter in the history of our times.

For one thing it is a reminder that we in the West can no longer always expect to occupy centre-stage. We are going to have to accept the fact that the various non-Western peoples are likely to come together with increasing frequency: that they are likely, more and more, to question the disproportionate share of the world's decision-making power and resources which we – and the Soviet Union – continue to enjoy. They may not succeed in putting an end to our supremacy, but they could, in the long run, make it less comfortable. From this point of view we shall be well advised to follow with some interest the expansion of contacts between all parts of the Third World. Will Brazil step up its growing economic role in Africa? Will the Arab states live up to the pledges they have made to use their oil wealth to give a political lead to the poorer developing countries? Will China and India eventually manage to settle their incessant border quarrels and discover common aims?

The Third World peoples will certainly have little hope of destroying our supremacy unless they can make a success of working together – not just as governments or companies but as individuals too. Absorbed in the complexities of our own relations with Asia and Africa, we in the West have so far taken comparatively little trouble to examine how the peoples of those regions have got on among themselves. Most of the time we have been content, in our books and television documentaries, to scrutinize each culture separately, as an exotic but isolated unit, Chinese or Indian, Arab or African, South-east Asian or Japanese. But attempts to make sense of a people tend to be limited in value if there is no contrasting set of attitudes and aspirations to throw theirs into relief. And by treating each culture as an isolated unit we miss out on that whole part of the human experience which consists of different peoples impinging and reacting upon each other. The encounter which has taken place in the last thirty years between the 1,050 million people of China and the 350 million people of sub-Saharan Africa is an instructive case in point.

I had long been intrigued by that particular combination. Academic studies and professional work had involved me with China for years. I had also travelled a number of times in different parts of Africa, and had followed the continent's travails with a keen, if amateur, interest. Dramatic, and little known outside specialist circles, the political and economic dealings between these two unlikely regions forced themselves on my attention. As time went on, however, it seemed to me increasingly that the vital issue was not so much a political or economic one as one of human relations. What was the human essence of the encounter between this formidable Eastern people, buoyed up by two thousand years of political unity, bureaucratic, introverted, resistant to foreign culture, and the disparate communities of Africa, bombarded by foreign influence and plagued by inner doubt, yet at the same time lively, outward-looking, and groping, however uncertainly, for a new identity of their own? Had the values of their societies harmonized, or grated on each other? How had the Chinese experience of Africa differed from that of the West? Had the Chinese comported themselves in Africa better or worse than Westerners? In either case, why?

This book is an attempt to answer those central questions. In search of an answer I travelled through a variety of African countries, covering, in clockwise order, Somalia, Kenya and Tanzania, Mauritius, Madagascar and Zimbabwe, Cameroon and Nigeria, the Ivory Coast, Mali and Senegal. I spent two months in China, exploring different aspects of the subject with ministries, research institutes and foreign aid bureaux, and paid a short but illuminating visit to the Portuguese colony of Macao. I consulted government archives, insofar as these were accessible, and worked my way through a number of Chinese and African political journals going back twenty to thirty years. But above all, I talked to people: diplomats and civil servants, professors and journalists, former politicians and retired guerrillas, engineers and doctors, traders and students and ordinary citizens. I broadened my survey, where possible, by talking to Africans from countries I had not been able to visit, and to Chinese who had worked in those unvisited countries. Interviews were, of course, a delicate instrument to rely on. The Chinese whom I encountered generally delivered themselves of a careful official line. Their remarks were pleasingly consistent, but also premeditated, and the most valuable thoughts often lay hidden in subtle nuances, or unexpected asides. African thoughts were vivid and spontaneous, but also haphazard. Different officials in the same government, even in the same department of the same government, sometimes gave a sharply contrasting picture of the relationship – and their varying recollections had to be weighed with care. But the interviews were essential: partly because of the relative lack of documentary evidence, but more important, because of my overriding concern with human exchange.

This concern has shaped the book in a number of other ways. In the first place, it seemed to me that the historical dimension of the subject couldn't be ignored. China didn't suddenly start to exist with the Com-

xvii

munist revolution, nor Africa at independence. Much could be learned by examining the patterns of behaviour manifested by Chinese and African people in the course of the great Ming landfalls, and of the various other exchanges, both formal and casual, which took place between them in the centuries before the Portuguese empire-builders appeared on the scene. Even the colonial period was worthy of attention. Under the impetus of the Western global expansion, individual Chinese and Africans, labourers and traders, were picked up and swept together at many different times; and their meetings were sometimes recorded with a peculiar vividness in the old colonial archives. Those two early periods of contact were consequently allocated one chapter apiece.

Secondly, my treatment of the modern contacts has been thematic rather than strictly chronological. The last four chapters contain what seem to me the essential data on the political and economic relationship which has grown up between China and Africa since the end of the Second World War. But I have deliberately grouped the material in such a way as to bring out, in each chapter, a particular human theme. Chapter Three, consequently, is the story of China's challenge to European rule and influence in Africa, and of Africa's response to China as an alternative source of ideas. Chapter Four explores the subject of China's private reasons for its African endeavour, and of the changing mood among Africans as China's purposes gradually became apparent to them. Chapter Five deals with the Chinese attempt to develop Africa: with the strengths and weaknesses of Chinese economic aid-giving and the formidable strain it imposed on the Chinese aid personnel. Chapter Six, finally, looks at the informal side of the relationship, the ignorance of Africa which still prevails among ordinary Chinese citizens, and the efforts which their leaders have made to overcome it in recent years. This structure seemed to me clearly to be preferred to a year-by-year chronicle, which would not only make dull reading but would blur my intended focus on the interplay of cultures and casts of mind.

Thirdly, I have defined the peoples I am surveying according to ethnic rather than political criteria. Most of my attention in the four modern chapters has, naturally, been given to the impact made on Africa in recent decades by the People's Republic of China. But I have also given a little space to the doings of representatives of the Nationalist regime on Taiwan, and of the small trading communities which migrated from the neighbourhood of Canton and settled in parts of south-eastern Africa in colonial times. They too were ethnically Chinese, and it seemed to me appropriate that their activities should also occasionally be taken into account. By the same reasoning I have taken Africa to exclude the Arab states in the north. The people of those states are distinguished not merely by cultural and linguistic differences from their sub-Saharan neighbours but by one conspicuous difference in the collective memory: they were not subjected to slavery. And their modern preoccupations, with issues like the conflict with Israel and Arab unity, seem to me to place them in an altogether different world. I have consequently referred to countries such as Egypt and Algeria only when events there affected Chinese relations with the peoples further south. I have on the other hand included the various offshore islands of the western Indian Ocean such as Mauritius, Madagascar and the Comoro group, which lie athwart the Chinese route to the continent, contain significant populations of African or partly African origin and provided the setting for a number of early Chinese meetings with mainland Africans. And I have also paid some attention to the 'black diaspora' of the Caribbean and the United States. Leaders of this diaspora played a major part in stirring the growth of resistance among educated Africans to European colonial rule. And it was they who first suggested to the fledgling statesmen of independent Africa that China was their natural friend.

A Chinese officer who took part in the great Ming expeditions which appeared off the coast of East Africa in the early fifteenth century described his fleet as a Star Raft. He used the term to indicate that the fleet carried to exotic regions the star-like radiance of an ambassador from the imperial throne. The expression has been variously characterized by Western scholars as 'pompous' and 'romantic'. To a modern reader it smacks of science fiction. Yet it seemed to me a useful image in which to encapsulate the whole history of the Chinese encounter with Africa – an encounter which has taken the form of a series of descents made upon the continent in the course of many centuries, massive, sometimes brilliant, often benevolent, but so far oddly ephemeral. I have consequently indulged in a little plagiarism at the expense of my Ming dynasty predecessor, and borrowed the epithet Star Raft as the title for this book.

This book is not intended primarily for specialists, though it contains a certain amount of information which may be of value to them. It is meant, first and foremost, for the ordinary thoughtful reader with an interest in China, or Africa, or the developing world as a whole. Chinese and African readers will, I hope, find a reasonably accurate portrait of the relations between their cultures. At points they may find it gratifying. Sometimes they may also find it sombre, especially towards the end. But the darker side is not sketched in a spirit of criticism; merely as part of an attempt to arrive, so far as possible, at a balance-sheet of what has so far been achieved in their relations and what remains to be done. To the Western reader I have tried to offer a glimpse of two contrasting peoples, as different from each other as each of them is from ourselves. And I have hoped to lead him or her, through a study of the relations between those two peoples, to reflect on the shortcomings of the West's relations with both.

A Word on Nomenclature

Most Chinese names are rendered in the 'Pinyin' transcription which is now standard in China and increasingly used throughout the world. For example: Mao Zedong not Mao Tse-tung, Zhou Enlai not Chou Enlai, Zheng He not Cheng Ho. For simplicity's sake, however, I have left untouched one or two names which have always been familiar to Western readers in an older romanisation and would look baffling in Pinyin – notably Sun Yat-sen and Chiang Kai-shek. And I have made no attempt to tamper with the established spellings of Cantonese names like Leung Quinn. I have also preferred to keep the more traditional forms of three Chinese place names, Peking, Nanking and Canton.

The problem with African place names tends to be that they change so frequently. In general I have used the name which was current for a place in the period under discussion. For example, I have spoken of Southern Rhodesia when referring to the 1950s and early 1960s, Rhodesia when discussing the late 1960s and 1970s, Zimbabwe when talking of post-independence events. There has had to be one exception. In the colonial period there were two territories called the Congo, one Belgian and one French. Since independence the ex-Belgian Congo has been known, successively, as Congo-Léopoldville, Congo-Kinshasa and Zaïre. The ex-French Congo has been known first as Congo-Brazzaville and in more recent years as the Congo, or the People's Republic of the Congo. But to most Western readers 'the Congo' means the larger, ex-Belgian territory. To avoid confusion I have consequently referred to the ex-French territory as Congo-Brazzaville throughout the contemporary chapters of the book.

I have written Portugal's former West African colony in its Portuguese spelling, as Guiné, not Guinea, to distinguish it from Guinea, the former French colony, and Equatorial Guinea, the former Spanish one, and have distinguished it further, in post-independence references, by adding the name of its capital and calling it Guiné-Bissau. The railway built by the Chinese in Tanzania and Zambia in the early 1970s is locally known

xxi

as TAZARA (originally an acronym for the Tanzania–Zambia Railway Authority), but I have chosen to stick to the name by which most readers will recognize it – the Tan–Zam railway.

Chinese Columbus

If the Chinese, with the knowledge of the compass, had possessed the genius of the Greeks or Phoenicians, they might have spread their discoveries over the southern hemisphere. I am not qualified to examine, and I am not disposed to believe, their distant voyages to the Persian Gulf and the Cape of Good Hope.

Gibbon, *The Decline and Fall of the Roman Empire*, Chapter 40

About the middle of October 1415, as Henry v's army trudged through the mud of northern France towards Agincourt, a giraffe arrived in Peking. The giraffe came from Malindi, in Kenya, and not many animals in history have been so acclaimed. The Ming emperor received it at the gate of the inner palace. Prostrate officials congratulated their sovereign on its coming. And half a millennium later, in 1983, when the political and economic business of the modern world brought a prime minister of China to Kenya for the first time, a Peking newspaper hailed the giraffe for its contribution to the friendship between the Chinese and African peoples.

The giraffe bore witness that two unlikely peoples had converged. Its arrival was the climax of a slow growth of contact between imperial China and the scattered communities of the East African coast. This convergence took many centuries, and no one can be entirely sure at what point it began.

Modern Chinese scholars date the beginnings very early indeed. The Chinese set store by history. They live in a country which has remained, in spite of foreign invasion and domestic revolution, the same recognizable political and cultural unit for more than two thousand years. They have at their disposal an unbroken series of encyclopaedic records which successive dynasties have maintained throughout that time, and they draw eagerly on those records for evidence of past Chinese dealings with a particular foreign people. Such evidence, in their eyes, helps to justify China's dealings with the same people today, and the farther back the evidence goes, the richer and stronger they consider the modern relationship to be. Sometimes their evidence is rather abstract. Trade, for example, to the Chinese way of thinking, proves the existence of friendly ties between China and a foreign country, even when the exchange of goods is indirect and no human encounter has taken place. On these grounds the Chinese scholars maintain that their first rulers who traded long-distance, the Han dynasty at the turn of the Christian era (202 BC to AD 220), were already in touch with two of Africa's most imposing ancient states. At that period the kingdom of Kush, based at Meroë in the northern Sudan, is thought to have been styling its pottery and its bronze utensils after the fashion of goods from China which Indian or Arabian ships were bringing to its Red Sea ports. Southeast of Kush, in the Ethiopian highlands, the kingdom of Axum was trading through its port of Adulis with ships on their way from the Mediterranean to the Indian Ocean, and may have been the source of a cargo of goods with an African flavour, ivory, rhinoceros horn and tortoiseshell, which merchants from the Roman empire unloaded in south China in AD 166.

African scholars tend to take a rather more sceptical view. Most of them live in new nations defined by arbitrary frontiers which European empire-builders imposed on their continent a century ago, and they look back on their past across the gulf of European colonial rule. They have no voluminous records, but are faced, instead, with the basic task of reconstructing their disjointed history from oral memory, written genealogy and ruined stones. Their concern is rather to clarify the past than to justify the present: rather to discover their ancestors than to explore a possible encounter between their ancestors and other foreigners before the Europeans came. They are wary of such an encounter. They want solid proof that it happened. China, after all, is an ocean away. Long-distance trade through middlemen has little meaning for them. Contact, in their view, is no contact if the human dimension is missing. When did the first Chinese and the first African meet?

Dated by this criterion the convergence is likely to have started later than the Chinese scholars maintain – but not much later. Chinese and Africans had probably rubbed shoulders in an intermediate place nine hundred years before the Malindi giraffe appeared in Peking. By the middle of the sixth century AD the people of Axum had progressed to building ships of their own whose prows 'cut through the foam of the water as a gambler divides the dust with his hand'; and Kosmas the 'Indian Voyager', commercial traveller turned Byzantine monk, records in his *Universal Christian Topography* (AD 545) how Ceylon

> being as it is in a central position is much frequented by ships from all parts of India and from Persia and *Ethiopia*. ... And from the remotest countries, I mean *Tzinista* [China] and other trading places, it receives silk, aloes, cloves, sandalwood and other products, and these in turn are passed on to markets this side, such as Malê, Kalliana ... Persia and the Homerite country ... and *Adulis*.

Kosmas talks specifically of men from Adulis who came to Ceylon on business: he does not tell us whether Chinese traders accompanied their silk. For 150 years before his time, however, a succession of Chinese visitors had been coming to the island. Buddhism had spread into China from the Indian sub-continent, and a series of Buddhist converts had begun to make the overland journey to India in search of scriptures and relics. Some of these hardy pilgrims took the sea passage home, and stopped in Ceylon on the way. We do not know whether or not they met men from Adulis. But the earliest and best known of them, Fa Xian, stayed in Ceylon for two years before his return to China in 414, and referred in his memoirs, in general terms, to the foreign merchants he found there.

These are encounters that may have happened. We have a record of one that did. Halfway through the eighth century, when Offa of Mercia was building his dyke on the Anglo-Welsh border, a solitary Chinese set foot in Africa. His name was Du Huan. He was an officer of the Tang dynasty (618–907), whose military exertions in Central Asia brought China in 751 into disastrous conflict with the rising power of the Arabs at the Talas River near Samarkand. Du was captured in the battle. He vanished into the dominions of the Abbasid caliphate, reappearing in China twelve years later to compose a *Record of My Travels*. Most of this memoir is lost, but a passage preserved in an encyclopaedia compiled by his cousin tells of a country called Molin which he reached after 'crossing the great desert' in a south-westerly direction from a starting-point in the Levant. Molin was inhabited by black people. It was approached through mountains where a variety of religions were professed, Islam, Christianity and 'the Zemzem teaching'. It seems to have lain not far from the coast, as horses were fed on dried fish and dates were imported from Persia. The climate was not appealing. There was little grain and no vegetation, and malaria was endemic.

3

Du had probably made his way to the coastal fringe of the kingdom of Axum, the territory now known as Eritrea. This is the best explanation of the mixture of religions he describes. In Du's time the kings of Axum, Christian since the fourth century, were gradually losing their grip on the Eritrean coastlands to two different enemies. Moslem invaders were crossing the Red Sea from Arabia, and pagan Beja tribes, ancestors of Kipling's Sudanese 'fuzzy-wuzzies', were encroaching from the north. Persian traders are also thought to have had some influence in this region, and may even have imparted their Zoroastrian creed to some of the coastal people. Du's third religion, 'the Zemzem teaching', could refer to this creed, since 'Zemzem' was the term used by his Arab captors to designate Zoroastrians. Alternatively it might refer to the beliefs of the Beja, since the Arabs sometimes used 'Zemzem' as a term for pagans in general.

What Du was doing in Eritrea he does not disclose. It is possible he was attached to a deputation which the caliphate sent in 759–60 to escort a Nubian prince home to his kingdom at Dongola in the Sudan. Tributaries of the caliphate, the Nubians had been giving trouble lately, and the inclusion of a Chinese in the party may have been intended to awe them by exhibiting the vast range of peoples who were subject to Arab rule. Mission accomplished, the party would have taken a commonly used trade route from the Nile to the Eritrean coast, sailed out of the Red Sea and round the edge of Arabia, and arrived back at the caliphate's heartland in Iraq not long before Du's return to China in 762. At all events, Du has left us a first Chinese impression of Africa – the first report on Africa by a complete outsider since Nero sent his centurions to investigate the Nile.

He seems to have been rather startled. Not so much by the jostling religions (both Zoroastrianism and Christianity were known in the Tang capital in his day) as by the lifestyle of the local population. 'Their customs', he says, 'are uncouth.' As an educated Chinese gentleman he would have been brought up to regard as fundamental the values taught by Confucius in the sixth century BC: loyalty to the ruler and filial piety. In Molin, however, these values were plainly lacking. The local people, he tells us, 'do not pay their respects either to the king of the country or to their fathers and mothers'. There were signs of sexual licence. Chinese society frowned on consanguinity in marriage, but Molin was easy-going. The Zemzem 'practise incest, and in this respect are worst of all the barbarians'. Islam was helping to restrain that tendency in

4

the Moslem community but had not yet apparently dissuaded the care-free Molin people from consuming alcohol. 'When they drink liquor, they carouse all day long.'

Du came back from Iraq not on the land route by which he had originally been abducted, but on a merchant ship bound for Canton. It was a time of burgeoning trade. As Islam expanded through the Indian Ocean, Arab vessels were starting to make their way to China's southern ports. Within a century after Du's adventure Canton had become the home of an Islamic trading colony. Other Moslem traders made their way, in the same years, south-west from the Gulf to the fringe of East Africa, where they began to establish small settlements in the swamp-islands off the Kenyan coast. The islands were rich in mangrove wood, which the traders probably wanted to use for construction purposes in their desert towns at home. Little by little, as this merchant traffic grew busier, a link began to be forged between south China at one end of the ocean and East Africa at the other.

By the tenth and eleventh centuries Arab reports and Chinese trade figures indicate that large quantities of African products were reaching China. Some of these were luxuries. East African ivory is thought to have been popular because it was soft and easy to carve. Officials rode in ivory palanquins, and ivory belt-buckles held up their robes. Rhinoceros horn was also carved, and powdered rhinoceros horn was prized as an aphrodisiac. Other products were attractive for medicinal reasons. Tortoiseshell was pounded to a gum and used to treat consumption. Frankincense and ambergris, a wax-like substance secreted by whales, were valued by Chinese doctors as tonics to stimulate the circulation. Ambergris was also used as a scent to sweeten the air. Zhu Zicai, a poet of the Song dynasty (960–1279), wrote of the banquet-chambers where

at night the gilded lamps, *fed with ambergris*, shine like pearls.

In 1974 Chinese archaeologists recovered an ocean-going junk abandoned apparently in the 1270s as it was about to discharge its cargo in the great south-eastern port of Quanzhou. The cargo included small amounts of these last three imports, tortoiseshell, frankincense and ambergris. Each could have come from a number of sources: taken in conjunction they point strongly to Africa, and in particular the coast of Somalia where the 'Horn of Africa' juts out to the east.

In the same period, AD 800 to 1400, Chinese artefacts were making

5

an impact on Africa. The shores of East Africa are lined with a string of antique cities built up, over the centuries, by the coastal African people known as the Swahili, who had mixed with the early Arab settlers, absorbed them by intermarriage and adopted their religion. Some derelict, others still flourishing, these cities stretch southwards along the coasts and offshore islands of the four modern republics of Somalia, Kenya, Tanzania and Mozambique. And their soil and sub-soil are strewn, to a rather striking extent, with Chinese debris. Forty years ago, for instance, a peasant on the island of Zanzibar struck his crowbar into a pocket of coral containing 250 copper coins of the Tang and Song dynasties, punched through the middle with their characteristic square holes. Other finds have been made in the coastal towns of Somalia, and Chinese coins account for approximately 300 of the 500 pieces of pre-modern foreign currency which have been discovered in Kenya and Tanzania.

But the coins are a minor phenomenon compared with the porcelain. The archaeologist Sir Mortimer Wheeler declared on one occasion that he had never in his life seen so much broken china as he had on the Tanzanian coast. Right down the length of East Africa porcelain imports have left their mark. Fragments litter the beaches and the town rubbish dumps. Bowls and bits of bowls of grey–green celadon or the blue-and-white ware which succeeded it have been found adorning the walls and roofs of houses, circling the doorway or prayer niche in a mosque. Above all they have been found embedded, with a strange insistence, in the pillar-shaped tombs beneath which the Swahili people buried their dead. Over the last few decades the bulk of this tomb decoration has been plundered, sold to visitors or removed to museums. Even today, however, it can still be a little startling, wandering through the bush in the heavy silence of an African afternoon, to light all of a sudden on the dumpy stone pillar of Mambrui, near Malindi, crowned with the remains of a green vase and wreathed by an almost complete frieze of blue-and-white plates painted with birds and crayfish; or the tall obelisk at Kunduchi near Dar es Salaam, brightly ornamented with a great bowl incongruously bearing the Chinese word for 'long life'; or the domed mausoleum at Siu on the Kenyan island of Pate, empty of bowls yet pockmarked from roof to ground with the cavities where the bowls once stood.

Porcelain finds have not been limited to East Africa. Fourteenth-century sherds have been found at Aidhab, far in the north near the old

6

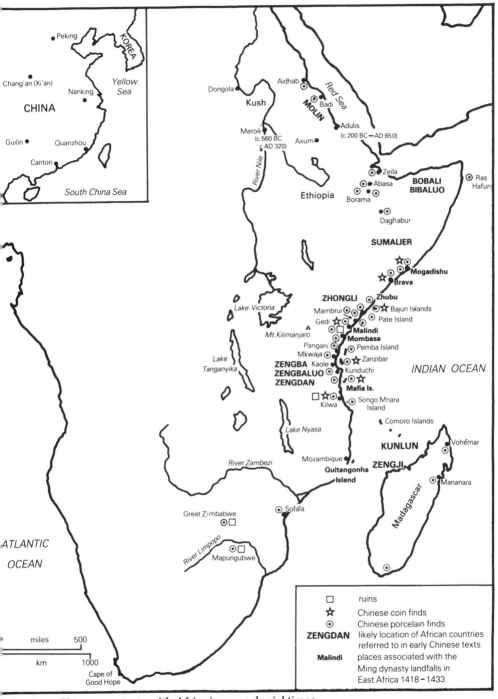

Map 1. Chinese contacts with Africa in pre-colonial times.

The map includes the following labels:

Peking
KOREA
Chang'an (Xi'an)
Nanking
Yellow Sea
CHINA
Guilin
Quanzhou
Canton
South China Sea

Dongola
Aidhab
Kush
MOLIN
Badi
Red Sea
Meroë (c.560 BC c.AD 320)
Adulis (c.200 BC–AD 650)
Axum
Zeila
BOBALI BIBALUO
Ras Hafun
Abasa
Ethiopia
Borama
Daghabur
SUMALIER
Mogadishu
Brava
ZHONGLI
Zhubu
Mambrui
Bajun Islands
Gedi
Pate Island
Lake Victoria
Malindi
Mt. Kilimanjaro
Mombasa
Pangani
Pemba Island
Mkwaja
Lake Tanganyika
Zanzibar
ZENGBA
Kaole
ZENGBALUO
Kunduchi
ZENGDAN
INDIAN OCEAN
Mafia Is.
Kilwa
Songo Mnara Island
Lake Nyasa
Comoro Islands
KUNLUN
Vohémar
Mozambique
ZENGJI
Quitangonha Island
River Zambezi
Great Zimbabwe
Sofala
Madagascar
Mananara
ATLANTIC OCEAN
River Limpopo
Mapungubwe

miles 500
km 1000
Cape of Good Hope

Legend:
□ ruins
☆ Chinese coin finds
⊙ Chinese porcelain finds
ZENGDAN likely location of African countries referred to in early Chinese texts
Malindi places associated with the Ming dynasty landfalls in East Africa 1418–1433

Sudanese port of Suakin, and Tang dynasty fragments have come from Badi, a port in Eritrea conceivably known to Du Huan. Slivers of celadon from the twelfth century or earlier have been uncovered on the southern tip of Madagascar. Far to the south and deep in the interior, half a dozen celadon dishes have been retrieved from the stone ruins of Great Zimbabwe, and celadon ascribed to the Song dynasty has been reported from an excavation at Mapungubwe, just inside the Transvaal.

All of this evidence points to a busy exchange of objects. It does not necessarily tell us that Chinese and Africans came together during these centuries, any more than they had done in the old days of long-distance traffic between the kingdoms of Axum and Meroë and the empire of the Han. There was no obvious reason for a Chinese merchant to travel to Africa. East African ivory and frankincense could be picked up from Moslem dealers in the ports of southern China, or at Palembang in Sumatra, nine months' journey there and back across the South China Sea. What was the point of sinking capital in a voyage to the far side of India which might take as long as two years? Most Chinese traders were probably content to let the Arab and Persian middlemen pick up their cheap export porcelain in places like Canton and hawk it as they saw fit in the distant African reaches of the Islamic world. Ubiquitous on the ocean, Arab and Persian vessels were the obvious carriers. 'The ships that sail the southern seas', says a Tang dynasty writer, 'are foreign ships.'

But the Chinese of this period were outward-looking and venturesome. Already in the Tang dynasty China was building ships which excited the awe of foreign contemporaries – vessels with two to three decks and crews that may have numbered several hundred men. Chinese merchants had the means to mount long-distance expeditions, and it is clear that they sometimes did so. Tang dynasty vessels were sighted deep in Islamic waters. Suleiman, a ninth-century Arab trader, refers to the presence of massive Chinese ships at Kulam-Malay in south-west India and at Siraf and Oman in the Gulf. Operations seem to have been curtailed in the confused tenth-century hiatus between the Tang dynasty and the Song, but revived with a vengeance in the latter part of the Song period (1127–1279). The Song rulers of this period, generally known as the 'Southern Song' dynasty, had lost half their territory to Tartar invaders from the northern steppes. To make up for their loss of revenue they promoted overseas trade. For the first time in its history China became a maritime nation. Chinese merchants travelled in ships 'like houses', with five to six decks, provisioned for ocean voyages with a year's grain supply, herds of pigs and jars of fermenting wine. Their navigators possessed the world's most advanced seafaring technology in the form of magnetic compasses, water-tight bulkheads, axial rudders, floating anchors and sounding lines. By the late twelfth century they were firmly back on the edge of the western Indian Ocean. They appeared in the Gulf, and off Yemen, but their vessels were too large to be accommodated conveniently in those shallow waters. A contemporary Chinese writer notes how 'when merchants on Chinese ships wish to go to Arabia, they have to change into smaller ships at Kulam-Malay and proceed from there'. This observation on the size of the ships may also tell us something about the movements of Chinese traders. It suggests that a good many stopped at India, but some went further, either to cut out the middlemen or to collect market intelligence at the far end of the trade route. Thirteenth- and fourteenth-century accounts confirm that this was the general pattern. Regular sailings to India, occasional sallies beyond.

One or two clues survive to raise the intriguing possibility that a handful of daring traders made their way to the African coast. Already in the ninth century the Tang prime minister and geographer, Jia Dan, knew of a sailing route which could be taken to the Gulf from a place called Sanlan in the 'extreme south-west' of Arabia, twenty days' voyage from the nearest settlements to the north. If Sanlan is twenty days' voyage away it is pretty remote; Jia gives ninety days for the entire journey from Arabia to Canton. A point in East Africa would fit the description.

Jia could of course have come by his information from Arab sailors. More difficult to explain away is the world map compiled between 1311 and 1320 by the Chinese cartographer Zhu Siben. This map depicts unmistakably, in the 'south-western sea', a triangular, southward-pointing Africa, at a time when both the European and, so far as is known, the Islamic world too still believed that the African coastline veered eastward to link up with Asia. Some of the data seem to be Arab. *Sanggu*, a Chinese attempt at *Zang*, 'the blacks', occurs in two different places, and *Zhebuluma*, probably from Arabic *djebel*, 'mountains', may echo Arab gossip about the Mountains of the Moon in the East African hinterland. But no known Arab knowledge can account for this Chinese rendering – rounded, slightly indented in the middle – of the coast of South Africa. A map based on the work of two other Chinese cartographers which

9

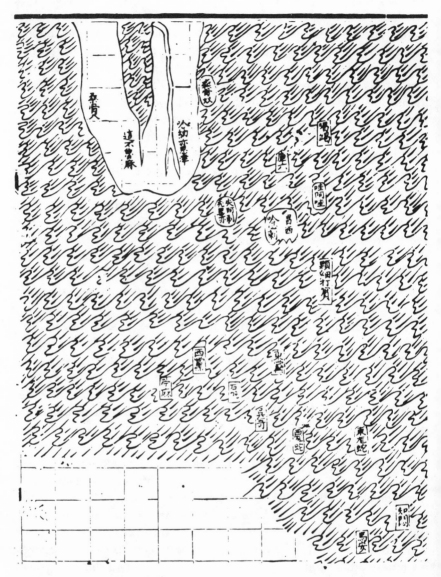

Zhu Siben's map of Africa (early fourteenth century). The island off the east coast is marked 'Zang slaves'. The huge body of water in the centre is reminiscent of the great 'Lake Uniamesi' of which Arab traders talked to the nineteenth-century European explorers on the eve of their search for the source of the Nile.

appeared in Korea in 1402 even adds a stream emerging on the continent's south-west coast in the approximate position of the Orange River. Both maps place the southern part of Africa immediately opposite the Indonesian islands, with a string of smaller islands in between and the tip of India tucked far away to the north. This could suggest that whoever supplied the data on southern Africa did not get there from the Gulf, by the established Moslem sailing route, but crossed from Sumatra and followed the chain of southerly islands, Maldive, Chagos and Mascarene, which stretch across the western Indian Ocean at conveniently short intervals all the way to Madagascar. An Oriental voyager: perhaps a Chinese. With sails designed for steering into the wind, Chinese navigators could in theory have travelled far down the African coast, undeterred by the trade winds which discouraged Arab seamen from venturing past the limits of the seasonal monsoon system to the south of Zanzibar.

Only a tiny number of Chinese are likely, at this period, to have visited Africa. But others talked about it. Chinese in Tang and Song times were curious, as they would not always be in later centuries, about the outside world. They wanted not only spices and ivory, but also information about the exotic regions from which such products came. A succession of writers set to work to satisfy this demand. Most of these men had never left China: they were purveyors of hearsay. Duan Chengshi, in the ninth century, was an 'unsuccessful bureaucrat and voracious dilettante'. Zhou Qufei, in the twelfth, was a retired administrator from Guilin in south-west China who grew tired of telling and retelling the curious tales he had gathered there and committed them to writing instead. But some of them certainly got their hearsay from traders. Zhao Rugua, a customs inspector, based his *Gazetteer of Foreigners* (1225) on details supplied by the Chinese and foreign merchants who underwent his scrutiny at the port of Quanzhou. As for Wang Dayuan, he claimed to have travelled right round the Indian Ocean on two merchant voyages in the 1330s, and is widely regarded by the Chinese nowadays as their first visitor to the East African coast. Some of these accounts may accordingly have been based on first-hand Chinese experience. What they certainly reveal is that the educated public of Tang and Song times were absorbing a good deal of knowledge about the continent, its products – and its people.

Our writers bring news of a series of lands which lie in the 'south-western ocean'. These countries are called, at different periods, Bobali and Bibaluo and Zengba and Zengbaluo. Bobali and Bibaluo both seem

11

to be Chinese versions of Barbarā, the loose Arab term for the Somali coast. Zengba and Zengbaluo, equally, appear to be names for the broad fringe of East Africa the Arabs knew as Zangibār, Coast of the Blacks. Zhao Rugua refers to a 'great mountain' west of Zengba: maybe some trader has caught an early glimpse of Kilimanjaro, but we cannot be sure.

Not surprisingly, our writers have plenty to say about trade. Ninth-century Bobali, for instance, is described with a touch of disappointment. This land in the south-western ocean only has ivory and ambergris. Bibaluo, in the thirteenth century, is regarded with more favour. It has big elephant tusks and big rhinoceros horns. The tusks, notes Zhao Rugua the customs officer, may weigh 100 catties* or more, and the rhino horns ten catties; and the tortoiseshells there are 'extremely thick'. Neighbouring Zhongli has frankincense, ambergris in lumps of three, five and ten catties, and a red gum resin called 'dragon's blood', while the land of Zengba offers, in addition to ivory and ambergris, fragrant timber and unworked gold. Sometimes we get news of the export side of the business. Zhao reports how the produce of Zengba is paid for by Arabs and Gujaratis with copper, white cotton cloth, red kapok fibre – and porcelain. Wang Dayuan, a century later, says nothing of Arabs or Gujaratis. He merely notes that any ship selling rice to the people of Zengbaluo makes a very big profit, that there is a market for ivory boxes and coloured satins. Goods with a Chinese flavour. Is Wang describing a transaction he took part in himself?

There is news of the landscape as well. With the same accountant's precision, our writers record the African wildlife. One animal in particular interests them. In Bobali there is a beast called the camel-ox, with a hide like a leopard's, hooves like a cow's, and no hump. Its neck is nine feet long and its body ten feet tall. A similar creature can be seen in the land of Bibaluo. Its front legs are five feet long, its hind legs only three feet. Its head rises high and is turned upwards, and its hide is an inch thick. Zhao Rugua calls it the zula, from the Arabic zurafa, giraffe, and describes it as one of three 'occasional variations of the camel'. The others are a mule with red, white and black stripes, probably a zebra seen rolling in the red dust, and the camel-crane, evidently an ostrich, with a body six or seven feet long and wings that enable it to fly, though 'not to any height'. Sometimes the careful records

* A catty is approximately 1⅓ lb.

12

are supplemented by touches of fantasy. Our writers pass on the myth known to mediaeval and Tudor England, that the ostrich eats iron, and indulge in accounts of the great *peng* bird which blots out the sun when it flies, preys on wild camels and has quills so massive they can be used to make water-buckets. The *peng* bird is plainly neither more nor less than the *roc* of the *Arabian Nights* and Marco Polo's *Travels*, which pounces on elephants and turtles and according to Marco Polo has a quill the width of two of his palms. But even the *peng* bird is not entirely marvellous. The *aepyornis maximus*, biggest of birds, ostrich-like but at eight to ten feet high the size of a young elephant, still lumbered at this period around the marshlands of its native Madagascar. It seems to have made an impact through these colourful if exaggerated tales on travellers in many parts of the western Indian Ocean before it became extinct, probably around the beginning of the seventeenth century. Our Chinese informant is unaware, like the *Arabian Nights* storytellers, that the *aepyornis* is flightless; but he at least knows, as they do not, that it comes from the neighbourhood of 'a large island'.

And here too, preserved down the centuries in the gossip of warehouse and dockside, are the Africans themselves. Chinese descriptions of African society are often clearer and more accurate than any surviving Islamic account. The people of Bobali, for example,

> do not eat the Five Grains, but only meat. They are given to sticking a needle into the veins of their cattle and drawing out the blood, which they mix with milk and consume raw. They wear no clothes, but merely use goatskins to cover the parts below their waists.

Here, in the ninth century, are recognizable East African nomads. Ancestors, possibly, of one of the various peoples, the Oromo, Darod, Dir and Masai, who still live today on a diet of blood and milk, or of the modern Somalis who are conspicuous for their relentless consumption of meat. Arabs, we gather, raid the Bobali nomads, and Persian merchants trade with them: the Chinese have chronicled the first appearance of Islam on the East African coast. By the thirteenth century Islam had a firm grip, and Zhao Rugua writes of Islamicized communities. The people of Bibaluo are Moslems: they 'serve Heaven but not the Buddha'. The people of Zengba are not only Moslems but settlers from the Gulf, and all the coastal peoples eat *shaobing*, a Chinese term for baked flour cakes which probably refers to the flat bread these settlers would have introduced from the Islamic world.

13

Contact with the Gulf had another major consequence for East Africa. From the late twelfth century onwards an elite who called themselves Shirazi gained control of settlements down the coast from Mogadishu in modern Somalia to Kilwa in modern Tanzania. These people may have been racially mixed, Africanized descendants of immigrants from the Shiraz region of Persia, or they may have been an essentially African group who claimed Shirazi origins as a source of prestige. At all events they maintained themselves, in some areas till the late nineteenth century, as a socially exclusive caste. They asserted their distinctiveness by building in stone and by enforcing on their subjects a set of sumptuary rules. Zhao Rugua has managed to discover the key features of their society:

> The people of Zhongli go with heads uncovered and barefoot. They wrap a cloth round themselves but do not dare wear jackets: only the chief ministers and the king's entourage wear jackets and wrap turbans round their heads as a mark of distinction. The king's residence is made of bricks and slabs of stone, the people's houses of palm fronds and thatch roofing.

The Shirazis took care to preserve a monopoly of divination, witchcraft and rain-making practices. Zhao goes on:

> Many people practise magical arts, and can change themselves into birds, beasts or sea-creatures, to frighten and delude the foolish commoners. If in their business dealings with a foreign ship a grievance arises, they cast a spell to bring the ship to a standstill, so that it cannot move forwards or backwards; and only when the crew have consented to make peace will they let them go.

Nonsense, but authentic nonsense. Magic transformation into animals is a stock piece of East African coastal legend, and tales of the magical becalming of ships still circulated in the Bajun islands of southern Somalia only half a century ago.

What did the Chinese make of these Africans whose customs and beliefs they report so faithfully? Much of what they saw or heard seems to have struck them as barbaric. Bibaluo, for example, consists largely of villages which 'contend violently with each other for supremacy'. One writer relates in gory detail how betrothal is celebrated there. The girl's family seals the agreement by severing the tail of a cow in calf, and the man's family responds by sending a severed human male 'tail' which is welcomed with delight and music at the house of his bride-to-be. Nomad food in particular is likely to have seemed outlandish to the

14

Artist's impression of the east coast of Africa as a Chinese official of the twelfth or thirteenth century probably envisaged it. All the details are derived from accounts of contemporary Chinese writers. Note the Islamicized coastal towns with their mosques, the incense-bearing trees of Somalia, the *peng* bird hovering with a captured camel to the north of Madagascar, and the cone of Mount Kilimanjaro in the middle distance. A Star Raft approaches from the east.

15

Chinese. Chinese are averse both to dairy produce and to uncooked food of any kind, and Duan Chengshi probably recorded the consumption of 'raw' blood and milk by the ninth-century Bobali herdsmen with a fascinated disgust. Yet the picture is not uniform. Zhongli is one place that is not wholly wild. It is an organized state 4,000 *li* (roughly 1,300 miles) in circumference, whose government, no doubt to the relief of merchants, has strictly forbidden the enchantment of ships. And the Chinese are more ambivalent than one might expect in their depiction of the wilder peoples. Women in Bobali 'are pure and upright'. Wang Dayuan thinks that the customs of the people of Zengbaluo 'have the uprightness of ancient times'. Cultivated Chinese, like cultivated Greeks and Romans, nursed a vague nostalgia for a golden age when men lived in harmony uncorrupted by knowledge and the desire for gain, and it seems they found something in the simpler African coastal communities which answered to that dream.

They also found a spirit of heroism. The tribesmen of Bobali, we are told, have never been subject to a foreign country. They have twenty myriad footsoldiers, make their weapons and armour from the tusks and ribs of elephants and the horns of wild oxen. Zhongli is a stronghold of Homeric warriors. When a man dies his kinsmen gather from far and wide. They brandish their weapons and ask the chief mourner to disclose the cause of death. '"If he was murdered," they say, " we shall kill the murderer in revenge with these swords." But if the chief mourner replies that no one killed him and it was a natural consequence of Heaven's decree, they throw down their swords and weep bitterly.'

Displays of bravado may have been typical of the patrician clans on the East African seaboard. It is also possible, however, that the authors of these accounts wrote of African heroism because their readers expected Africans to behave heroically. During these centuries of slow convergence, small numbers of Africans had been seen in China itself. They had come there by a route different to that of the gossiping merchants, and had worked their way into the Chinese imagination as embodiments of valour.

Dark-skinned people were talked of in China as early as the fourth century AD. They were known by the strange, pregnant name of Kunlun. First it meant primaeval chaos. Then it referred to a frontier tribe. Then it was used to signify a magical western mountain. By the fourth century it was attached, still with magical connotations, to the dusky seafaring peoples of South-east Asia, whose 'Land of Kunlun' lay not far from China's southern borders. By the great period of the Tang and Song dynasties it had yet another meaning. When an Arab delegation arrived at the Song court in 977 the Chinese recorded that 'their attendants had deep-socketed eyes and black bodies. They were called Kunlun slaves.' The first of these Kunlun slaves seem to have been presented to the rulers of China between the eighth and tenth centuries. Initially they were supplied from the Indonesian kingdoms of Sri Vijaya and Java. Traders from this region are thought to have started slaving out of Africa well before the Arabs did. By the ninth century, however, the Arabs were busy transporting East Africans to drain the clogged soil of southern Iraq. A few Africans were apparently brought overland to China from the Arab dominions and given employment in Tang dynasty households.

The Tang period was rich in short stories, and in several of these stories Kunlun servants appear. They speak Chinese, behave like Chinese and are treated by their Chinese owners with every sign of respect. The Kunlun are no common servants. They are unfailingly heroic and resourceful. One, Mo'le, is even celebrated as a traditional Chinese knight-errant in a story entitled *The Kunlun Slave*. Mo'le is a retainer in a late eighth-century household who helps his young master rescue a captive singing-girl. He begins by deciphering a coded appeal the girl has made to his master: 'This is a trivial matter. Why did you agonize about it instead of telling me?' He then goes into action, kills the fierce dogs that guard the girl's quarters, carries the young man to her chamber over ten encircling walls and, laden now with the young man, the girl and the girl's possessions, vaults safely out again. The girl's frustrated captor sends fifty men to catch him, but Mo'le dodges nimbly through a shower of arrows and vanishes from the common gaze. Ten years later, he is seen by some other members of the household selling medicine in the city of Luoyang. They come back reporting that 'his face and hair were as of old'.

Scratch the surface, and the Kunlun ooze magic. This magic is not always apparent at first sight. Sometimes it has to be summoned up by giving the servants nourishment, especially wine. Sometimes it only comes into play in the course of particular exploits. Two of the Kunlun, for instance, are brilliant divers, whose skill consists in fishing up treasure for their Chinese masters from rivers, lakes and wells. At other times, however, the magic seems to lie in their actual appearance. A maidservant troubled, according to one story, by pains in the back and waist is cured by an old man who visits her in her dreams and daubs the affected parts with 'a substance like black lacquer' rubbed off the palms of his attendant Kunlun. Black skin plainly is not believed to be real. Kunlun can be magical in an alarming way. Another tale describes how a Tang statesman is wakened in the night by an apparition which goes round and round him, looking like a Kunlun with large white teeth, and warns him of the imminent death of his mother. A traveller in a ghost story is approached in the candlelit hall of a derelict house by two Kunlun in black robes. Black clothes are part of the Kunlun aura. One Chinese child born freakishly with a 'shining black face' is presented to the local prince, who gives him the nickname Kunlun and a black suit to match. To mediaeval Chinese thinking, apparently, if you were black you should wear black.

It seems clear from the stories that these few uprooted African slaves, strong, a little frightening, utterly mysterious, excited in Chinese minds a mixture of admiration and awe. Possibly the Chinese hoped to harness their magic. In an early account of a lion dance, the ritual cavorting still practised nowadays to bring good luck at the time of the Chinese New Year, the performers who manipulated each pantomime lion from a distance, tugging it with ropes attached to their feet, are said to have been 'decked out to look like Kunlun'.

Three centuries later, in Song times, the slaves had grown familiar. We no longer find them in fiction, but in sober factual records. They came, we are told, from the land of Kunlun Zengji, a name which probably refers to Madagascar and the adjoining Comoro islands but also happens to combine the Chinese and Arabic terms for 'blacks'. 'Black as lacquer' and with 'tadpole' hair, they were lured with food and transported in countless numbers to the Arab countries. It is clear that a large number were brought to China too. Kunlun slaves were kept, according to a record of 1119, by 'most of the rich people in Canton'. These slaves did not necessarily belong to Chinese: many of the 'rich people in Canton' are likely to have been members of the Islamic trading colony which continued to flourish there. But the Chinese residents of Canton must have seen them daily.

At first glance the slaves described in reports of life at Canton do not differ that much from the old Kunlun in the stories. They are still very strong, able to carry weights of several hundred *catties*. They are still accomplished divers who can swim without blinking and are used, consequently, to caulk ships under water. They are still stalwart retainers, employed as doorkeepers. But there the resemblance ends. The Chinese tone has changed from awe to bleak realism. No longer either heroic or magical, Kunlun have turned into displaced nomads, tragically ill-adapted to their Chinese surroundings: 'They eat raw things. [Again that hint of revulsion.] If, in captivity, they are given cooked food, in a few days they get diarrhoea. . . . This makes some of them fall ill and die.' Unlike the resourceful Kunlun of fiction, 'their nature is simple and they do not run away'. In contrast to the Chinese-speaking Kunlun of fiction, 'their speech and their desires are unintelligible. . . . After they have been domesticated for a long time, they can understand human speech, but they cannot utter it themselves.' There is no getting round the implications of this last sentence. Kunlun are not considered to be human. They do not appear to be bound by the family ties which for Chinese are the essence of humanity: 'It is said that they have no longing for their kinsfolk.' They are called 'savages' and 'devil slaves', and their sexes are classified by Chinese terms used to denote the male and female of animals and some birds.

We can guess pretty much why the African image has changed so. These slaves at Canton are no longer being glimpsed through the blurred fancy of a short-story writer but scrutinized, for the first time, by the ordinary citizen. To understand his reaction we need only recall the impact of large-scale slavery in Europe. Europeans in mediaeval and early modern times looked on Africans respectfully as inhabitants of hazy but imposing lands. When the African slave trade reached its peak in the seventeenth and eighteenth centuries they ceased to feel that respect. They saw at close quarters African victims of slavery, helpless and therefore contemptible; and they extended their contempt in due course to Africans in general. In China, fortunately, the African slave trade never spread. There is no sign of mass slavery anywhere except in Canton, and no sign that the presence of slaves in Canton affected Chinese attitudes to Africans who were not slaves themselves. The same writer who described the capture of hapless slaves by the Arabs also left us the sketch of the stately kingdom of Zhongli.

One group of Africans found in China a very different reception to that experienced by the Canton slaves. In 1071 and again in 1081–3, visitors came to the Chinese court from a country beyond Oman, 160 days to the west of China. The country was called Zengdan, a name meaning Land of the Blacks. Its emissaries were treated with honour.

Their leader, Zengjiani, was accorded a Chinese title, Lord Guardian of Prosperity: during his second visit, boats were arranged to facilitate his progress along the waterways from south China to the capital, and the Song emperor lavished on him, in recognition of his long journey, gifts that included 2,000 ounces of white gold.

Zengjiani and his party were honoured, almost certainly, as the first Africans to take part in the curious symbolic charade with which China received foreign merchants. Such merchants, in the traditional Chinese view, brought 'tribute'. Their goods were an acknowledgement by their country of origin of China's universal sovereignty, and the goods given them in return were rewards bestowed on their country for its gratifying submission to the Chinese emperor. Zengjiani's group were ambassadors, in the eyes of the Song court. In fact they may well have been private traders, but it rather looks as though they puffed themselves up to fulfil Chinese expectations, to present themselves as ambassadors and ambassadors of an imposing state at that. Their ruler, they declared, was the 'prince of princes', and their nation's pedigree went back five hundred years. They had a code of laws and a coinage, and their nobles rode horses and elephants. The goods their country produced included not just the usual spices and wild animals, but a number of extra items untypical of East Africa, pearls and glass, camphor and buffaloes. We may guess that some of this information was bogus. No doubt the canny traders had decided to embellish their account of Zengdan a little by portraying as their own the customs and products of one or two other countries they had visited on the long ocean voyage.

All the same, Zengjiani's mission was a major development. Africans, for a change, were reaching out to China. As their coastal city-states grew more organized and more affluent, they were beginning to seek business across the ocean to the east. By the late thirteenth century Mogadishu was trading actively enough to attract the attention of Kubilai Khan, the Mongol (Yuan) ruler who conquered south China and put an end to the Song dynasty. Kubilai sent envoys to learn about Mogadishu and treat for the release of an earlier envoy who had been held captive there. In 1342 the Arab traveller Ibn Battuta met in an Indian port a man from Mogadishu who had been in China. His name was Sa'id. There is no indication he had been there on business, but we do know he was a devout Moslem and an Islamic doctor of law. Religion was as powerful a reason as trade for these Islamicized African towns to extend their contacts eastwards. Friendly Moslem communities stretched all the way to the south China ports. What did the Koran say? 'Seek knowledge, even as far as China, if need be.'

By the beginning of the fifteenth century the slow trickle of knowledge and contact had done its work. The convergence was complete. The time was ripe for a grand conjunction. In East Africa the coastal towns were reaching the height of their prosperity. Their harbours were busy with foreign ships: their own ships were busy in the western Indian Ocean. In China the great days of the merchant venturer were over. After the Mongols completed their conquest of China in 1279, they began to impose restrictions on private overseas trade, partly to discourage the chronic piracy which had battened on it. The Ming dynasty which drove out the Mongols and restored native Chinese rule in 1368 tightened the restrictions further. But China was still on the seas, since the Ming government still had a naval force and the will to deploy it.

What followed was colossal.

In 1414 a Chinese fleet pushed into the western Indian Ocean. It was commanded by Zheng He, Grand Eunuch of the Three Treasures. Three times already since 1405 Zheng He and his ships had descended on the ports of Indochina, Indonesia, south-west India and Ceylon. Now they were advancing into more distant regions, covering in the process a larger total quantity of water than any seafaring people had before.

Zheng He was the Chinese Columbus. He has become for China, as Columbus has for the West, the personification of maritime endeavour. Yet he differed from his Western counterpart in a number of major ways. Three-quarters of a century before Columbus crossed the Atlantic, this Ming dynasty admiral had at his disposal resources which make the Genoese explorer look like an amateur. Columbus had three ships. They had one deck apiece, and together weighed a total of 415 tons. Zheng He had sixty-two galleons, and more than a hundred auxiliary vessels. The largest galleons had three decks on the poop alone, and each of them weighed about 1,500 tons. They had nine masts and twelve sails, and are said to have measured 440 feet long by 180 feet wide. With a force of perhaps a hundred men, Columbus might have been grateful for the company of

868 civil officers, 26,800 soldiers, 93 commanders, two senior commanders, 140 'millerions' [captains of a thousand men], 403 centurions, a Senior Secretary of the Board of Revenue, a geomancer, a military instructor,

21

two military judges, 180 medical officers and assistants, two orderlies, seven senior eunuch ambassadors, ten junior eunuchs and 53 eunuch chamberlains

who travelled in Zheng He's retinue, along with an unspecified number of signallers, interpreters, scribes, professional negotiators, purveyors, Chinese and foreign navigators, helmsmen, military and civil mechanics, naval captains, common sailors and cooks. Columbus's crew, whose diet included dirty drinking water and flour baked with sea water, might also have appreciated the abundance of grain, fresh water, salt, soya sauce, tea, liquor, oil, candles, firewood and charcoal which Zheng He brought with him in his attendant supply ships and water tankers.

Zheng He's voyages differed from Columbus's not only in scale but in kind. Each voyage was a huge collective operation, a state undertaking in the fullest sense. Zheng He was not just financially sponsored, as Columbus was, by a sympathetic government: he and his captains, eunuchs of the palace, were the agents and chosen personal servants of their emperor. He was not in the smallest degree an entrepreneur.

Nor, in fairness to Columbus, was he strictly an explorer. The real Chinese explorers were the anonymous merchants who slipped across the Indian Ocean centuries before Zheng He's time. The Grand Eunuch's crews advanced, as they later described it, through sky-high waves to the westernmost lands of the west and the northernmost lands of the north, far-off regions screened by a blue transparency of light vapours. But they cannot have shared with Columbus's men a dread of the unknown. They knew, in principle, what lay ahead. Calmly, bureaucratically, the Chinese had prepared themselves for the Moslem world beyond India. Zheng He himself was a Moslem. His father and grandfather had been to Mecca, and he was probably chosen admiral largely on the strength of his familiarity with the customs of Islamic countries. He in turn recruited Moslem translator–interpreters, a mullah called Hassan and another Chinese Moslem called Ma Huan who later wrote a memoir of the expeditions.

Far from being an exploration, this great outreaching of Chinese seapower was inspired by the most inward-looking of motives. On the Ming throne at the start of the voyages sat a new emperor, Yong'le (1402–24). Yong'le was a hardened soldier who had come to power by deposing a gentler relative, in a manner curiously reminiscent of his exact contemporary, Henry IV of England. Like Henry IV he was not entirely secure on his throne, and had to contend with rumours that his predecessor was still alive. The hunt for this predecessor, said to be at large in the southern ocean, was the formal reason for mobilizing the fleet. It is hardly conceivable that the hunt was still in progress when the fleet passed beyond India ten years later. Prestige was probably the main consideration by now. The Ming as a newish dynasty may have needed prestige: Yong'le as a usurper certainly did. Prestige, as we have seen, was conferred through the arrival in China of foreign visitors with goods which the Chinese received as symbolic 'tribute'. The farther afield the fleet sailed, the greater the influx of 'tribute' bearers it could attract to Yong'le's court. Supreme under heaven in their own opinion, the Chinese were none the less in quest of a sort of diplomatic recognition.

They also wanted trade. The great days of the merchant venturer were over, but the Chinese business instinct was still very much alive. Zheng He and his fellow eunuchs were scouring the Indian Ocean for luxury goods which the imperial court could consume and retail at a profit, and their galleons were called Treasure Ships for the wealth they carried home. Treasure Ships also carried Chinese export produce, and the eunuchs probably had the task of developing new outlets for handicrafts like silk and porcelain which China was now manufacturing to saturation point. They may just have thought of Africa. The rich East African coastal towns had dramatically expanded their imports of chinaware since their supplies of Islamic pottery were disrupted in the thirteenth century by the Mongol devastation of the Middle East. By the mid-fourteenth century porcelain from China was used in every important coastal settlement and was sometimes edging Islamic goods out of the market.

Still, when Zheng He's fourth expedition sailed beyond India in 1414, it was headed not for Africa but for the Gulf. No one so far as we know planned the conjunction of China and Africa. Fate intervened, through the most unlikely of instruments.

The great voyages were punctuated by a number of lesser missions, and shortly before Zheng He sailed into the western Indian Ocean one of his junior eunuchs took a flotilla to Bengal. There, unexpectedly, he found a giraffe, recently brought from East Africa by envoys of the young city-state of Malindi. A new king had just come to the throne of Bengal, and the creature may have been a gift from the ruler of Malindi to a Moslem fellow-sovereign. Or Malindi may even have been in the business of exporting giraffes. Whatever the truth, giraffes were fascinating, and the Chinese wanted this one. The Bengali king was persuaded to part with his animal, and the Chinese shipped it off to their emperor, a present from Bengal. Probably they installed it in one of the 'horse-ships' the fleet used for transporting wildlife. Shipping large animals, even in a 'horse-ship', was a risky business, however, and the Chinese apparently decided to arrange for a back-up just in case their acquisition failed to survive the journey. Someone at some point persuaded the envoys from Malindi to go back home for a second giraffe, ferry it to a suitable rendezvous on the Gulf or the coast of India, and bring it on board a 'horse-ship' of Zheng He's returning fleet.

So it was that in October 1415, flanked by ambassadors from Malindi, a giraffe arrived in Peking.

A contemporary hymn to the throne reveals why the Chinese greeted this animal with such rapture. They took the giraffe for a unicorn. The unicorn was a sacred animal, and by Confucian tradition

when a sage possesses the virtue of the utmost benevolence so that he illuminates the darkest places, a unicorn appears. This shows that Your Majesty's virtue equals that of Heaven: its merciful blessings have spread far and wide so that the harmonious vapours have emanated a unicorn as an endless bliss to the state for a myriad myriad years.

Here was a chance not merely to heighten Yong'le's prestige, but to exalt him as a practitioner of Perfect Government, unequalled since the sage emperors of the legendary past. When the Bengal giraffe arrived a year earlier Yong'le had refused to accept congratulations. 'Even without unicorns there is nothing that hinders good government.' The second giraffe was a miracle too great to be ignored. He agreed to receive it with all due ceremony, still giving, however, what is usually regarded as a bluff, Canute-like response to the flattery of his courtiers. 'It behoves Us even more than in the past to cling to virtue, and it behoves you to remonstrate with Us about Our shortcomings.' Behind the mask of modesty, we may suspect he was thoroughly gratified. Still more giraffes were brought to China. The animal from Bengal had its portrait painted and a poem written in its praise, and a giraffe was stationed during feasts and sacrifices on the east side of the imperial throne.

Zheng He's fourth expedition probably went no further than the Gulf, but that was far enough to bring it into contact with the lively East African world. We have already come across Mogadishu, chief city-state of the Somali coast and centre for many years of a flourishing overseas trade. Somewhere on his cruise, perhaps in the same Gulf or Indian

24

port where he collected the ambassadors from Malindi with their wonderful animal, the Chinese Columbus met a party of merchants from Mogadishu and invited them to organize a mission to Peking. The merchants complied with vigour. In 1416, the year after Zheng He's return to China, envoys from Mogadishu arrived at the Chinese court, bringing with them for good measure a deputation from Brava, the nearest state to the south. Visitors from no less than three African territories, Malindi, Mogadishu and Brava, had now made the tremendous journey to the foot of the Ming emperor's throne. Their devotion called for a response. It is basic Chinese courtesy to see a departing guest on his way, but Yong'le went further. The Grand Eunuch was to set out once more, to escort these men home and bestow rewards on their rulers. A formal visit would be made to Africa, 450 years before the first Chinese envoys reached Europe.

Africa, then, was the final destination of the fifth great voyage of 1417–19. Some time in the second half of 1418, East African coastal communities had their first 'close encounter' with a Chinese fleet. Two others followed, on the sixth expedition of 1421–2 and the seventh of 1431–3. The written records the Chinese made suggest that they spent most of their time at the northern end of the coast, in what is now Somalia. They visited not only Mogadishu and Brava but also Zhubu, a little settlement thought to have lain by the mouth of the Juba River near the modern Kenyan border; and they entered into relations with 'Sumalier', probably a collective term for Somali nomads from the hinterland. These records, however, may not account for the full extent of Chinese activity. There are hints that some ships pressed south. A nautical chart published two centuries later but generally agreed to have been used by navigators on either the sixth or the seventh voyage shows a long strip of African coastline, liberally strewn with place names. Some of the names are vague ('Black Kids'), but others are plainly transcribed from the local languages, and several can be identified without much difficulty. There is Malindi, Mombasa, probably Mafia Island off southern Tanzania, possibly Quitangonha Island off northern Mozambique.

Even that may not have been the end of it. A map prepared for the Portuguese court in 1459 by the Venetian Fra Mauro contains a bizarre footnote based on information supplied by an unidentified traveller, about a 'ship or junk of the Indies' which 'about the year 1420' sailed two thousand miles to the west and south-west of capes Sofala, in Mozambique, and Diab, in Madagascar, before adverse weather drove

25

it back. The crew landed at Diab and found a roc's egg there. Fra Mauro's statement, made at a time when no European had been anywhere near Mozambique or Madagascar, is illustrated by a recognizable sketch of a Chinese junk. This unexpected European testimony is supported by another footnote, on the Chinese chart, telling of an extreme point called Habuer where heavy storms stopped the fleet going further. It is plainly a possibility that a far-flung squadron of the Chinese Columbus, tempted for once into a piece of pure exploration, edged past the southern tip of Africa and gazed into the south Atlantic three-quarters of a century before the caravels of Bartolomeu Dias and Vasco da Gama appeared from the other direction.

What did the Chinese find in their grand descent on Africa? Some idea is given by a man named Fei Xin. Drafted into military service, according to Ming custom, to expiate a crime of his father or grandfather, Fei travelled west with the fleets, a reluctant soldier. At the end of the final voyage he wrote an enthusiastic memoir, probably designed to charm the government into restoring him to civilian life. Fei didn't go as far as East Africa, but he spoke to other Chinese who did, and his memoir, published only three years after the end of the last expedition, describes the Somali coast as they saw it. Life changes slowly in the traditional coastal towns, and a visitor to Mogadishu or Brava today can still see, like Fei Xin's shipmates, houses of 'heaped up stones', with their 'kitchens, lavatories and reception rooms all on the upper floors'. The fields round Mogadishu are still 'barren', the crops still 'few', and the wells still 'very deep'. The men of Brava still wear 'a short jacket and a hanging cloth around their waists', their women still sport 'gold earrings', and the community still 'makes its living by catching fish'.

Fei's memoir tells us not just what the Chinese saw, but something of what they thought. To judge from the verses he sprinkles through his text the first glimpse of the Somali coast came as a shock:

> Your eyes rove round to meet only sighs and stares –
> Desolation, the whole country nothing but hills!

But the spirits of the Chinese revived when they saw what the coastal towns had to offer:

> Rare spices and rare beasts evoke a sigh of admiration.

Fei lists with relish the goods displayed. Ambergris, myrrh and gum copal. Lions, rhinos and oryxes. Money-leopards, so called for the coin-like blotches on their fur. The *fulu*, or Auspicious Deer, which appears in a Chinese painting as a familiar creature with black and white stripes and perhaps got its name from *fero*, the Somali word for zebra. Ostriches, which redoubled the excitement of the courtiers back in Peking:

> All of them craning their necks looked on with pleasure, and stamping their feet they were scared and startled, thinking these were things that were rarely heard of in the world and that China had never seen their likeness.

The Treasure Ships lost no time in proffering in exchange Chinese porcelain, silks and satins, gold and silver, pepper, rice, grain and beans.

But the fleet was a Star Raft. *Triumphant Tour of the Star Raft* was the title of Fei Xin's book. A Star Raft was an expedition which carried to exotic lands the star-like radiance of an imperial ambassador, and the object of its voyage was to win for the emperor the allegiance of distant peoples. The exchange of goods was laden in Chinese eyes with a symbolic significance far outweighing the value of the goods themselves. By trading with the fleet the African coastal states were paying the Ming emperor the homage they owed him as sovereign of the world. Fei sums up happily. One by one the chieftains of Mogadishu, Brava and Zhubu have 'accorded with the Rites', 'looked with longing on our gracious gifts', 'felt our Transforming Power' – and 'presented their tribute'.

Africans are unlikely to have seen it quite that way. Even a single Chinese squadron of, say, ten or twelve Treasure Ships, flanked by auxiliary warships and supply boats and packed with some thousands of heavily armed and exotic-looking men, must have loomed up in their harbours as vast and unsettling as a visitation from Mars. What did these strangers want? We know there was a language barrier, that 'double translation' was needed, Chinese into Arabic into Swahili or Somali. The Chinese must have attempted through a series of interpreters to obtain from the coastal peoples a formal expression of allegiance to the Ming throne. We may guess that the coastal peoples had trouble understanding the request: some of them probably balked at it.

Bland though he is, Fei Xin drops a hint. The small settlements, Brava and Zhubu, are 'pure' or 'simple'; African arcadias again. Mogadishu is more prosperous and socially complex, but also more bellicose. Its rulers drill warriors and practise archery, and 'their customs are quarrelsome'. Fei leaves it at that, but a later Chinese author, whose novel about the voyages appeared in 1597, fancies he knows what happened.

27

福鹿

An Auspicious Deer, or zebra. Ming dynasty painting.

28

In his version Zheng He encamps on the coast and seeks 'letters and tokens of submission'. The kings of Brava and Zhubu are ready to supply these, but Mogadishu's ruler pleads sickness and stalls. Zheng He's officers are for besieging Mogadishu with breastworks, catapults and 40,000 men, but the Chinese Columbus opts for patience. 'How can we presume to dominate them by relying solely on intimidation?' Mogadishu sends an archer to spy out the Chinese camp. Zheng He divines his purpose, but decides that the best course is to let him see as much as possible of China's superior armaments and military skills. Awed by a dazzling display of martial arts, the archer is sent back to advise his king that a formal submission 'won't cost him much, and will avoid any trouble that might otherwise arise, causing him a dilemma which it would be too late to regret'. Mogadishu none the less puts up a resistance, but Chinese ingenuity wins the day and the episode ends with all three states submitting and paying tribute and the Grand Eunuch dispensing hospitality and reassurance to their kowtowing kings. Much of this account is fantasy. The author has taken Fei Xin's report and expanded it into a romance spiced with monsters and miracle-working Buddhist monks. He may however preserve a memory which Fei has preferred to veil: a memory that the great squadrons were not welcomed everywhere, immediately, with open arms.

How different all the same these Chinese visitors were from the Europeans who arrived in Africa seventy years later. Travelling in thousands, armed to the teeth, the Chinese were not aggressive. Unlike the Portuguese they stormed no cities and conquered no land. Even if the sixteenth-century novelist was right to describe an initial conflict, he also makes it clear that the Chinese were tactful, anxious to avoid disturbing the small coastal states any more than was necessary to achieve their basic ends. Unlike the Portuguese they refrained from plunder. Instead they coaxed the coastal rulers into trading by presenting them with gifts of coloured silk. They did not burn, as the Portuguese would, with the urge to impose their religious convictions, to lay siege to African souls. All they sought from Africans was a gesture of symbolic acquiescence in the Chinese view of the world. Mogadishu and Brava, for their part, were happy enough with the relationship to send their envoys to Peking three further times while the Chinese Columbus was on the seas. The Chinese were accepted, because the Chinese treated a weak and strange people with courtesy and restraint.

Why did the Chinese behave better than their Western successors?

29

Two reasons seem likely. First, they had no need to assault Africa. They did not come to conquer, simply to garner prestige and profit for the emperor in Peking: and this they could perfectly well achieve through their placid traditional system of exchanging imperial favours for foreign 'tribute'. Second, the Chinese would never in any case have thought Africa worth assaulting. The impoverished Europeans of the early Renaissance preyed on Africa because they approached it on something like equal terms. Portuguese soldiers glimpsed gold in cities richer than their own. Portuguese priests noticed heathens, benighted in their ignorance but for all that men like themselves whose souls cried out to be saved. Such thoughts would never have occurred to the Chinese, for whom China was the centre of the world. They would never have lusted for African gold because China had gold in plenty, and most other forms of wealth. Africa was a patch of the surrounding outer darkness, distinguished only by its possession of a few rare spices and animals. The Chinese would never have concerned themselves with African beliefs because Africans, like all non-Chinese, were barbarians, and extensive contact with barbarians was neither desirable nor necessary. One Ming writer urged his contemporaries to 'treat the barbarian kings like harmless seagulls'. Zheng He and his captains surveyed Africa from far too lofty a standpoint to think of disrupting the flow of African life.

The Chinese descent on Africa differed from the European descent in one other important respect: the Chinese left. The seventh expedition was the last. After eighteen years of comings and goings, when contact was at its height, the Chinese turned their backs on Africa and withdrew, abruptly and completely, from the Indian Ocean. We know the basic reasons why. The civil servants who ran the day-to-day administration of Ming China rose up in protest at the strain of an abnormal endeavour. As practical-minded men they felt that the voyages were no use. The crews had died in their thousands, and money and grain had been invested out of all proportion to the value of the goods acquired. In fact the Star Raft probably paid its way, but the charge of extravagance must have seemed increasingly convincing as the navy's lines of communication stretched four thousand miles to Africa and zebras came back in return for gold and silver and silk.

The voyages seemed all the more of a strain because they were, in a sense, an anachronism, a maritime spectacular staged at a period when China was moving away from the sea. The Chinese government had largely stifled private overseas trade: now it was beginning to wonder if it really needed a navy. For Ming China, like modern China, the strategic priority was to defend the northern land border. The Mongols had been evicted but they might yet return. Yong'le, that vigorous monarch, was game for exertions both landward and seaward. His successors, increasingly, would not be.

There were solid arguments against the voyages: there was also an undercurrent of intrigue. The civil servants had not been content to await the result of the expeditions before passing judgement on them. On the contrary, they had agitated against the Star Raft from the very first time it sailed. They viewed the whole venture with an implacable prejudice. In their eyes it was a racket, consecrated to trade, which as followers of the Confucian doctrine they had been brought up to consider a wasteful and frivolous activity. Worse, it was a racket organized by the palace eunuchs, whom the regular bureaucrats disliked and feared as dangerous rivals for power. They wanted it stopped. When Yong'le died in 1424 the civil servants persuaded his immediate successor, Hongxi (1424–5), to call a halt to the expeditions. The Star Raft's attractions were still sufficiently great to induce one more emperor, Xuande (1425–35), to sponsor the seventh voyage, but from then on the bureaucrats had their way. By 1479 they were strong enough to suppress the very memory that the voyages had taken place. In that year another powerful eunuch hoped to emulate the Chinese Columbus and mount an expedition of his own. He asked for the files on Zheng He's voyages. The bureaucrats had had enough of both eunuchs and navigation. They announced that the files had been 'lost'.

It was a triumph of introversion. In withdrawing from Africa the Chinese were also rejecting the entire outside world. China was moving inland. In 1421 the capital was shifted from Nanking to Peking, six hundred miles to the north. Southern Chinese who might have had some contact with foreigners were replaced in the civil service by men whose outlook was formed wholly in the interior. As Yong'le's successors turned away from the sea, shipbuilding and seafaring, once so lively, were curbed to a point where people began migrating from the southern maritime provinces, and within a few decades there were virtually no Chinese on the oceans at all. China's doors closed for four hundred years, till the Europeans forced them open in the nineteenth century. It is no accident that today, when China is once more opening up to the world after a phase of withdrawal, the Chinese Columbus is remembered as a hero, and his expeditions to Africa, launched in the teeth

31

of bureaucratic hostility, as a praiseworthy effort at 'learning from foreign countries'. Zheng He stands for that questing impulse which has so often battled with introversion in the Chinese spirit.

At the same time we cannot fully understand the end of the expeditions if we forget that the Chinese Columbus was himself, by Western standards, a voyager of an introverted kind. His interest in Africa was limited. He came simply to fill his ships with animals, spices and tokens of allegiance, and once he had done that he had no reason to stay. By the time he returned from the final voyage in 1433 we may guess that the Chinese had seen as much of Africa as they wished. There was nothing much they had got from Africa they could not get somewhere else, nothing at least that warranted the trouble of going to fetch it. With perhaps one exception. The Ming court in the sixteenth century spent ten years conducting a futile search for ambergris. They had forgotten where it came from.

At first glance it would seem that Zheng He's squadrons left little visible mark on Africa. The east coast of the continent is strewn with Chinese debris, but only a tiny fraction of it can plausibly be connected with the great descents of 1418–33. Six coins of Yong'le's reign have been found at Mogadishu. At Gedi in Kenya and at Mafia Island off Tanzania two identical late-fourteenth-century porcelain bottles have come to light. Traced with copper–red chrysanthemums and ringed with bands of blue, funnel-necked, exceptionally fine, they could perhaps have been special souvenirs brought by the squadrons to gratify the coastal potentates. That is the total extent of likely material relics.

The fleet left no settlers. Its passengers seem to have left no offspring by local women, even in spite of the fact that, to judge from the Ming descriptions, they travelled unaccompanied by women of their own. In 1602 a French navigator, Pyrard de Laval, landed on Madagascar and met, by his own account, Chinese whose forbears 'were on a ship which was lost in this place'. It is tempting to suppose that these men were the descendants of castaways from a stray vessel of Zheng He's. More likely, however, they were representatives of the Merina people from the central plateau of Madagascar, who are remarkable for their Asiatic features and are nowadays generally agreed to be of Malay or Indonesian extraction. The first European explorers of Africa tended to attribute Chinese origins to people like the Merina and the yellow-skinned Khoikhoi (Hottentots), whose appearance didn't fit their preconception of what an African should look like.

Various other attempts have been made to identify Chinese settlers or descendants of Chinese settlers on parts of the African coast. Some of the coastal clans of the modern Swahili people have hankered after a lineage grander than that of mere Afro-Arabs. An elder of the Shanga clan on the Kenyan island of Pate told a researcher in 1980 that according to a centuries-old tradition their ancestors came from Shanghai ('This is actually where the name of Shanga came from'). Some modern Chinese scholars have cited rumours of old houses in the bush near Mombasa where Chinese used to live, of Zheng He's village, camp and monument on the outskirts of Brava. There is, indeed, a ruin connected with the Chinese at Gedi, near Mombasa. The connection was made, however, not because Chinese lived there but because Chinese coins were found there; and the ruin is labelled, suitably enough, the House of the Chinese Cash. 'Zheng He's monument' is an uninscribed monolith on the Brava sand dunes which seems, alas, to have been put there not by the Chinese Columbus but by the Italian Duce some fifty years ago. None of these theories of settlement will stand up to close inspection. And none, in the end, is as startling as the simple fact that for once in African history an armada of foreigners came, did their business and went away again.

In spite of its transient nature, however, the great Ming landfall had a lingering impact on Africans. They did not forget so easily. Africans outlasted the Chinese on the seas. Early in the sixteenth century the arriving Portuguese found them, way east on the Malay coast in the seaport of Malacca. Men from Ethiopia, Mogadishu, Malindi, Mombasa and Kilwa, they came in their own ships, and they came to trade. The goods they bought included silk and porcelain which are thought to have been Chinese.

What seems to have happened is that the Chinese created a market. All the way down the East African coast patrician clans went on demanding the silk which Zheng He's fleet had once been accustomed to lavish on them. When the Portuguese reached East Africa they found people swathed in silk. From Malindi and Mombasa south to the towns of Mozambique courtiers wore satin turbans and silk below their waists. Monarchs approached beneath silken canopies, and the rooms and couches in their palaces were draped with silken cloths. Some of this silk may have been made locally and some was certainly bought from Indian cities: but those cities supplemented their own production with

Chinese silk imported through Malacca, and China is likely to have remained an ultimate source of supply. Right into the seventeenth century gifts of Chinese silk were a sure way to the heart of an East African chieftain.

More tenacious still was the appetite for porcelain. Porcelain had been imported in bulk long before the squadrons descended, and it went on being imported after they left. On and on it came, dwindling after the mid-nineteenth century but never quite dying out. What was the charm of this porcelain that gripped East African coastal peoples for more than a thousand years? Often it just served a straightforward practical purpose. Chinese plates and bowls were the day-to-day tableware off which wealthier citizens ate their millet, rice or fish. Chinese vessels were handy containers for objects of every kind. Swahili townsfolk on the coastal fringe of Kenya used Chinese snuff boxes and inkwells to store kohl for women's eyelids, ginger jars to carry pens and trinkets, and big jars like the ones in the Ali Baba story to hold perfume or oil. They stuck little Chinese bowls in the base of their cisterns to ensure that even when the cisterns were empty a small supply of water would remain for the fish which they kept there to prevent mosquitoes breeding. Cups and saucers from modern China are still sold today for their functional value in Kenyan coastal shops. Some of them, by a quaint coincidence, bear the brand name 'Kunlun'.

But porcelain also conferred prestige. It lent grandeur to mosques, tombs and houses. Chinese tableware was brought out to honour a distinguished visitor. Chinese plates, cups and jars lined the alcoves in the chamber where a bride was viewed by the wedding guests for two hours after her marriage. In the town of Pate, soon after 1800, the Swahili poet al-Inkishafi described a time when the citizens had prospered, when

> Their feast-tables were spread with ware from China,
> Each drinking-vessel traced with fine engraving.

But the glory had departed and

> Where once the porcelain stood in the wall-niches,
> Now wild birds nestle their fledglings.

And porcelain probably had a whiff of the supernatural. Mediaeval East Africans may have shared the Middle Eastern idea that the greenish celadon vessels would sweat or crack if poison was placed in them, or fancied that the chime they extracted by rapping the vessels could call down spirits to earth. The vast popularity of blue-and-white ware may be connected with the absence of blue dye anywhere south of Ethiopia: did people without a word for blue in their languages, unused to seeing blue except in the sky, perhaps regard blue porcelain as part of heaven, as magic? One Portuguese chronicler relates how a tribe in sixteenth-century Zululand rubbed their bodies with a china bottle in the hope that it would cure their ailments. Was prestige really the only reason for the compulsion to fix Chinese vessels in the surface of tombs? At one place in southern Somalia sixty years ago the dead man's spirit was thought to come and drink rainwater from the bowl. Old superstitions may have survived as unexplained rituals. Modern Chinese bowls are still sometimes added to tombs on the Somali–Kenyan border; and when an office building was completed in Malindi in 1979 eight blue-and-white china plates were fixed to the wall as a matter of 'ancient custom'.

For a while Africans apparently remembered not just Chinese products but the Chinese themselves. When Vasco da Gama and his Portuguese rounded the Cape of Good Hope and anchored off the Mozambique coast in 1498 they had a disconcerting experience. The two African dignitaries who boarded their flagship were distinctly blasé. Though given food and clothes they 'did not seem to prize anything'; and they volunteered, in a mixture of sign language and bad Arabic, the information 'that towards the rising sun there were white people who navigated in vessels like ours, which they had seen going up and down that coast'. They added, according to the Portuguese poet Camões, that these white navigators had sailed their sea

> Even from the rising of the sun, until
> The land makes southward a full point, and so
> Back from the south to east. . . .

Sixty-five years had passed since Zheng He's last expedition left East Africa. No time in the collective memory of a pre-literate people, let alone a people who had witnessed an event as momentous as an extraterrestrial landing would seem to us. The remarks which greeted da Gama could in theory have referred to light-skinned Indian traders. But the Indians themselves told da Gama, when he reached their country four months later, of beardless white people with armour, cannons and a weapon like 'a sword on the end of a spear' who had visited them regularly about eighty years before to buy spices in return for 'very fine linen cloth'. There is, consequently, good reason for thinking that these Africans remembered a Chinese squadron which had cruised off Mozambique in their fathers' day.

Memory might linger, but the future of Chinese–African contact had passed into the hands of the Europeans with their small ships and their unimpressive goods. Much of the old trade filtered now through them. Chinese porcelain came to Africa by courtesy, successively, of the Portuguese, Dutch and British fleets. In 1719 African lions were again being caught for an emperor of China – by the Portuguese Jesuits of Mozambique. It was also the role of the Europeans to bring Chinese and Africans together for the first time since the Chinese Columbus withdrew from the ocean. In circumstances, however, of a harshly different kind.

The Advent of the Celestial

'Why, Xiangzi!' she exclaimed. 'Did a wolf run off with
you, or did you go to Africa to mine gold?'

Lao She, *Rickshaw Boy*, Shanghai, 1937

I n the course of one generation the Europeans imposed their will
on the world of the Indian Ocean. The Portuguese who arrived
in the ships of Vasco da Gama were bent on acquiring gold and
Eastern spices. Trade in these goods, however, was monopolized by
the infidels, by Arab and Indian Moslems, and the Portuguese soon
realized that the old, peaceful trading network had no place for them.
Their response was to rip it apart. Between 1500 and 1530 they seized
a series of entrepots which controlled the trade in different parts of the
ocean, and smashed the two Moslem fleets which were mustered to
oppose them off the Indian coast and the Malay Peninsula. The Moslem
middlemen quickly appreciated that their days of tranquil dominance
had come to an end. 'Devil take you,' said an Arab to the first Portuguese
who set foot in the Indian port of Calicut. 'What brings *you* here?'

The middlemen were the immediate, but not the only, victims. At
either end of the ocean the Portuguese were anxious to establish permanent trading and naval bases. Before very long they were knocking at
both African and Chinese doors. Wealthy but disunited, the Swahili
towns of East Africa offered little serious resistance. Sometimes the Portuguese won admission by playing on local rivalries, and sometimes they
stormed ashore. Mombasa was sacked twice, in 1505 and 1528, and force,
or the threat of force, was used to establish forts at the points controlling
the gold trade with the African interior, Kilwa, Sofala and Mozambique.

China, where the first Portuguese arrived in 1513, was a different
proposition. It was a monolithic and still formidable empire, little disposed to tolerate the intrusion of piratical foreigners. In 1521–2 a Portuguese squadron was ignominiously defeated by the Ming dynasty's
coastguard fleets, and a visiting Portuguese envoy was imprisoned in
Canton. But in China, too, the Portuguese eventually took root. By the

middle of the century they had succeeded, with the connivance of local officials, in setting up a trading post at Macao, on the tip of an island in the Canton delta. The emperor in Peking gave his reluctant sanction to the arrangement, and in 1573 the Chinese grudgingly confirmed their acceptance of Macao's colonial status by walling it off.

Right round the Indian Ocean the Portuguese had helped themselves to the first small slices of local sovereignty. Over the coming centuries the Dutch, French and British would be arriving for their share. Ruling the ocean and encroaching, at either end of it, on both Chinese and African territories, the Europeans barred the way to formal contact between the peoples of those territories for four hundred years. Yet the Europeans were also, paradoxically, a powerful mingling force. As the ships of Portugal and Holland, France and Britain pressed on from continent to continent, individual Chinese and Africans were picked up and swept together. Time and again we meet them, slaves, servants and concubines, bit parts in the chronicles of Western discovery, flotsam deposited at random by the European typhoon.

The Portuguese started the mingling. Portugal's population was too small to run an empire unaided, and to make up for their continual shortage of manpower the Portuguese relied heavily on the help of auxiliaries of every kind. From each of their subject territories they brought home slaves. African slaves toiled in Lisbon side by side with Europe's earliest Chinese cooks. The Portuguese shuffled their subject peoples from one overseas province to another. From each place they gathered young men who they hoped would absorb and transmit their blazing zeal for the Roman Catholic faith. At Goa in India, Portugal's overseas headquarters, Jesuit fathers in 1556 imparted Latin and theology to a strange assortment of seminarians that included six Ethiopians, three East Africans and five Chinese.

The Portuguese also brought Africans to China. They had African slaves in their retinue from the earliest days of their presence in Macao, and they went on bringing them in. It is easy to understand why. The Portuguese priests and merchants who settled in Macao were perched insecurely on the edge of an alien empire. Barely tolerated by the Ming authorities, they could not count solely on Chinese to protect and look after them. African slaves were more likely to have their interests at heart, if only because they were as strange and as unaccustomed to China as the Portuguese themselves.

Macao in the early seventeenth century had a distinctly African flavour.

In 1635, for example, it was said to contain some 7,000 inhabitants: 5,100 were slaves, and most of the slaves were African men and women. These Africans did much of the work on which the colony's well-being hinged. Many of them were assigned to the hard, coarse labour of crewing the great trading carracks which sailed from Macao to Portugal's outposts in India and Japan. Others, the more fortunate ones, were employed in the Jesuit residence, the charity hospital and the various private households. An English visitor, Peter Mundy, wrote of the Portuguese gentlemen of the town 'each having their Negros or Caphers, Cladd in Dammasks, an ordinary wear here for slaves and servaunts'. African slaves were a vivid part of life. When Macao in 1642 celebrated the end of a spell of Spanish rule in Portugal, Africans dressed in scarlet paraded by torchlight through the streets.

In one celebrated crisis the slaves gave the Portuguese dramatic proof of their loyalty. Macao had no garrison, but when the Dutch, rival empire-builders, attacked the Portuguese there in 1622, they met with an unexpected rebuff:

> Many Portuguese slaves, kaffirs and the like, having been made drunk, charged so fearlessly against our muskets that it was a wondrous thing to see. ... The slaves of the Portuguese at Macao served them so well and faithfully that it was they who defeated and drove away our people there last year.

A black woman brandishing a halberd laid about her with a zest that reminded the Portuguese of a mediaeval heroine of theirs who killed seven Spaniards with a shovel. Africans had played a decisive role in the only battle ever fought between Europeans on Chinese soil.

Close by in Canton the Chinese authorities watched the result attentively. They found it convenient to display a new consideration to the Portuguese settlers. But they knew who had done the fighting. The presiding magistrate at Canton sent the colony a gift of three hundred bushels of rice to be distributed among the victorious slaves.

Some of the slaves evidently detected in China a chance of a better life. They fled from Macao to serve under Chinese commanders. Three hundred of them were organized into a bodyguard for Zheng Zhilong, a retired coastal pirate who had accepted the job of suppressing other pirates on behalf of the failing Ming dynasty. When the dynasty collapsed in 1644 and Manchu invaders moved south into China, one of their priorities was to capture Zheng Zhilong. To achieve this, however, they

39

had first to disarm his African bodyguard, who put up a brief but gallant struggle in which a hundred were killed. The rest enlisted under the Manchus at Canton, where they distinguished themselves during a siege by Ming loyalists in 1647. Their war-cry was *'Santiago!'*

Zheng Zhilong made his peace with the new Manchu dynasty, but his son, Zheng Chenggong, known to the West as Koxinga, mounted a resistance in the south-eastern province of Fujian that plagued the Manchus for years. Koxinga was also able to attract the allegiance of an African bodyguard, a force composed of 'giants' whom he bought from Macao and equipped with muskets inlaid with silver. Popular tradition in Fujian still remembers Koxinga's warriors. They were known as the Black Daredevils, because of the fearlessness with which they undertook the dangerous task of firing a cannon. In 1661 they helped Koxinga to establish himself in a more secure headquarters by driving out the Dutch who had occupied the nearby island of Taiwan. Fighting their way round the creeks and headlands of seventeenth-century China, the slaves from Macao had given a new lease of life to the legend of the heroic Kunlun.

Some of the Africans left in Portuguese service also displayed an occasional tendency to make common cause with the Chinese. One Manchu document speaks of black slaves at Macao who entice Chinese to steal the goods of the European barbarians. For the most part, however, the Africans did little to alarm their colonial masters. In later centuries, when growing turbulence in China threatened to spill over into Macao, the Portuguese began to maintain there a garrison of some two thousand soldiers from their African provinces of Mozambique and Angola who patrolled the town and guarded its border with the hinterland. Black troops paced up and down the climbing cobbled streets beneath the Latin balconies and the jostling Chinese shop signs. They were used right down to the time when Portugal's African empire began to disintegrate twenty years ago. They led isolated lives, and a visitor to Macao today is reminded of them only by the appearance on a few restaurant menus of 'African chicken' and 'Angolan steak'.

Other European powers moved their subject peoples in the opposite direction.

While the Portuguese turned Macao into a centre of trade and religion, the Dutch and French were beginning to settle on the southern tip of Africa and the islands round its flanks. The environment they confronted was a very different one. They found here no town, and no formidable empire: just tracts of open country, ungoverned, sparsely populated or not populated at all. They did not need servants to cosset and protect them personally so much as labourers who could grapple with the land and supply them with the food and shelter to keep their settlements alive. Jan van Riebeeck, founder in 1652 of the Dutch colony at the Cape of Good Hope, had been there no more than a fortnight when he began to hanker after 'industrious Chinese'. Local Khoikhoi (Hottentot) hunters did not seem likely to provide him with efficient labour. Van Riebeeck had seen Chinese in the East: they could plant rice and sugar, work as carpenters, masons and potters. The idea, in other words, was to bring Chinese to Africa to shoulder tasks which Africans were unable to perform. Or unwilling. The French in the eighteenth century set out to tame the wild islands of Mauritius and Bourbon on Africa's eastern flank. They hauled slaves across the water from Madagascar, Mozambique and the Guinea coast of West Africa to help them cultivate sugar. But the slaves refused. They ran, continually, into the forests. A French admiral, the Comte d'Estaing, thought that he could compensate the colonists of Mauritius for the fecklessness of the local labour force by bringing in 'hardworking and thrifty' Chinese to till the soil.

But how to obtain the Chinese? Africa had for decades been a prolific source of slave labour. Not, as is often supposed, because African rulers were happy to sell their own people, but because they were prepared to traffic in prisoners captured in conflicts with neighbouring states in exchange for European manufactures like firearms and cloth. But China was not a slave market. The Chinese empire was relatively seldom in conflict with its neighbours, and where conflict did take place the Chinese were not in the habit of enslaving prisoners of war. As for domestic slavery, that had been extinct in China since at least the thirteenth century. Far from being prepared to offer its citizens to foreigners, the new Manchu government strictly forbade them to emigrate. The Dutch and the French had minimal chance of creating a Chinese slave trade.

Chinese labour was, none the less, conscripted – in conditions that amounted to slavery in all but name. By the seventeenth century the European powers had established a string of trading stations round the coasts of South-east Asia. Many thousands of impoverished Chinese had slipped illegally out of the teeming southern provinces of their empire and journeyed to these European outposts in the hope of scraping a living. Once there they could be removed to colonies farther afield.

41

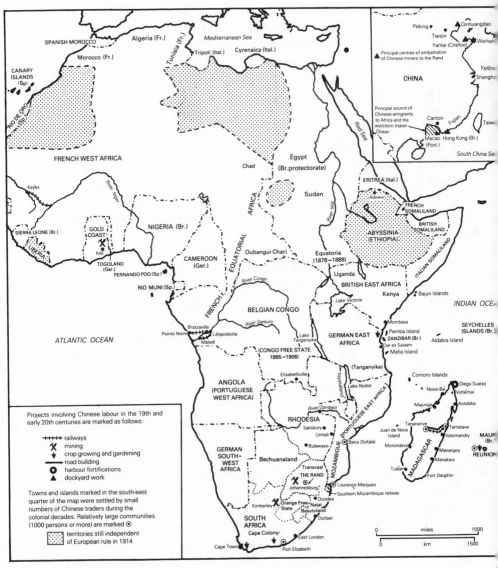

Map 2. Movement of Chinese labourers and traders to Africa in the colonial period. (Bord
are those of Africa in 1914.)

42

Some had fallen foul of the authorities, and were consequently fair game. Van Riebeeck's successors at the Cape of Good Hope helped themselves throughout the late seventeenth and eighteenth centuries to a supply of Chinese convicts who had been flung into chains in the Dutch East Indies for crimes such as counterfeiting money. Several hundreds of these men, Chinese recorded by strange Netherlandish versions of their names (Oempinko, Loquanko, Gouwhouko), were transported over the decades to the Cape of Good Hope, a Dutch Siberia where the settlers put them to work as basket-makers, gardeners and fishermen. Some of them were organized with the free black inhabitants of Table Valley into a kind of emergency service to deal with fires and stranded ships. The Comte d'Estaing in 1760 tried his hand at a similar operation. He abducted three hundred Chinese from the port of Bencoolen in Sumatra and took them to Mauritius to start a new life in the fields. At this point, however, the Europeans ran up for the first time against a layer of Chinese obstinacy. Where the Africans had bolted, the Chinese resisted head-on. They were traders, they said, not labourers, and they were not going to work. The colonists were reduced to coaxing. An official of the French East India Company wrote plaintively to his superiors how

> I put them in a wing of the barracks courtyard and sheltered them from the ravages of the weather: short as we were of meat for our hospital I had them supplied with beef. ... They had their rice ration regularly and on top of that, whenever possible, salt pork and even brandy. I issued them with a little money and the togs they needed. In a word, I spared no effort to treat them gently and win them over.

To no avail: the Chinese still wouldn't work, and the following year the French capitulated and sent them back to Bencoolen.

D'Estaing had made a stupid blunder. Within a few decades, however, genuine Chinese labourers were proving themselves to be every bit as truculent as the kidnapped traders had been. In the early nineteenth century the governments of Europe were moving to abolish slavery in their African possessions, and the colonists anticipated, rightly, that as soon as their chains were struck off the freed slaves would leave their work sites and never come back. Cheap Chinese labour, it was conjectured, could fill the gap. Dirt-poor Chinese could perhaps be enticed by the offer of meagre but contractually guaranteed wages to toil for a fixed period of three to eight years in the plantations and dockyards

43

the slaves had left. The British, who appeared on the scene in the Napo-leonic wars, seizing Mauritius from the French and the Cape of Good Hope from the Dutch, were leading exponents of this new form of recruit-ment that became known, after the pigtails worn by Chinese at this period, as the 'piglet trade'. In 1829 they tried, like the French before them, to set a band of Chinese working on the Mauritius sugar plan-tations. They were no more successful. Within weeks the 'piglets' revolted, and the Europeans couldn't cope. 'The Chinese play pranks. People begin to get tired of their services, which are almost nil. . . . This means the end of their introduction. . . . The multiplied arsons show how dangerous they are.'

The 'piglets' do not appear to have felt any particular solidarity with the African slaves they replaced. They revolted, in fact, precisely because they were not prepared to be treated like the Africans. The European sugar planters had failed to notice any difference. They viewed the Chi-nese as slaves, and worked them like slaves. But the Chinese wouldn't take it. Dirt-poor they might be; they were free men. Several more decades would elapse, and several more disappointments, before the European colonists began to appreciate dimly how the Chinese regarded themselves.

In spite of these disasters, however, the appetite for Oriental labour continued to grow. In the late nineteenth century the colonists were advancing from the fringe of Africa, its coasts and offshore islands, and conquering huge territories in the continent's heart. They were eager to girdle these territories with railways and to tap their resources with plantations and mines; but they couldn't expect much help from the people they had conquered. African resistance was still widespread. The French colony of Niger, for example, and the British colony of Somaliland were not wholly 'pacified' until as late as the 1920s. Even where the resistance had been overcome few African peasants were willing to work for Europeans or to submit to the unfamiliar discipline of large-scale economic projects. The colonists usually had to resort to rounding up Africans by force. Chinese labour, on the other hand, was increasingly easy to gather. From 1840 onwards the Europeans had been using mili-tary force to extract from the weakening Manchu dynasty permission to instal their traders in ports along the coast, and in 1860 they forced the dynasty to lift its ban on emigration. Contract labourers could now be lured from China itself, from the new 'treaty ports' and the coastal provinces surrounding them. Deep in the swampland of the southern

Sudan, which a British explorer had annexed on behalf of Egypt in 1871, the governor of the new Egyptian province of Equatoria, Eduard Schnitzer, alias Emin Pasha, German and Moslem, doctor and naturalist, linguist and recluse, explained to a correspondent what needed to be done:

> I cannot get over the conviction that if it is possible for Central Africa to be opened up, *it can only be accomplished by means of the Chinese*, and that our beautiful country, with all its rich resources, and with the possibility which is offered of *establishing good communications between each settlement by means of such workmen*, would repay a thousandfold such an undertaking. The idea has been one of my dearest projects for four years. . . . Will you convince the Belgians that *a few hundred Chinese established in any suitable place* – under the direction of practical Europeans – would form a better nucleus for the colonization of Africa than any number of Indian elephants and ironclad steamers?

The Belgians needed no convincing. Their king, Leopold II, had managed to play on the determination of his more powerful European neighbours, Britain, France and Germany, to keep each other out of Central Africa. He had won by general European consent the right to exploit, as his own private property, the entire forested mass of the Congo river basin with its tremendous potential wealth in timber, rubber, palm oil, ivory and minerals. Leopold had been advised by his hired explorer, Henry Morton Stanley, that the Congo without a railway was 'not worth a penny', and in 1889 his agents set to work driving a railway inland, parallel to the course of the river, from Matadi near the Atlantic coast to the future capital of Léopoldville. Africans living along the route proved unwilling to cooperate in any work other than porterage, and Leopold's steamers shipped in thousands of conscripts from all over West Africa, Yorubas from Lagos and Dahomeans from Whydah, 'Accras' from the Gold Coast and 'Krooboys' from Liberia, Sierra Leoneans and Senegalese. But the numbers were never enough, and the Belgians consequently set in motion one of Leopold's pet schemes. Five hundred and fifty Chinese were recruited at Macao and pitchforked into the Congo to work side by side with the African contingents. Strange meetings indeed for these gaunt figures, haled from their homes in the West African and Chinese coastlands and marched towards each other at a forest construction site like the Roman legions described by Gibbon in which 'the Iberian, the Arab and the Goth gazed on each other in mutual astonishment'. Hundreds of Africans had already died from

45

smallpox, dysentery and beri-beri, and the Chinese soon began to succumb in their turn, racked by the fevers of the alien rain-forest. Within weeks over half the newcomers were either dead or in full flight eastwards through the jungle, driven perhaps by some vague hope of getting back to China. The hardiest reached the neighbourhood of the River Sankuru, almost halfway across the continent, and there they abandoned the exodus and settled down. A minority continued to work on the railway, debilitated and useless for any but the lightest tasks.

Yet the Europeans persisted. Chinese helped to lay many of Africa's earliest railway lines. The Portuguese shipped several thousand labourers in from Canton to build their first railway through the still 'unpacified' southern part of Mozambique. The French deployed 'exotics', as they called them, on a line from the town of Kayès to the River Niger in the West African hinterland, and a line linking the capital and the eastern coast of a large, empty kingdom they had just subdued, the island of Madagascar. In colony after colony administrators and travellers repeated Emin's verdict. Only the Chinese could develop Africa. Indians were also in demand, but Britain alone had access to a ready supply of Indian labour. The Germans in Tanganyika, German East Africa, judged Chinese coolies 'the only possibility' for their coffee and tobacco plantations.

Sick and refractory though they often were, the Chinese still seemed more reliable than local African labour. They continued to enjoy a reputation for competence. At Uitenhage, for instance, in the Cape Colony of South Africa, imported Chinese farmhands won general respect for their skill in cultivating land which had been regarded as useless. In addition workers in China were getting exposed to the new efficiencies of the Industrial Revolution, as railways and mines began to be opened in their country by European entrepreneurs. The idea began to gain ground that Chinese could show the Africans – new-caught, sullen peoples – how to work.

Britain in the early twentieth century had achieved, for the first and only time, a complete political predominance in South Africa. In the South African war of 1899–1902, the British had defeated, at terrible cost, the fellow-Europeans who disputed their mastery of that rich country, the farming people known variously as Boers or Afrikaners, whose Dutch ancestors had arrived 250 years earlier at the Cape of Good Hope. They had conquered the two independent Boer republics, the Transvaal and the Orange Free State, and reduced them to the status

46

of British colonies, governed from London in the same way as Britain's two older South African possessions, the Cape Colony and Natal. Most important, they had secured, by conquering the Transvaal, control of the great Witwatersrand goldfields, commonly known as the Rand, in which millions of pounds of British capital had been invested since gold was first discovered there in 1886. Gold-hungry British settlers were free at last of the threat of being harassed by a Transvaal government composed of hostile Boer farmers, and British industrialists hoped that with the war now over the Rand mines would flourish as never before.

But their hopes were turning sour. The mines depended on African labour, and African labour was evaporating. African miners scattered by the war were not coming back to the Rand in numbers high enough to guarantee a satisfactory level of output, partly because they were not prepared to accept the reduced wages which the mineowners hoped to impose on a reviving postwar labour market. They protested, in their usual quiet way, by staying in their homes. The result was chronic depression. Costs were rising, while production was static or falling. Profits were declining, and investment was on the point of collapse. Thoughts turned promptly to the usual standby. 'The importation of Chinese', said the *Daily Telegraph*, 'is the condition of keeping South Africa a white man's country.' John Buchan thought Chinese should be brought to the Transvaal. Rider Haggard saw no reason why they should not be. Winston Churchill felt that such assistance would have to be invoked 'if the mining industry was to be resuscitated, and South Africa was to turn her back upon the dark past'.

Proponents of the idea maintained that the Celestials, as they called people from China, the 'Celestial Empire', would set an example of industriousness to the African labour force. 'The advent of the Celestial' would 'make the native work for the first time in his life'. If the Chinese presence failed to inspire the recalcitrant Africans who continued to withhold their labour, it would at any rate frighten them, by the brutal logic of competition, into coming back to the mineshafts on the mineowners' terms.

No time was lost. The Conservative government in London worked in tandem with the colonial authorities and the mineowners to engineer an experiment in Chinese contract labour far larger than all the previous experiments put together. This time labour was going to be gathered not just from the European enclaves on the China coast but from the depths of the Chinese interior. China was divided into three great catchment areas, north, centre and south. Local European trading firms and their Chinese sub-contractors scoured the countryside for recruits and emerged, in the end, with a grand total of 63,695.

Unlike the ordinary coolies of the day, who were slight, frail men from south China, most of these recruits were big peasants from the northern provinces of Shandong, Hebei and Henan. Some had worked in the north China coalmines. Some had helped to build a railway through Manchuria for the benefit of the Tsar and consequently, and unhelpfully, spoke Russian. Few knew what to expect on the Rand, and many must have nursed wild hopes: 'gold digging in Africa' became proverbial in the northern country districts. For two and a half years, from May 1904 to November 1906, they were herded to the main Chinese ports, where Transvaal emigration agents waited to inspect them and supervise their embarkation. After a four-week voyage on steamers 'fumigated by the Clayton process', they were landed at Durban, mustered briefly at Jacob's Camp – the world's first concentration camp, where the British had corralled their Boer prisoners during the war – packed into railway cars and swept onward, in their billowing trousers and pigtails, to Johannesburg and the mines.

The colonists had decided, by this time, that Chinese and Africans could not be regarded as absolutely the same. Africans were conquered tribesmen, who counted for nothing, but the 'pigtails' at least had a country of their own. It was, to be sure, a laughable country, a corrupt and disintegrating empire at the mercy of the European powers. But it was a country and it had a government, whose permission the colonists had to ask before they went hunting in its territory for people to work in their mines. To win a free hand for the Transvaal authorities to recruit large numbers of miners, Britain had been obliged to negotiate an Anglo-Chinese Labour Convention with the Manchu empire. This treaty guaranteed the coolies certain theoretical rights. They were to be issued with detailed contracts spelling out their destination, transport arrangements and conditions of work. They were to be entitled to legal redress if their persons or property were harmed, and a consul, the first Chinese consul in Africa, was to be sent to Johannesburg to look after their welfare. In addition the coolies were promised a variety of minor creature comforts. They were to get time off on the major Chinese holidays, and Chinese theatre troupes were to be brought out with them to keep them entertained. Overseers on the Rand reported with pride on the steps their companies had taken to make the newcomers feel at home. The

Chinese, they noted, would have 'quite good' living quarters, 'ample' hospital accommodation, 'excellent' food, including daily rations of meat, rice, vegetables and tea, and at one mine a kitchen where 'they can prepare any special article of diet which they may fancy'. Showers and lavatories, to the general amazement, were installed for the first time. It had never occurred to anyone that the African miners might have welcomed such things.

Any benefits that these measures appeared to offer were counteracted, however, by sheer European dread. White farmers, traders and artisans were terrified that the wily Orientals would take root in their territory, buy their land, capture their businesses and jobs. To calm such anxieties the mineowners had written into the contracts fifty-five kinds of skilled labour in which the miners were forbidden to engage, and had stipulated that when the contracts expired every last miner would be sent home. It still did not reassure Sir William Butler: 'Johannesburg must in the near future become practically a Chinese town – a town in which Chinese will be the most important language.'

The upshot was that the incoming Chinese were subjected to a regime of ferocious segregation. Escorted by mounted police, they were marched straight from the railway sidings at Johannesburg into the harshest quarantine. To forestall the possibility that they might slip into the cities and compete for jobs with Europeans, they were penned for the duration of their three-year contracts in compounds ringed with sentries, corrugated iron and wire fencing. Miners who grew restive in these claustrophobic surroundings were promptly and savagely disciplined. They were flogged with the *sjambok*, the rhinoceros-hide whip of South Africa, and had their heads stuck in the Chinese pillory, the *cangue*. Local courts mostly ignored their complaints: the main concern of their consul, Liu Yulin, was to help the Europeans keep order. Some of the miners died from their floggings, and in one year fourteen were hanged.

Predictably the coolies struck back. They had not come to Africa to be treated like convicts. Even the lowliest 'pigtails' were filled with dignity and an inner toughness by the sense that they were Chinese, heirs to an ancient civilization, infinitely superior, because they were Chinese, to the burliest European overseer. The European way with colonial labour was not good enough. By the middle of 1905 bands of several hundred Chinese were breaking out of their compounds and roaming round the *veld*, launching raids on the homesteads of isolated Boer farmers at Klipfontein, Hekpoort, Brakpan. Most of the fugitives were simply frightened and famished men struggling to keep alive in an utterly strange environment. They lurked out of sight of the roads, killed calves in the open fields, broke into houses and lashed out when they were caught. But there were also one or two acts of what we should now call terrorism which it seems impossible to explain except as the product of an overwhelming sense of grievance and frustration. Some miners dynamited a store at Boksburg. Others descended on the railway line at Driefontein and copied a technique which the Boers had invented in their war with the British: they unfastened the iron fish-plates used to join the rails together and strewed them on the line to derail passing trains.

The result was, improbably, that the presence of Chinese in Africa became a major issue in a British general election. Word had begun to spread to Britain of miners subjected to unspeakable atrocities in conditions close to slavery. Prominent members of the Liberal Party like Lloyd George and Sir Charles Dilke had for some time been expressing their misgivings over the fate of the Chinese miners, and now, in January 1906, they made the Rand experiment, presided over by a Conservative administration, a central theme of their election campaign. The campaign resounded to the cry 'Pigtail!' The streets were filled with posters of Chinese being maltreated and with sandwich-men dressed up as Chinese slaves. The public were incensed, not so much by humanitarian feelings as by a vague notion that the government had permitted an important British territory to be submerged in a Chinese flood. A Conservative MP lamented that the 'awful tide of abuse, misrepresentation and falsehood' had cost his party sixty to seventy seats in the 200-seat Liberal landslide which followed, and modern historians reckon that Chinese labour did as much as any single issue to propel into power the great reforming government of Campbell-Bannerman, Asquith and Lloyd George.

In the Transvaal itself the Boer leader, General Botha, deplored the existence of a 'state of unrest in the countryside such as has not been known within the memory of man'. The Boers had never shared the British enthusiasm for Chinese labour, and they were, at the same time, worried by the persistence of 'native troubles'. The Zulus who inhabited the neighbouring colony of Natal had been lords of their own proud kingdom till a generation before, and they were by no means reconciled to European rule. In May 1906 a Boer deputation called on the British governor-general. One of their spokesmen voiced the most visceral terror of all:

CHINESE LABOUR.

C.-B.—*(Radical Delegate visiting Transvaal).* "My poor man, I suppose those dreadful Chinamen have taken away all your work?"

British Workman.—"Don't you make any mistake, guv'nor. For every ten coolies there's a white man gettin' £1 a day to boss 'em. What I say is—*LET 'EM ALL COME!*"

Conservative cartoon of April 1905. The Macmillan-like figure is Sir Henry Campbell-Bannerman, then leader of the Liberal opposition. The Conservatives are rebutting the opposition claim that the arrival of Chinese labourers in South Africa would threaten the livelihood of the British settlers there.

51

They did not know what the end of the Natal native troubles might be, but *he feared a general rising*. In such a case he did not fear that the Indian coolies would ally themselves to the Kaffirs, *but he feared that numerous Chinese labourers would join the natives.*

Actually there was little sign of such an alliance. The tormented Chinese rampaged on their own account, and their frenzy was vented without distinction on anyone, European or African, who crossed their path. As for the Africans, they seem to have been almost as unsettled by the Chinese influx as the Europeans themselves. Chinese were being brought to the mines to frighten them into working, and frightened they were. The Chinese had scarcely begun to arrive before an increase was reported, first 'appreciable', then 'gratifying', in the numbers of African miners re-engaging for further service. African anxiety was not confined to the mines. South-west of the Transvaal, in the Cape Colony, the franchise at this time was based on property, and some relatively prosperous Africans consequently had a vote in the local parliamentary elections. A poll was imminent at the precise time, 1903–4, that the Transvaal authorities were enacting the legislation necessary to bring Chinese miners to the Rand, and the views of Cape Africans on the 'pigtail question' were a focus of much attention. The governor of the colony, Sir Walter Hely-Hutchinson, wrote how 'the native vote will turn the election, and the natives see, or think they see, that Chinese immigration will reduce the rate of their wages throughout the country'. These Africans apparently shared the white settlers' dread of a Chinese deluge. They were said to be afraid that the ultimate purpose of bringing the Chinese in was to drive them out of the land. In the end the Progressive Party won the election by publishing a draft bill designed to prohibit the immigration of Chinese from the Transvaal into the Cape.

Day to day, on the Rand, there was little fraternization. Clergymen in Britain had cried out in horror that the Chinese and African miners could not be mixed. If Chinese were more industrious, Africans were morally purer, and the corrupt Celestials could not be permitted to infect the native workers with their addictions to gambling, opium smoking and 'Oriental' vice. The mineowners had their own reasons for keeping the two groups separate, since African labour was paid a lower wage. The result was a rough and ready segregation of the workforce, Africans employed on the surface of the pits and Chinese underground. When the contingents did meet there was sometimes friction. A fight which broke out on one of the mines began with some Africans 'pulling a coolie's queue while bathing with him in a dam below the compound'. Africans on the Rand do not seem to have felt any instinctive sympathy for the newcomers, and sometimes they actually took the European side. When the first Chinese rioted, their African co-workers tried to help the white overseers, and at the New Primrose mine in August 1905 Zulu police armed with knobkerries dutifully held back a crowd of Celestials watching a fire.

There was, none the less, one form of collusion which the colonists had never in their wildest nightmares foreseen. Miscegenation, at least, they were sure could not happen. 'The national customs of Kaffir and Celestial alike are absolutely fatal to any such union; and nothing in the past history of either of them renders it possible that those consequences could ensue even on the smallest scale.' In effect they imprisoned 60,000 young male Chinese for three years, and expected nothing to happen on the rare occasions when they allowed them out. Great was their horror to observe, mere weeks after the first Chinese were landed at Durban, that friendships between Chinese men and African women had already sprung up. 'You may see them walking about together in the villages on the Rand.' There was a squawk of panic in the newspapers, dire prophecies of a 'new racial amalgam' which 'would at no distant date drive the white man from the Continent'. 'Are we prepared to surrender this land, which should be the inheritance of our own children, to a swarming posterity of this description?'

European fears in the end put paid to the great experiment. By late 1906 the new Liberal government in Britain had granted autonomy to the Transvaal, reversing, for practical purposes, the result of the Boer War. The Boers had promptly formed an administration, the first step in their recapture of political power in South Africa. The Boers, always anti-Chinese, wanted the coolies out. They were supported by the Liberal government for humanitarian reasons, and their case was made stronger by the economic facts. The Chinese had done what they were brought for. Output at the mines had been revived and expanded, and the Rand had been restored to its original position as the world's leading gold producer. African labour was streaming back for a reduced rate of pay. Recruitment in China was accordingly stopped, and in February 1910 the last of the Chinese departed. They left no lasting memory except, apparently, on the work-site itself. African miners in the 1940s were unwilling to go near the old mineshafts on the Rand. They were haunted, it was said, by the ghosts of the long-gone Celestials.

So far as the Rand was concerned the worst colonial terrors had proved, in the end, to be groundless. European rule had not been threatened by an alliance of truculent coolies and disgruntled tribesmen. In the Congo, twenty years later, there were signs that such an apocalyptic menace might possibly take shape. The French were endeavouring to build a railway through their territory on the north bank of the Congo River, from the colonial capital of Brazzaville to Pointe Noire on the Atlantic coast – a route roughly parallel to that of the old Belgian line on the southern side. As usual the local peasants were reluctant to take part in the proceedings. Some had to be dragged to the project by a rope about their necks. Many armed themselves and fled their villages rather than be carried to the rain-soaked construction sites where pneumonia, dysentery and sheer hunger were rumoured to be notching up 'a death for every sleeper'. The recruiters tried forcing in hunters and farmers from the northern plains of Chad, but these soon succumbed to lethal depression in an unfamiliar landscape of mountains, decaying humus and impenetrable trees. So there was nothing for it but the old remedy. In 1929 the French signed up 786 Chinese from the streets and gambling dens of Canton and Hong Kong. The bottom of the barrel, they reported disconsolately: croupiers, barbers, old soldiers and even intellectuals. As usual the Chinese proved unwilling to jump to European orders. The authorities had to placate them by laying on unprecedented amenities – beds and mosquito nets, motion pictures, bean paste and prawns. Even then they wouldn't work, but resisted the overseers with sabotage and 'insolent inertia'. They showed, it must be noted, no great love for the Africans whose lot they were fated to share: their first act on disembarking from the steamer at Pointe Noire had been to ransack the town and thrash the black gendarmes. The difference, this time, was that the African workers started picking up ideas. The French observed with dismay that the labourers collected from Chad and Oubangui-Chari 'were all the more surprised that we bore everything without reacting, and *they began to imitate the Chinese*: there was a rash of strikes and disobedience to the training personnel'. These Africans showed signs of learning from the Chinese that head-on opposition to the European masters was as effective as hiding or flight. The French got nervous. They doubled the police, issued cartridges to the sentries and repatriated 190 Chinese ringleaders. Perhaps after all the unruly Celestials were more trouble than they were worth. Other Westerners had already come to the conclusion that Chinese labourers in Central Africa 'would indubitably introduce an element hostile to the development of a sound and stable African civilization'.

European mastery of the fringes of China and Africa and the shipping lanes between them made possible another kind of more spontaneous mingling. Traders as well as labourers were attracted out of China by the chance of making a living in the European settlements overseas. The French, as we have seen, foolishly tried in 1760 to force a contingent of these traders to work as plantation labourers in their new island colony of Mauritius. Chinese traders were not going to work for the Europeans: they were men of a better quality than that. Their idea was not to serve the colonial system, but to make it serve them.

By the mid-1780s several thousands of Chinese craftsmen and merchants were coming to Mauritius of their own free will. Mauritius was fast becoming one of the main revictualling stations between Europe and the East, and there were good prospects for men prepared to work as cobblers and blacksmiths, tailors and carpenters. A small Chinatown, the 'Camp des Chinois', began to take shape in the island's capital, Port Louis. Its members were not exalted, but they had from the outset a definite idea of their position in society. They avoided mixing with the slaves from Mozambique and Madagascar and sought the company of the whites.

Europeans on the island regarded these immigrants with some approval. Unlike the turbulent labourers they were industrious, inoffensive and socially useful, and the policy for many years was to encourage them to move in. The French shipped them unobtrusively out of Canton, and the British who took over Mauritius in the early nineteenth century augmented their numbers still further. The results were spectacular. By the mid-1840s Chinese traders dominated the Port Louis market. By the 1860s they had spilled into the countryside, and an English visitor was reporting that 'in every out-of-the-way nook and corner of the island' you found 'a Chinaman's shop'. Some of the white settlers began to call for a curb on the Chinese influx, but Mauritius was blessed with a series of humane and thoughtful governors, and one, Sir John Pope-Hennessy, sprang to the traders' defence in a speech delivered in 1886 to the colonial assembly. At a period whose records reveal so much that is ugly and narrow in European attitudes to other peoples, it is refreshing to discover in his remarks a nobility worthy of the best of the Romans:

55

Go into the little shops of the Chinese in this town, and what do you see? At the end of the shop you will see in the evening – you will notice it in the evening, but it is there all day – a little lighted lamp. That is a lamp before their altar. They have their own forms of religion. It is not for us to stigmatize their religion because we ourselves may believe that we have a purer form of faith. . . .

We all know that at almost all the cross-roads of the island are to be seen the well-built stone residences and shops of the Chinese that have sprung up within the last few years; and those Chinamen undoubtedly manage to sell to the poorer classes of this community cheap and simple goods which the poor people wish to buy. . . .

They are a class that assists in distributing the food which the population requires.

For these reasons I could not vote for any motion which would have the semblance of supporting a policy of restriction or of inflicting any disabilities on the Chinese.

By the late nineteenth century, however, it was becoming clear that some of the traders would have to move on. The Mauritius market was saturated: there were too many Chinese, and the community leaders were anxious to encourage onward migration. At the same time word began spreading that the African mainland was opening up. Europeans were shipping in Celestial labourers to help develop their new colonies, giving the traders a chance to hover round the work-sites and sell their compatriots Chinese goods. And South Africa had struck gold. One small but constant incentive to moving, finally, was the lure of the sea-cucumber, trepang or *bêche-de-mer*. Less respectfully known as the sea-slug, this grey–black, quivering, carbuncled creature, somewhat revolting to Westerners, is none the less an essential dish at the best Chinese banquets – and the western Indian Ocean had an abundance of sea-slugs which poor Chinese emigrants could harvest and export home. The first Chinese settler on Madagascar is said to have got there rather in the way the first Vikings reached America, blown by a chance storm while gathering sea-slugs off Mauritius; and gradually the promise of new fishing grounds drew adventurous newcomers on from one desolate atoll to another, till about the turn of the century they reached the East African coast and began advancing northward by way of Zanzibar.

Little by little hardy Chinese traders pressed forward into the southeast quarter of Africa, taking advantage of the great colonial steamship services like Messageries Maritimes and the Union Castle Line. Often they arrived in the newly conquered African territories hot on the heels of the Europeans themselves. British colonists had been installed in Rhodesia no more than a decade when the first seventeen Chinese pioneers trekked across the frontier, six weeks' journey on foot and in ox-wagons from the coast of Mozambique. More substantial groups took root in South Africa and Madagascar, where their descendants still live today in communities approximately 10,000 strong.

In one or two places the traders continued to encounter the kind of tolerant welcome that had awaited them in Mauritius. In May 1898 the administrators of the 'Congo Free State' set up by King Leopold II of the Belgians concluded an agreement with the Manchu court stipulating that Chinese should have the right to settle in the Congo, buy fixed and moveable assets, practise their professions and change their jobs. In spite of its dignified name the 'Congo Free State' was a colony like any other; but modern China has been sufficiently impressed by the liberal terms of this protocol to endorse it as the first formal Sino-African treaty.

More often the reception was harsh. In territories like South Africa and Rhodesia the Chinese found themselves regarded as unsavoury interlopers. Celestial immigrants were forbidden to own land or property or to compete in business with Europeans, and were channelled into the lowly occupations of laundrymen or cooks. The restrictions irked them. Sometimes they managed to devise ways of beating the system. Amenable Europeans could now and again be persuaded to go 'out in front' as the nominal heads of enterprises which were in fact Chinese-controlled. Two Chinese families based in the Rhodesian town of Bulawayo contrived in this manner in the 1940s to run a cattle ranch, a maize mill and a 'Sun Yat-sen Gold Mine' which survives to the present day.

At other times the traders fought back with typical Chinese fire. In 1907 the Boer authorities in the Transvaal set out to curb their activities through an Asiatic Registration Act, which provided that the colony's Indian and Chinese shopkeepers should be subjected to finger-printing as though they were criminals. The head of the local Chinese community, a man called Leung Quinn, responded by forging an alliance with the larger body of Indian immigrants which was organizing itself to resist the measure under the leadership of a young lawyer named Mohandas K. Gandhi. For four years Leung Quinn played a vigorous part in Gandhi's campaign of defiance. He peddled cheap goods illegally in the streets of Johannesburg, led his fellow-Chinese in the burning of trading licences and registration certificates, fought every legal skirmish open to him and got, for his pains, four successive prison sentences which eventually broke his health. It was a gallant protest against an early form of *apartheid*. There is not, however, the least sign that these Chinese traders felt any sense of unity with the subjugated African tribesmen who were destined to bear the brunt of the future *apartheid* policies. Their objective was just the same as it had been in the early days on Mauritius: to climb up the ladder of colonial society till they reached the European level. Leung Quinn's position was proud. China, he maintained, was an independent country in alliance with Britain, and Chinese in British territory should consequently be entitled to the same privileges as those enjoyed by any British citizen in the Manchu empire. He rejected legislation which reduced Chinese 'to a level lower than that of the natives of South Africa and other coloured people'.

Grand though their social ambitions might be, however, the traders soon realized that they had to mix with the African subject peoples. In Mauritius, for example, Africans were their obvious customers. The abolition of slavery had created there in the 1830s a new class of African freedmen living from hand to mouth as fishermen and market gardeners. European merchants were not interested in such impoverished clients, and only a handful of Indians had so far set up shop. Chinese petty traders filled the gap in the market. For decades they supplied the struggling freedmen with the inexpensive goods they needed: rice, groceries, matches and cloth. The poor people whom Pope-Hennessy praised the Chinese for looking after were 'Creoles' – descendants of African slaves.

In the harsher colonies to which the traders advanced from Mauritius, Africans were not only their customers but their only possible neighbours. Chinese and Africans were thrown together by European contempt. 'Have you never realized', Cecil Rhodes's voice booms down the decades, 'that you might have been a Chinaman or a Hottentot or that most degraded of men, a Mashona? But you are not, you are an Englishman and have thus drawn the greatest prize in the lottery of life. . . .' Shunned by the white settlers, the Chinese had no choice but to concentrate on meeting African needs, and they did so with intelligence and vigour. They ran tea shops and food shops for Africans in the segregated black townships, carried salt and sugar, canned foods and woollen jumpers to the bush villages and the tribal reservations. Europeans were astounded by the readiness of Chinese traders to muck in. 'A Chinese', marvelled a white Rhodesian settler in 1924, 'will go and live for a few days at a native kraal and drink beer with the natives to bring off a deal. *We* can't do this.' In the remotest hamlets of eastern Madagascar, where Europeans never went, barefoot Chinese toured among their clients, slept under the stars or in Malagasy huts. 'Remarkable', wrote the French, 'is their business sense and their adaptation to the native mentality. Inexhaustible is their patience. . . .' Chinese traders introduced the peasants of Madagascar to the concepts of money and credit. It was Chinese money-lenders who, in the absence of social security, provided the peasants with funds in emergencies and in the long months before harvest-time. When the vanilla and coffee were harvested the Chinese stepped in as middlemen, buying up the crops for resale in the towns. The Chinese grocer was so universal that household shopping became known in Madagascar as *'aller chez les Chinois'*.

In South Africa Chinese immigrants even laid on a form of public entertainment. Cross-examined by the police in 1937, Chief Agent Kwang of the Cantonese Club of Johannesburg gave details of the lottery games which Chinese syndicates up and down the country had organized for the African population. Most Africans on the Rand, women and children especially, gambled on *fah-fee*, a form of roulette, while *pa-ka-pu*, a bingo-like game based on Chinese characters instead of numbers, had hundreds of African adherents in Johannesburg and others scattered as far afield as the Cape Province and Natal. Five hundred to a thousand African runners collected the bets for the ninety-eight Chinese syndicate offices, and guards were provided to see the winners safely home. Roused to their usual concern for African moral purity, the authorities disapproved. Such pastimes would 'contaminate' the natives, who were 'not gamblers'.

In several colonies, finally, the traders displayed a willingness to mix with the subject people in a more fundamental way. They lived with the native women, and had children by them. Chinese are sometimes said to be exclusive in their attitudes, indisposed to marry or form relationships with people of different origins. Sir Arthur Gordon, another of the enlightened British governors who served in Mauritius in the last decades of the nineteenth century, had a very different impression:

The Chinese, who are thorough citizens of the world, have no such prejudices of race [as the Indians], no such eager desire (for the most part) to return to the homes they have abandoned: they rapidly assume the manners, dress and (in name at least) the religion of the country they inhabit; and a reference to my dispatches from Trinidad in 1867 or 1868

59

will show how frequently they intermarried with Creole women in that colony.

Here . . . the same rule holds good, that *the connections of Creole women with Chinese are more numerous than those with the Indians.*

Up till the early decades of the twentieth century, Chinese emigrants generally travelled without their women. Most Chinese women were physically crippled by the practice of foot-binding, and the custom in any case was to leave the women behind to look after their parents-in-law. So the traders needed partners, and they found, in Mauritius, readily available partners in the local Creole girls of African descent. It was partly a business investment. Creole girls spoke French and English. They could teach the traders the local languages, smooth their way into society and help them to win the beginnings of a clientèle.

Strictly speaking the relationship usually amounted to cohabitation rather than marriage. But it was often more real, as an expression of human affection, than the formal marriage with the Chinese wife at home. Traders in Madagascar, where such partnerships were widespread, sometimes asked the French colonial authorities for permission to formalize a long-standing tie. The partnership could endure till death, or even beyond it: Chan Sion Weng and Marie Ramizavelo, to select a random couple, lie together in the cemetery in the Malagasy port of Tamatave. The phenomenon was especially marked in Madagascar, and it is possible that the Malagasy people, with their admixture of Malay or Indonesian blood, had a particular attraction for the Celestial immigrants. But relationships were formed on the African mainland too. When the Belgian Congo became independent in 1960, the new state's first president, Joseph Kasavubu, a pale-skinned, slant-eyed, calculating man, was generally believed to be descended from the union of a Chinese trader with a local woman of the Bakongo tribe.

Unlike the Indian Moslems who migrated to Africa at this period, Chinese were prepared to accept the children of such unions as part of their families. The only condition they sometimes imposed was that the children should be sent back home to be immersed in China's language and customs. The criterion for acceptance, in other words, was a cultural and not a racial one. Skin colour itself was not a barrier, though it was felt to lend some urgency to the task of sinicization. In the small Chinese community which grew up in Southern Rhodesia particular trouble was taken to sinicize the darker-skinned children who looked least Chinese. The curious consequence has been that some African-looking people in today's Zimbabwe speak Chinese fluently, while others who look entirely Chinese speak almost none.

Africans looked on these efforts to cultivate their society with somewhat ambivalent feelings. From an African point of view the Celestial traders were employers, and sometimes competitors. In 1932 a villager called Tangi, from Machui in Tanganyika, petitioned the British colonial government for a concession to catch sea-slugs. Africans already dived for sea-slugs in the service of Chinese firms: why should they not go into business on their own account? The government said no, this was a Chinese speciality and Tangi would have to be content with a sub-contract. Envy was accompanied by bafflement, and occasional fear. There were whispers in South Africa that the Chinese ate people.

For all that it did not go entirely unnoticed or unappreciated in Africa that the Chinese, unlike the European settlers, were willing to mix. Peasants in Madagascar paid tribute to the traders' politeness, to their lack of ostentation and to their readiness to perform small services for their neighbours. No doubt the Chinese swindled them, but they swindled them affably. In 1947, when the Malagasies rose in a brief but bloody revolt against their French colonial masters, the traders got their reward. The rebels largely refrained from molesting them, and even rescued one or two of them from vindictive French troops. In South Africa the relations between the traders and their customers were never as intimate; but even in South Africa the Chinese succeeded in making a certain mark. Philanthropists in Johannesburg discovered in the 1950s that the undernourished Africans of the city were prepared to accept hand-outs organized from Chinese food shops which they would not take directly from Europeans.

By the turn of the nineteenth and twentieth centuries the Europeans had reached the farthest limit of their global advance. They controlled not only the edge of the Indian Ocean, but most of the hinterland. India had fallen to Britain, and Indochina to France. The Dutch ruled the East Indies. In the far west of the ocean Africa was being divided among the conquering European empires. China, to the east, was being informally cordoned off into European spheres of influence, and there too it seemed possible that a full-scale partition might soon be organized. But in lunging for empire, the Europeans went too far. The underdog peoples began to fear for their very identity. At the height of European triumph, the first coherent voices of protest began to be heard.

Chinese resentment was mounting on two separate counts. Many Chinese were incensed by the steady European erosion of their country's sovereignty. At the same time they were turning against the alien and discredited Manchu dynasty which had ruled them since the seventeenth century, and whose weakness had been largely responsible for letting the Europeans in. These sentiments found an outlet in such dramatic outbreaks of violence as the anti-European rising by the League of Harmonious Fists (the 'Boxers'), which convulsed north China in 1900. Significantly, however, they were first given a coherent shape and purpose not in China proper but in the Western colonies outside China where Chinese traders had taken root. It was here that the Chinese were exposed most directly to European arrogance, and here too that they picked up from Europe, and turned against it, its own heady doctrine of nationalism. The Chinese nationalist leader Sun Yat-sen (1866–1925) spent several of his early years in the British and Portuguese entrepots of Hong Kong and Macao. Subsequently he travelled throughout the world whipping up anti-Manchu feeling among the various Chinese trading communities. Funds and support for his cause poured in from the large communities of Chinese emigrants in South-east Asia and the United States – and also from the little enclaves in the south-east corner of Africa. In 1896 a collaborator of Sun's visited the Celestial traders in South Africa and the western Indian Ocean on a tour intended to foster the creation of revolutionary cells.

By the following decade Chinese national consciousness was growing fast. In 1904–5 Tsarist Russia was unexpectedly and totally defeated in war by Japan. The secret was out that the whites were not invincible, and the news galvanized Chinese all over the world. Even in Africa the whites became less cocksure. In 1906, as the pigtailed Chinese miners rampaged around the Rand, a European speaker pointed out apprehensively to a public meeting in Cape Town how Japan's success had aroused in China a new feeling of 'China for the Chinese'. He hoped it would not become 'South Africa for the Chinese'. Five years later, in 1911 'China for the Chinese' began to become a reality. The Manchu dynasty was overthrown by a revolution and replaced by a home-grown republic. The most articulate political force which emerged to compete for power in the new republic was Sun's Chinese Nationalist Party. The Nationalist Party aimed to annul the 'unequal treaties' which the Europeans had imposed on the enfeebled Manchu court, and it was hostile to the principle of European colonial rule anywhere in the world. Some of its most enthusiastic backing came, once again, from the overseas diaspora – and once again that included Chinese trading communities in far-flung parts of the globe. By 1921 the Nationalist Party had a branch on Madagascar, and by 1930 it was sending cabled directives to the Madagascar Chinese. French officials in the colony suspected that this activity was directed against them. They observed with disquiet how the ordinary Chinese trader had 'acquired more assurance, more confidence in himself'.

Chinese unrest was sharpened, as this awakening gathered momentum, by a growing awareness of the plight of other peoples whom the Europeans had subdued. By mingling their subject peoples together in the colonial entrepots, the European powers had given them the opportunity to make some dangerous comparisons. Some Chinese intellectuals were conscious, for example, of the presence in Macao of black domestics brought there from Portuguese Mozambique. Others had actually passed through the colonial outposts in Africa on journeys to and from Europe, and had glimpsed at first hand the process of European expansion on the continent. They were roused to agitation by a sense of the imminent danger which the European conquest of Africa portended for their own country. The reformer Liang Qichao (1873–1929) deduced that this was the prospect which awaited a people who failed to modernize. 'The area of Africa', he observed, 'is four times that of Europe, and its interior, apart from a belt of desert, is rich in plants and domestic animals. But because the native people have been unable to develop, they have had to give way meekly to more powerful enemies.' Sun Yat-sen pointed with dismay to the carve-up of Africa agreed on by the European powers at Berlin in 1884–5. Here, he declared, was evidence of the demented Western appetite for acquiring new land. For Chinese intellectuals the fate of Africa was a cautionary tale.

A similar awakening was taking place in these years among people of African stock. Once more the need for change was glimpsed most clearly from the outside. Africa was a patchwork, politically fragmented and ethnically diverse, and few people on the continent had any sense of a common identity. In the New World, however, the black diaspora created by centuries of slaving was beginning to produce a nucleus of intellectuals who looked on Africa as their ancestral and rightful home. One man in particular led the way. Dr William Edward Burghardt DuBois (1868–1963) was born in Massachusetts five years after Abraham Lincoln proclaimed the abolition of slavery in the United States. Of racially mixed, middle-class parentage, he enjoyed a relatively comfortable upbringing. He was educated at Harvard, and later occupied a professorial chair at Atlanta University in Georgia. Appalled, however, by the continued wretchedness of the black condition in the American South, he spent the bulk of a prodigious lifespan studying, writing and campaigning in an effort to rouse in Africans both inside and outside their continent a sense of collective purpose. DuBois was the dominant spirit at a 'Pan-African Conference' which was held in London, barely noticed, in the final year of Queen Victoria's reign. In 1919 a more ambitious gathering, remembered today as the first Pan-African Congress, was organized in Paris. DuBois came down to Versailles at the head of a party of African and New World Negro leaders to present the startled Western statesmen busy settling the First World War with a list of ways in which they might consider improving the lot of their colonial subjects. This congress was followed over the next quarter-century by a series of other meetings in European and American cities. Delegates from the African colonies gradually became more conspicuous than their black American and West Indian counterparts; names like Nkrumah and Kenyatta began to be heard; but always DuBois was the patriarch.

DuBois, like the Chinese reformers, meditated on the hardships of other peoples besides his own who had been subjected to the rule of the Europeans. But whereas the Chinese had taken an interest in the fate of other peoples chiefly insofar as it seemed to hold a useful lesson for themselves, DuBois looked round the world with a sweeping compassion. European tyranny, in his view, was a shared misfortune which bound all of its victims together. 'In Africa', he wrote in 1935, surveying the world's sorrows, 'a black back runs red with the blood of the lash; in India a brown girl is raped; in China, a coolie starves; in Alabama seven darkies are more than lynched; while in London the white limbs of a prostitute are hung with jewels and silk.' 'Your nearest friends and neighbours', he told his African listeners, 'are the coloured peoples of China and India, the rest of Asia, the Middle East and the Sea Isles. ... Your bond is not mere colour of skin, but the deeper experience of wage slavery and contempt.'

Other prophets of the African awakening voiced the same all-embracing sympathy for the non-white peoples of the world. One was the Jamaican Marcus Aurelius Garvey (1887–1940), who, like DuBois, influenced the thinking of many English-speaking West Africans. Garvey was the founder of the 'Back to Africa' movement for resettling the New

World diaspora in Liberia, Africa's solitary independent republic which freed slaves from the United States had founded in 1847. A harsher figure than DuBois, he countered the white racialism of his day with an equally rigid insistence on black racial purity; but he too advocated a 'unity of the darker peoples' which included the Chinese. China was part of a fellowship of humiliation.

Different though their viewpoints were, Chinese and African leaders were beginning to be drawn together by a common anxiety to preserve their independence from complete annihilation at the hands of foreign powers. Not counting Liberia, Africa still had one independent state. In 1896 the Emperor Menelik II, ruler of Ethiopia, or Abyssinia as it was generally called at the time, had unexpectedly stemmed the tide of European conquest by defeating an invading Italian army at the battle of Adowa. Menelik seems to have been intrigued by the venerable Asian empire which continued, like his own, to maintain its freedom precariously in the teeth of the European advance. He is said to have asked one traveller, 'What progress does industrial development make in China? Do they make guns?' By the 1920s many Ethiopians had reached Liang Qichao's conclusion that modernization was the key to survival. Negadras Gabré-Hiwot Baykedagn, a statesman allied to Menelik's successor Haile Selassie, pressed for modern education and warned that other ancient countries such as China were introducing the reforms necessary to preserve their independence far faster than Ethiopia was.

Actually China was in a scarcely better predicament. After years of turmoil and sporadic civil war the Nationalist Party had finally, in 1926–7, fought its way to control of the greater part of the country under the leadership of Sun Yat-sen's successor, Chiang Kai-shek. But its resistance to foreign domination was only half-hearted. The Nationalists made some attempt to overturn the 'unequal treaties' with the European powers, but did not try to any noticeable degree to free China from the subtler grip of Western finance and Western culture. And within a few years China under their rule fell victim to another Asian country which was bent on beating the European empires at their own game. In 1931 the armies of imperial Japan poured into the Manchurian provinces of north-east China. Hungry for colonies, Japan was soon beginning, as Churchill put it, to devour China 'like an artichoke, leaf by leaf'. By 1935 the Japanese were preparing the way for further annexations by forcing the Chinese Nationalist government to withdraw its troops and administrators from large parts of the territory around Peking.

At precisely this juncture Ethiopia also faced invasion. Greedy for empire and impatient to avenge the defeat suffered at Adowa forty years before, the Fascist Italy of Mussolini was busy concocting the excuse it needed to plunge its forces into Haile Selassie's domains. It was the final indignity. The last traditional African state, clinging forlornly to its ancient customs, and the new republican China, just beginning to grope for a few shreds of international respect, found themselves menaced simultaneously by military assaults designed to wipe them off the map. Chinese and African spokesmen looked at each other's countries with a quickening sympathy. In May 1935 *World Knowledge*, a left-wing periodical published in Shanghai, pointed out that the Italian designs on Ethiopia and the Japanese designs on China were the same. The difference was that Ethiopia could be expected to put up a fight. 'Although the Abyssinians are pitch-black they are not like China, ready to preserve peace at any price.' Haile Selassie's warriors could fight on regardless of the cruel heat of the desert, and their marches, in spite of all exhaustion, were 'immensely prolonged'. They would be helped, furthermore, by the black community in New York, who were forming an air squadron and had organized a boycott of Italian goods. 'This shows the mutual assistance among black people and the national awakening of the peoples of Africa.'

The prognosis was too optimistic. In October Mussolini's troops went in, and by June 1936, overwhelmed by Italy's air force and fire-power, Ethiopia had gone the way of China's Manchurian provinces. China and Ethiopia, thought George Padmore, had been shamefully let down by the outside world. Padmore was another of the great African prophets. Born in Trinidad, he had seen in the Russian Revolution of 1917 the best hope for bringing a rapid end to colonial rule, and was employed in Moscow in the early 1930s as chairman of the Negro Bureau of the Trades Union International. He had even been co-opted on to a committee set up to investigate a failed uprising launched against China's Nationalist government by Li Lisan, a deposed leader of the youthful Chinese Communist Party. The seasoned black revolutionary had frowned on the thirty-year-old Chinese: 'in my opinion, fundamentally a young romantic adventurer with an addiction to putschism'. Now he contemplated China with a sudden access of goodwill. Not even the Soviet Union had come to Haile Selassie's aid. 'Not one rouble was sent to Abyssinia; not one bandage; not one ton of wheat.' In China, however, 'the anti-imperialist forces were on the side of their black brothers'.

66

A Shanghai cartoon of 1935 satirizes Mussolini's rape of Abyssinia (Ethiopia). The caption reads, 'I Want To Make You Civilized, My Love'.

This growing sense of unity was given vigorous expression by a Chinese writer of the time. The writer was a colleague and rival of the deposed Communist leader Li Lisan. He was a practitioner of guerrilla warfare who had been inspired, some years previously, by the resistance of 'Abd al-Krim al-Kattabi to Spanish rule in Morocco. Recently he had conducted across China a force which shrank from 120,000 to 7,000, strafed by the Nationalist government on a march which was, as *World Knowledge* described the campaigns in Ethiopia, 'immensely prolonged'. Mortal foe of the Nationalist Party, he stood for a far more fundamental challenge than the Nationalists had ever been able to pose to European domination in China and the world. Currently he was preparing to spearhead the resistance of north-west China to the invading Japanese. In a lecture prepared for his followers he examined the significance of Haile Selassie's defeat. It was, without doubt, a setback. Ethiopia had suffered 'extinction', and 'extinction' was the doom which Chinese patriots in the first half of this century most feared for their country. But the writer was undaunted, every sentence filled with the soaring confidence which Europeans had begun to notice in very much humbler Chinese:

> Why was Abyssinia extinguished? First, it was not only a weak country, but also a small country. Second, it was not as advanced as China; it was an ancient country passing from the slave to the serf system, had no capitalism, no bourgeois political parties, much less a Communist Party; had no army like China's, much less an army like the Eighth Route Army.

Ethiopia had had to fight on its own, and its leaders had made mistakes: not a failing to which this writer was prone to confess himself liable. China, he assured his followers, would never be subdued. Even for Ethiopia he had not, in the long run, abandoned hope. 'Quite a large-scale guerrilla war still persists in Abyssinia, and if the Abyssinians can only persevere, they will be able to reoccupy and revive their fatherland in a future fluctuation of world affairs.'

The writer was Mao Zedong.

3

The Chinese as Missionary

Ofeyi began to apologize for the late visit but Ahime
stopped him. 'I was not asleep. At most I sleep four hours
in the night. At my age, sleep becomes less and less
essential.' He laid aside the book he had been reading. 'I
like your Mao,' he commented. 'You can see I have been
reading things to make sure I can meet you on your own
ground. He is unique this Chinese isn't he? A man of
simple truths and a large experimental farm. For the first
time I feel like undertaking a journey to meet a man I have
only encountered on the pages of a book. After all, it is
the time of life to travel . . . .'

Wole Soyinka, *Season of Anomy*, 1973

The portrait of a 'Young Chinese Missionary' – gaunt, inspired,
in a scholar's long gown – is said to have hung for some years
in the Vatican before it was discovered to be a representation
of the youthful Mao Zedong pacing the hills of his native province of
Hunan. The Vatican was mortified, and the portrait was removed. But
perhaps the cardinals had not really blundered. Mao was the prototype
of a new, evangelical variety of Chinese. After twelve years of war,
first against the Japanese invaders and then against the American-backed
Nationalist regime of Chiang Kai-shek, Mao and his Communist Party
finally won control of China in 1949. It was a victory, in their eyes,
not so much for Communism as for China itself. 'The Chinese people
have stood up,' Mao assured his followers: 'from now on no one will
insult us again.' The Chinese Communists exulted in the certainty that
they had put an end to China's century of humiliation at the hands
of foreign powers. In driving foreign influence forcibly from its territory,
China, they maintained, had set an example which other subjugated
nations should and would follow. They were fired by a missionary urge
to spread the news.

If this was the mission, where was the mission field? The obvious answer seemed to be, on China's periphery. All over southern Asia were territories formally ruled, as China had never been, by European colonial governments. During the Second World War the peoples of these territories had seen their European masters reeling under the onslaught of imperial Japan. Japan had been beaten in the end, but the myth of European invincibility had been shattered once and for all. The subject peoples had been willing to help drive out the Japanese invaders, but now that the war was over they wanted their liberty. They were not prepared to tolerate a resumption of indefinite Western control.

Yet Asia was not, in fact, an entirely promising field for Chinese evangelism. In the first place, Mao and his colleagues arrived on the scene a little late in the day. Their gospel was independence. But in the four years that elapsed between the end of the Second World War and the Communist victory in China, several Asian countries had already obtained independence. The British had pulled out of India, Burma and Ceylon, and the Dutch had, more hesitantly, relinquished their claim on Indonesia. So far as these states were concerned the game was already won. Secondly, Asia failed to conform, in certain basic respects, to the thrust of the Chinese message. China insisted on the need for violent insurrection. Some of the peoples in the region had, duly, taken up arms. The Vietnamese fought the French, and the ethnic Chinese of Malaya rose up against the British. In the majority of countries, however, violent insurrection was either thwarted or never took place at all. Instead the colonial powers yielded their authority peacefully to local politicians and princes. China advocated a wholesale purge of Western influence once freedom had been secured. But few of the new Asian governments were disposed to lend an ear to China's anti-Western preaching. Some, in Malaya and the Philippines, were fearful of China and Communism and remained obstinately attached to their former Western masters. Others, in India and Burma, were neutral, cool to the West but pricklyproud and determined to find their own way.

Africa was another matter.

The problems of Africa were far from the minds of the Chinese Communists in the earliest years of their rule. In September 1950 Mao sent a cable to South Africa protesting against the laws with which the new Afrikaner Nationalist government was beginning to build its edifice of racial segregation; but the main point that seems to have struck him was the effect those *apartheid* laws would be likely to have on the lives of South Africa's Chinese traders. As the fifties wore on, however, the

Chinese discovered to their excitement that Africans were following in their path. Africans were not independent, but were agitating for their freedom. Violent resistance – just what the Chinese prescribed – had broken out against the European rulers in several parts of the continent: against Britain in Kenya, against France in Algeria and the West African colony of Cameroon. To the Chinese, Africa seemed to be re-enacting their own recent past. In a memorandum issued in 1961 to the commissars of their army the Chinese leaders drew attention to a whole series of parallels they had noticed:

> At present some parts of Africa are going through experiences similar to those we underwent in China in the Boxer uprising sixty years ago. Some of the events are like those which occurred during the revolution of 1911, while others resemble what happened around the time of the May the Fourth [cultural renaissance of 1919].

It was China's duty, plainly, to encourage the Africans by explaining these similarities to them. In the dark century before 1949, Chinese intellectuals had drawn lessons from the misfortunes of Africa and other colonized parts of the world. Now, confidence returning, the Chinese felt ready to give lessons to others. The Chinese are a didactic people: they have a profound faith in education, and they delight in giving instruction to the uninitiated. Teaching was the essence of their African mission:

> We must tell them, in order to help them, about the experience of the Chinese revolution, pointing out the significance of the Taiping uprising, the Boxer uprising, Dr Sun Yat-sen, and the revolutionary experience of the Communists in this generation.

At the same time the Chinese Communists were missionaries of a strangely passive kind. They did not rush outwards with their gospel like the revolutionaries of earlier years. They were content, like their serene Ming ancestors, to proclaim themselves a model and wait for disciples to arrive for teaching, secure in the conviction that, as one of their leaders put it, 'no country in this world has had more experience than we'. Their urge to teach Africans was kindled by the spontaneous interest that Africans were showing in them.

African attention was focused on Asia, in the aftermath of the Second World War, by the success of Eastern peoples like the Indians and Indonesians in wresting independence from the victorious but fatally weakened Europeans. Africans had noticed China too, but only as one of

71

a number of countries which were downtrodden like theirs. All that was changed by the Communist victory of 1949. Far away on the coast of East Africa thirteen Somali leaders who were busy campaigning for freedom from Italian rule took time off to draft a 'letter to the Chinese people'. China had become overnight an outstanding object of interest. Not because it was Communist, but because it seemed to Africans a case of a non-European country that had broken with the West completely and won independence in the fullest sense. In the early fifties Africans watched this transformed China hold its own for three years against Western military technology when it intervened on the Communist side in the Korean war of 1950–3. The war coincided with the start of a great African rebellion against the British rulers of Kenya. This 'Mau Mau' rebellion took place for reasons wholly unconnected with the conflict in the Far East. It expressed the resentment felt by the Kikuyu farming people of central Kenya against the small population of European settlers who had taken over the territory's most productive land, and its fighters were recruited by the ritual oaths of Kikuyu tradition. Yet one of its leaders thought it appropriate to assume an Asiatic *nom de guerre* – Waruhiu Itote became 'General China'.

There was little chance to learn about China in the colonies themselves. Now and again, in the classroom, young Africans picked up clues from the sour accounts of European schoolteachers. They were intrigued: they asked awkward questions. In Communist countries, their teachers told them, all wives belonged to the state: did that apply to Mao Zedong's wife too? The pupils got their knuckles rapped. Some young people, however, were beginning to go abroad. Most of the European powers were conceding by now that independence must come sooner or later, and making an effort to prepare some of their African subjects for it by giving them the chance of a higher education in the mother country. Once abroad, lively-minded, restless students began getting access to anti-colonial and Marxist publications. They read about the exploits of the Communist Chinese. Some of them travelled further. They procured themselves invitations to the conferences of youth, trade unionists and women which were held under Soviet auspices in neutral and East European countries, and there for the first time they met representatives of that steadfast Soviet ally, the China of Mao Zedong.

Right from the start it is clear that the Chinese were determined to treat these African wanderers better than any Europeans had ever done. Africans were entertained at elaborate parties and invited to travel onwards, expenses paid, to Peking. On they came, in ones and twos and small delegations, to a welcome fit for heroes. They were carried shoulder-high, showered with flowers and confetti and bombarded with the din of traditional rejoicing, gongs and cymbals and fire-crackers. They were led before microphones to voice their demands for freedom to applauding crowds half a million strong. They were borne round in limousines like ministers and seated beside the Chinese leaders at rallies and parades. With startling frequency, they met the leaders. Chinese as a rule are intensely hierarchical. They receive foreign visitors at the exact level the visitors' status is judged to warrant. Age and seniority are all-important, and a veteran Chinese official finds it unbearably demeaning to be thrust into the company of foreigners below his rank. All this went by the board. *Amour-propre* was stifled: protocol was waived. Very humble Africans, unknown young men and women, were received with honour by the greatest personalities in the land. One group from Southern Rhodesia got a special invitation to journey to the northwestern city of Xi'an for a dinner with Mao and his wife. Other visitors found themselves closeted, almost as a matter of course, with Mao, his Prime Minister Zhou Enlai, his Foreign Minister Chen Yi; or all of them.

Understandably it took their breath away. Walter Sisulu of the African National Congress of South Africa, who made the trip as early as 1953, felt that he had been treated, for the first time in his life, as a dignified human being. His colleague Lilian Ngoyi, who came two years later, was 'swept by a rush of feeling that the world was on her side'. The best hotel in Johannesburg, to which she could never have been admitted, seemed to her like a doss-house by comparison with the Peking Hotel. Sometimes euphoria was mixed with a certain awe. The leader of one group of young pilgrims, truants on the run from colonial Uganda, told his hosts shyly,

> This country is proud to be a friend of your people. In representing this country we are afraid of committing the slightest error which would diminish the weight of the message that we have been designated to bring. ... If the expression is inadequate to convey faithfully the sentiments of our people on your side, I would like you to accept at least the sincerity with which we shall try to convey them.

Eager, a little unsure of themselves, these visitors were ideally suited to receive the Chinese teachings.

The increase in contact was prodigious. At the beginning of the fifties no Africans went to China; in the last three years of the decade eighty-four groups of pilgrims made the journey from the Belgian Congo alone. As the European will to empire flagged and Britain and France began to hand over control of their colonies to nationalist politicians, the Chinese were also beginning to meet African rulers for the first time since the fifteenth century. At first Africa's new states were mostly Arab ones to the north of the Sahara; but in 1957 Ghana became the first black African territory to win its independence. The governments of Ghana and the other new sub-Saharan countries were inhibited from dealing with China to begin with by fear of the disapproval of their former European masters who regarded China as a menace. They were encouraged, however, by their own elder statesmen – by DuBois, for instance, the venerable prophet of African liberty, who came from the United States to spend his last years in Ghana breathing free African air. In 1959 the old man celebrated his ninety-first birthday in Peking. In a speech at Peking University he told the new governments of Africa to single China out for special attention and study: 'China is flesh of your flesh and blood of your blood.' By the early sixties a small nucleus of countries had taken the risky step of establishing formal diplomatic relations with Peking. In doing so they gave the Chinese the opportunity of bringing their gospel of independence to African soil.

The gospel was brought by Zhou Enlai in person. Supreme diplomat and manager of his country's foreign policy, the Chinese prime minister stepped into Africa with an entourage of fifty in the last weeks of 1963. Great tracts of the continent were still under European rule. Most of the independent countries had barely emerged from European tutelage, and few of them felt secure enough to defy the Europeans by welcoming an Asian revolutionary leader. Africa was edgy, and Zhou knew it. His movements were exploratory, even improvised. The visit began as a tour of six states which already had ties with China: the Arab northern tier of Egypt, Algeria and Morocco, and a trio of maverick West African countries, Ghana, Guinea and Mali, which the Chinese economically called 'Jiajima', a portmanteau term made up by combining the first syllable of the Chinese version of each of their names. Calls on four other states, Tunisia, the Sudan, Ethiopia and Somalia, were negotiated while the tour was actually in progress: the first three of these lasted just forty-eight hours apiece, and the stop in Ethiopia was so discreetly handled that most of the country's citizens were unaware of it. Journeys to three new East African countries, Kenya, Uganda and Tanganyika (later Tanzania), were arranged, then cancelled when army mutinies

74

broke out in all of them: the Tanzanian visit was made good the following year. It is tempting to think of Zheng He's squadrons, first putting in at the enterprising African ports whose merchants had met them in the East, then nudging their way gently to points further afield.

Zhou's first task was to reassure the governments which received him that they were not setting any shocking precedent by doing so; that China had a perfect right to be in their midst. In characteristic Chinese style he based his case on history, drawing attention to Zheng He and the long record of early Chinese contact with the East African coast. His delegation came, he informed the Tanzanians, to 'renew acquaintance with old friends': they 'did not find themselves in a strange land'. It was, incidentally, a neat way of rousing African pride, paying tribute to the grandeur of past Swahili culture of which few Europeans had even heard. Julius Nyerere, the Tanzanian leader, was happy to concur. China and Africa, he observed, were 'merely resuming a connection which had been broken off'.

It was no part of Zhou's purpose, however, to play down the historic importance of his visits. He stressed it, appropriately, in the Somali capital of Mogadishu, the old Islamic town which had once been Zheng He's principal port of call. 'We feel', he declared, 'that our present visit to Africa is somewhat belated. But after all we have arrived. . . .' With Zhou's coming the Star Raft had recrossed the African horizon.

And Zhou brought not peace, but a sword. He came not simply to soothe timorous governments, but also to fulfil the expectations of the countless individual admirers whom China had accumulated in the past fifteen years. He had a second, more provocative historical argument. China and Africa were brought together, he insisted, by their common experience of oppression at the hands of the colonial Europeans. In the Sudan he hit on a convenient symbol, the Victorian general Charles George Gordon, who had started his career helping to suppress the 'Taiping' rebellion of Chinese peasants against alien Manchu rule, and ended it as the victim of an African uprising, speared by the Mahdi's dervishes in the governor's palace at Khartoum. The Sudanese people, said Zhou, had 'finally punished' General Gordon.

Fortified by history the Chinese prime minister turned to Africa's present condition with a single, reverberating diagnosis: 'Revolutionary prospects are excellent throughout the African continent.' He was making, as he later explained it, two points. Africans in territories not yet independent were fighting for their freedom. Additionally, Africans in indepen-

75

dent countries were working to eliminate residual foreign control. Zhou proceeded to spell out a set of principles which he said would govern China's relations with Africa. China would be the champion of subjugated Africans against European rule and of free African governments against European influence. Zhou was not thrusting China forward. The whole point of his message was that Africans had the right now to take their own initiatives. China would lend a hand, but only if it was asked to. It was up to Africans, if they wanted, to come to China for tangible support. Still, the invitation had been issued. Zhou's coming heralded a season when China would glide to the foreground of African affairs. The West heard his message with foreboding. His diagnosis was popularized in an English version no different in meaning, but significantly more ominous in flavour. 'Africa is ripe for revolution.' A fruit which is ripe, after all, is awaiting a hand to pluck it.

Rebels from white-ruled Africa had already begun to turn to China for help. The first step was to get out of their territories. Providing they could reach the border undetected they were likely to be safe: borders were long, desolate and difficult to police, and the rebels could generally walk across them and make their way to a refuge previously arranged on the other side. Most of the white-ruled territories, by the early 1960s, had independent countries next door, and a number of these independent neighbours were willing to give the fugitives shelter and money. Some of them also housed a Chinese embassy. The Chinese were known to be warm partisans of the cause of African freedom, and one or two of their embassies had staff specially assigned to handle approaches from the independence movements to which the rebels belonged. From 1960 onwards a series of movements presented themselves at Chinese embassy doors. Some wished to put an end to the rule of the European settlers in the southern tip of the continent. There was the African National Congress (ANC) of South Africa, the South-West African People's Organization (SWAPO) from the South African protectorate of South-West Africa or Namibia, and the Zimbabwe African People's Union (ZAPU) founded in Southern Rhodesia by Joshua Nkomo. Other movements appeared from the colonies of Portugal, last and most obstinate of the European empires: the Popular Movement for the Liberation of Angola (MPLA), the Front for the Liberation of Mozambique (FRELIMO), and from a small Portuguese enclave in West Africa the African Party for the Independence of Guiné and Cape Verde (PAIGC). The Chinese supported, in particular, groups which had turned their backs on any negotiation with their European adversaries and were determined to fight. Some of the principal movements were still ambivalent on this score, and angrier factions had broken away from them. They included the Zimbabwe African National Union (ZANU), destined under Robert Mugabe's leadership to become the major rebel force in Rhodesia, and the Pan-Africanist Congress (PAC) of South Africa, which was vociferous but never managed to occupy centre stage. Breakaway factions like these turned to China as their natural patron.

The Chinese responded with many kinds of material assistance. They had arms left over from their wars with the Japanese and Chiang Kaishek, and more arms that they had learnt to produce in the fifties when China was an ally and technical apprentice of the Soviet Union. Boats containing Chinese emissaries and their cargoes of weapons crept down the coast of independent Tanzania to the frontier of Portuguese Mozambique. In Mozambique and other lands of southern Africa guerrillas began to prowl the bush equipped with Chinese mortars and bazookas, machine-guns, assault guns and hand grenades. Sometimes the equipment was not entirely suited to its surroundings – termites in Rhodesia ate away the wooden cases of Chinese anti-vehicle mines – but the efficient Chinese version of the Soviet AK-47 Kalashnikov automatic rifle became a standard guerrilla tool. The Chinese gave funds. Seldom amounting to more than a few thousand pounds at a time, this money could none the less be crucial: the MPLA of Angola, for instance, got donations which sustained them in the vitally important period at the beginning of the sixties when their first blows against Portugal were being prepared. The Chinese gave food and medicines and lorries. Now and again guerrillas fought in Chinese uniform.

Breakaway factions like ZANU and the PAC were kept going for years by Chinese hardware and money. Most movements, however, got no more than a useful trickle of material aid. For China was poor. It lacked hard currency; it needed arms to defend itself. Its main contribution to the cause of African independence was made in a different and more characteristic form. The Chinese were teachers.

China specialized in training batches of Africans in the arts of guerrilla warfare. Every movement at some stage got trained by the Chinese. The numbers trained at a given time were never very large, sometimes only four or five and seldom more than fifty. They included, however,

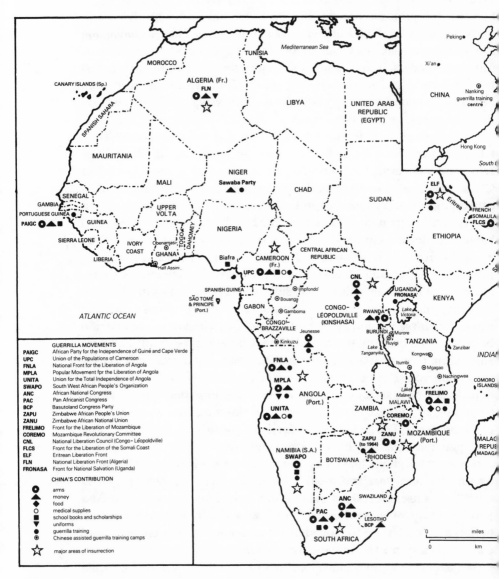

Map 3.   Chinese support for African insurrections since 1949. (Borders are those of Africa in 1968.)

78

the men whom the movements meant to serve as their future field commanders, and sometimes their political leaders as well. Great African
heroes like Samora Machel of FRELIMO and Amilcar Cabral of the PAIGC
had their spell of Chinese schooling. The Chinese were running, in effect,
a kind of teacher-training college, training the elite of each movement
to train the rank and file.

In the beginning this training was administered at a military academy
in the city of Nanking. One guerrilla remembers the academy as 'China's
Sandhurst or Aldershot'. The journey to Nanking was an adventure
in itself. For one young recruit dispatched by ZAPU of Southern Rhodesia
it compensated for the missed excitements of an adolescence spent
behind the walls of colonial detention centres. His team, travelling without passports, were held up in Pakistan: the Chinese embassy came
to the rescue, paid their hotel bills and gave them pocket money, and
even looked on indulgently when they decided to spend that pocket
money on a sightseeing trip to India. The path to Nanking was cloaked
in secrecy. On another occasion two prospective trainees from FRELIMO
and ZANU met by chance on the journey east. Each asked the other
where he was going, and each lied vigorously about it all the way to
Hong Kong, where both of them boarded a China-bound train. They
looked sheepishly at each other across the gangway.

The Nanking Military Academy turned out to be an agreeable institution. Trainees had simple but comfortable rooms, and their beds were
made for them daily. There was English food for English-speaking Africans, and French food for French-speaking ones. One recruit felt there
was almost too much comfort; that it softened them up. But the basic
purpose was achieved. They arrived with hatred for their European
rulers, and at Nanking they developed it.

As time went on the training shifted to camps dotted round remote parts
of independent African countries like Ghana and Tanzania. Guerrilla
leaders increasingly preferred to have their young men trained in 'local' conditions. The Chinese complied cheerfully, sometimes sending as many as
twenty instructors to a particular African camp. They did not fight themselves, but they earned some kudos by coming to the scene of battle.
Laurens van der Post, the South African-born author, has given an artist's
impression of a Chinese instructor and his charges as they might have
appeared to a young European settler who stumbled on them in the bush:

Somebody must have been seeing to the fire for soon an immense spire of flame soared up into the sky showing François every detail of the scene. He saw the men themselves and, as they crowded round the fire, every line of the expressions of bitter, determined, unhappy if not utterly tragic faces of men of many different tribes.

Yet it was not the faces of the Africans which caught François's attention but that of one man squatting calmly and serenely in an Oriental fashion beside the fire. There was something reminiscent of the Bushman about the colour, high cheekbones and slanted eyes of this face. But the long, sleek hair, neatly brushed back, showed it to be the face of a man infinitely more sophisticated, and in the circumstances more sinister than that of any Bushman of Africa could have been. There was no mistake about it, François knew that he was looking at a Chinese, moreover a man who, compared with the desperate, uncared-for look of his companions, appeared centred, assured, fastidious, self-respecting and inwardly at home, though he was there some ten thousand miles at least from his native land.

Training courses varied in length from a fortnight to two and a half years. 'Economic development', it said on the students' forms at Nanking. The label was something of a euphemism. There were lessons in shooting and in handling new weapons like bazookas and submachine guns. At a slightly more advanced stage, there was sabotage, referred to in another Chinese euphemism as 'special engineering'. We know how this subject was presented, for on one occasion the Chinese somewhat audaciously used the pages of a magazine to give a lesson in sabotage to a wider African audience. The lesson took the form of an interview conducted by a Chinese correspondent with a certain Li Yong who had fought as a guerrilla against the Japanese invaders of China in the Second World War:

> The mines employed by Li Yong and his men had cast iron cases shaped like pineapples. The charges were black gunpowder, which the militia made with locally produced sulphur, charcoal and saltpetre. Charcoal of the castor-oil plant, or any wood that crackles loudly under fire, has the best blasting properties, according to Li Yong. . . .
> The militia around Fuping made mines with hollowed-out stones later. But they were not used because the Japanese never dared to invade the area again. Such mines were used on an enormous scale by militia units all over north China towards the end of the war.
> One big advantage of the stone mines, said Li Yong, is that they can be made in large numbers from materials available in the countryside. Even teenagers can learn how to make them.

Weapons training, however, was not the main point. The Chinese approach was conceptual. The instructors spent up to 75 per cent of their time expounding to their pupils the principles of strategy, tactics and topography, and teaching them how to analyse the political conditions in which they would have to fight. The pill was sugared ingeniously. At Nanking, in the evenings, trainees would be taken to see a play, film or opera depicting the history of the Chinese Communist Party and more especially the mistakes it had made on the road to power. The performance gave the trainees a chance to relax, but was used at the same time by the instructors to point to similarities with the African experience and to hammer home lessons taught earlier in the day. Some of the African pupils found it difficult to fathom how you could sit through a three-hour drama of landlord–peasant conflict without laughing once; but they were impressed all the same by the thoroughness with which, at the end, their questions were called for, researched overnight and answered the following morning.

The central message the Chinese were attempting to convey was Mao Zedong's theory that guerrillas operating in a backward country must win the support of the local peasantry if their rising were to succeed. It too was introduced with subtlety. On the first day of a course organized at Nanking for the PAC of South Africa, the lecturer began by asking, 'Are there any Zulus here?' The Chinese had managed to acquire a copy of *The Washing of the Spears*, an American account of the wars of Shaka, the great Zulu conqueror of the early nineteenth century. A Zulu who identified himself was promptly asked to give a description of Shaka's campaigns, in particular the device by which the twin 'horns' of the Zulu war-host surrounded and entrapped an enemy army. 'This', said the lecturer at the end, 'is what you must do in South Africa.' This, he explained, was how, in Mao's teaching, a rebel force based in the countryside would encircle the enemy-occupied cities. The lecturer had got to the heart of his subject by way of a deft appeal to his listeners' ethnic pride. The pupil who gave the discourse remembers that his political commitment had previously been a little suspect in the eyes of the Chinese; but 'they forgave me because I was a Zulu'.

Chinese tuition was not trouble-free. Some pupils grew restive. Less harsh as a rule than the African sergeant-majors, Chinese trainers were none the less sticklers for parade-ground drilling. ZANU recruits in Tanzania were unable to see the point. Most of them came from the Shona people, who set little store by hierarchy; yet here were the hierarchical Chinese insisting that they salute their seniors. Chinese insistence on instilling theory and yet more theory was also a trial for young Africans anxious to get back to their countries and take up arms. 'We felt we were already late starting this thing,' said one group impatiently. 'After our political orientation everybody was able to understand the situation at home.'

Convinced as they were that current events in Africa were no more than a replay of their own recent history, the Chinese sometimes showed an introverted tendency to refight their old campaigns. Back in the fifties, when the Cameroonians of West Africa were in arms against the French, Mao is said to have presented one of their leaders with a copy of his own work *Problems of Strategy in the Guerrilla War against Japan*, inscribed with the greeting, 'In this book you can read everything which is now going to happen in the Cameroons.' In the same way the Chinese prescribed how to tackle South Africa. Black South Africans should go home and carve out for themselves defensible areas of land: revolutionary 'liberated zones' in the countryside similar to those which Mao's Red Army had founded in mountainous parts of China in the late twenties and thirties. Fresh from Nanking, and faithful to their instructions, a band of PAC fighters set out in 1968 to ignite the rural Transvaal. Most of them were wiped out by the Portuguese troops on their way south through Mozambique, and the few who reached South Africa were rounded up quickly in the flat open spaces of the inhospitable *veld*.

Some of the more thoughtful recruits felt compelled to protest. South Africa was not the same as pre-revolutionary China. It was short of mountains, and, more important, it was industrialized. The bulk of the people lived in the cities, and the countryside was a patchwork of tribal reservations closely guarded by pockets of government troops and police. PAC strategists began to advance the heretical proposition that the answer in South Africa might be something quite new – a guerrilla war launched from within the cities of an advanced society. They were not entirely comfortable about challenging their Chinese mentors: one of them preferred to explain their idea as an extension of Mao's teachings, a new way of encircling the enemy and hitting him in his weakest spot. Amilcar Cabral, the West African leader, rejected the Chinese guidelines for another reason. Cabral observed frankly that in his country of Guiné the peasants were not revolutionary in the sense that China's had been. They had no history of revolt: they did not suffer either from land hunger or scarcity of food. Cabral had no hesitation in striking out on his own. Rather than embed his forces in permanent rural bases to concentrate

on wooing the peasantry as the Chinese Communists had done, he preferred to fight the Portuguese with little mobile units, flitting round
the country from one forest arms cache to another. 'We did not invent
guerrilla warfare,' Cabral conceded; but he went on defiantly, 'we
invented it *in our land.*'

The Chinese did not expect to have their recipes challenged. They
made a point of inviting criticism, but they seem, initially, to have been
taken aback when it came. Who were these critics? Reactionaries? Gradually, however, they began to appreciate, and even encourage, African
initiative. By the early seventies they had instructors training Angolans
of the MPLA not out of Chinese texts but out of texts prepared by the
Angolans themselves which the instructors had adapted.

After their Chinese training was over the guerrillas went back to launch
the first assaults against the white-ruled territories. The impact of their
training was quickly and inevitably diluted. Fellow-guerrillas they mixed
with had been trained by other countries in other parts of the world.
Often the independent African states that gave them shelter had their
own ideas on how the campaigns should be fought. Most of all the
guerrillas learnt from the trial and error of their own experience in the
bush. Yet the Chinese missionaries had not wasted their time. They
transmitted to a number of movements a distinctive and useful legacy.

Many movements addressed the population, to begin with, through
communiqués written in a turgid and woolly style. Chinese instructors
helped them to simplify their language, showed them how to change
their style, as one PAC guerrilla puts it, from long-winded 'Oxford English' to 'Fowler's Modern English Usage'. Many movements also started
off without an adequate vocabulary in which to express their political
ideas and emotions. But the movements read Mao. And Mao's writings
are full of catchy phrases. Africans began to borrow these phrases and
recast them for their own use, often with an exuberant extra twist. Mao
had said that reactionaries were paper tigers: African guerrilla journals
stigmatized their enemies variously as 'an emasculated paper tiger' and
'a paper tiger which shall not escape being crushed to pulp'. Mao in
a famous poem had praised Chinese militia women who 'prefer the
uniform to red silks': 'daughters of Zimbabwe', declared ZANU's magazine, 'love their battle arrays, not silks and satins'. Mao, paraphrasing
an ancient Chinese historian, had said that to die for the people was
weightier than Mount Tai but to die for the oppressors was lighter than
a feather. His remark caught the imagination of a Mozambican named

Luchwachwa, who turned it into verse, replacing Mount Tai with an appropriate local landmark:

> To die for one's country
> defending the people's interests,
> This death is heavy, weightiest of all,
> like Mount Gorongosa.
>
> But he who dies fighting
> against the will of the people,
> He is disgraced.
> His death is light, nothing – as light as a feather.

The discourse of some guerrillas was enriched with a curious layer of sinological erudition. They spoke familiarly of the stratagems of Sun Zi, Chinese military theorist of the fourth century BC, and the treachery of Zhang Guotao, a Communist commander who defected in the thirties to the Chinese Nationalist side. Mindful of the need to protect their families from the attention of government security forces, they disguised themselves, sometimes, in Chinese names. ZANU's ranks, for example, included several Maos and several Zhou Enlais. One Mao, Patrick Tavengwa, was a thoughtful character, like his prototype, good at explaining the objectives of the Rhodesian war. He fought in tandem with a more extrovert captain who went under the pseudonym of James Bond. Both were killed in 1974, but their leaders remembered them with affection: 'James Bond was a commander and Mao was a political commissar and the two made a sensational team.'

Movements also carried back from their Chinese classrooms some practical ideas for waging war. They grasped, in principle, the importance of discipline. Several guerrilla forces adopted the injunctions first drawn up by Mao in 1928–9 to ensure that the Chinese Red Army won popular support through its courteous and considerate behaviour. Mao's *Three Main Rules of Discipline and Eight Points for Attention* reappeared in the bush of Angola and Rhodesia as *Three Rules and Eight Points* or *Three Rules and Nine Points*. FRELIMO's and ZANU's guerrillas, like Mao's, were expected to take from the masses 'not even a needle or a piece of thread', and visitors to ZANU's camps in the sixties were struck by the simplicity and good order of the movement's Nanking graduates as they took their turns at the cooking-fire. Unfortunately discipline was apt to break down. By the late seventies, with many of their leaders in prison and an unmanageable torrent of raw recruits pouring in, ZANU's forces were getting better known for indiscipline, not to say mayhem. The same weakness afflicted one or two other movements. The leaders got trained effectively at their Chinese seminars, but were not always able to pass the content of their training down to the ranks.

Chinese strategy, however, made a deep impact. The peasants must be won over. Movements incessantly echoed Mao's dictum, 'the popular masses are like water and the army is like a fish', and several of them accepted, after their first dose of Chinese tuition, that they had to spend a period quietly learning how to 'swim'. ZANU's was the most dramatic case. ZANU began their campaign in Rhodesia disastrously, taking their fellow-Africans' support for granted and hurling bands of raiders into costly pitched battles with the superior forces of Ian Smith. In late 1966, however, their commanders returned from Nanking with word of a new and more thoughtful approach. Four years were spent digesting it at their camps in Tanzania under the supervision of a Chinese infantry expert known as Comrade Li. In December 1972 the time came to move. ZANU embarked on a new type of offensive, a slow, methodical encroachment, mixing with villagers, asking their grievances and putting the case for a rising against the Europeans. By the time the war ended seven years later ZANU's forces controlled two-thirds of the Rhodesian countryside and were well placed to make sure, in the elections which were held to decide the country's future rulers, that the peasant vote went their way.

As important if more intangible was the Chinese gift to morale. ZANU's offensive was launched into Rhodesia from bases set up in the forests of neighbouring Mozambique. There the guerrillas lived for years, huddled in a strange country, far from their families, not knowing if they would ever see them again. They were homesick, and some of them ran away. China supplied a doctrine, relevant and not too complicated, to hold them together. Robert Mugabe and his colleagues actually declared that their creed was the thought of Mao Zedong, and set up an Ideological College to instil it among their fighters. Other groups made similar professions of faith to please their Chinese sponsors, but ZANU's veterans deny that they were motivated solely by opportunism. The Chinese taught patience. They preached, sternly, that the war would not be won in three days, or won by a single skirmish, that only the second generation might see the end of it. At the same time they insisted that patience would get its reward. 'Chairman Mao teaches us', proclaimed ZANU's rebel radio, '*that the revolution will be successful*'. Never mind, said the Chinese, if your weapons were inferior: numbers and willpower would decide the issue. Brimful of confidence in the aftermath of their own revolutionary triumph, the Chinese Communists succeeded to a significant extent in passing that confidence on.

Africans paid some handsome tributes to China's role. In 1975, on the eve of Mozambique's independence from Portugal, the FRELIMO leader Samora Machel looked back on China as a 'great and reliable strategic rear area': his main backer in independent Africa, President Nyerere of Tanzania, added a few years later that if it hadn't been for China Mozambique might still be under Portuguese rule. ZANU's leaders acknowledged frankly that Chinese teachings had turned the tide of their war. In 1981, in London, a student from the new republic of Zimbabwe met a girl student from Peking. The Zimbabwean was anxious to invite her home for a meal, but he wanted due warning: China had helped his people so much that he had to make proper preparation.

A curious back-handed tribute to the effectiveness of the Chinese mission was also paid by the movements' European adversaries. They scrutinized Mao's writings and even used Chinese phrases themselves. One Portuguese captain defended his decision to raze a Mozambican settlement on the grounds that the villagers deserved it 'because they are to terrorism what water is to fish'. Some of the white commanders prided themselves that they could beat the guerrillas at their own game, winning over the peasants with largesse in the form of hospitals and schools. General C.A. Fraser, the head of South Africa's Joint Combat Forces, told his cadets grimly in 1968 that the Chinese Communists had no monopoly on patience and 'staying power'.

The European settlers maintained that China was their ultimate enemy. White-ruled Africa, they argued, was the victim of a long premeditated Chinese scheme. A police chief explained to an audience in Bloemfontein how the overthrow of the free world had been planned by Communists in Shanghai in 1926: 'arrows were drawn on the map of the world and one of the biggest pointed to Africa'. The colonists even claimed that the Chinese were physically fighting them, and a Portuguese conscript in Mozambique who changed sides and attached himself to FRELIMO's forces was surprised not to run into Chinese soldiers as his officers had led him to expect. It is likely in some cases that the Europeans were manufacturing a Chinese bogey in the hope of rallying domestic and international support for their cause. But they also seem to have been genuinely filled with an atavistic terror. The

86

nightmare which had haunted the Boers in turn-of-the-century South Africa was coming true at last: Chinese really were helping Africans to rise up against their masters. One white farmer who had moved to Rhodesia after the Kenyan troubles in the fifties noted that the ZANU rebels were using much more sophisticated weapons than their Kenyan predecessors had done. He was in no doubt why. 'I would call it Mao Mao rather than Mau Mau.'

Independent Africa presented the Chinese with a more complex challenge.

The Chinese Communists had expected Africa to relive China's recent history and drive foreign influence violently from its soil. But history in most of the continent had failed to repeat itself. The transition to independence was as disappointingly peaceful as it had been in Asia. The Europeans quietly relinquished their power to local rulers; and European influence remained. The African politicians and civil servants who took over were trained in Europe. They wrote, spoke and even thought in European languages. To an extent that the Chinese had probably never visualized, they also had European friends. European socialist politicians took a sympathetic interest in African causes. European expatriates continued to teach on African campuses and sit as advisers in African government offices. Now the Chinese, in the person of Zhou Enlai, had set themselves up as the champions of independent Africa against any further European meddling in African affairs. How were they to pursue their mission? Were they to wean Africans gently off European influence, or attack it with a bludgeon?

The Chinese leaders quickly noticed that the new African governments were not all alike. The differences reminded them of another, earlier period of Chinese history. In 1961 they explained the analogy to their army commissars:

> Africa looks like the seven powers of the Warring States [403–221 BC], with its Nasser, Nkrumah, Hussein [Hassan], Sekou Touré, Bourguiba and Abbas, each with his own way of leading others. In general everyone is trying to sell his own goods.

The different regimes broke down, for practical purposes, into two major categories: a minority which showed some sign of heeding the Chinese message, and a majority which had no inclination to receive it at all.

A number of the new African leaders were discontented in varying degrees with the political and economic system they had inherited from the Europeans. They included, in West Africa, Kwame Nkrumah of Ghana and the rulers of a handful of former French colonies, Guinea, Mali and Congo-Brazzaville; to the east and south, Julius Nyerere of Tanzania and Kenneth Kaunda of Zambia. They did not necessarily want to eradicate European influences, but they did want at least to modify the Western legacy and make it harmonize better with African tradition. This made them potentially disposed to listen to what China had to say.

It did not mean, however, that they were ready to open their arms to all that China stood for. Mao Zedong's China had a number of features which disturbed them. First of all it propagated a rigid Communist doctrine which was supposed to be valid for every country on earth. These African leaders were just discovering what it was like to be free. They did not want to replace an alien Western system with an equally alien Eastern one: they wanted their countries to have doctrines of their own, never mind if those doctrines were mutually conflicting or even embryonic. Secondly, China was regimented. Husbands and wives, for example, were split up to work hundreds of miles apart in the interests of the state. These leaders represented peoples who had no tradition of an all-powerful state and gave their deepest loyalty to the family. Maybe, they mused, regimentation was needed in a crowded country like China, where citizens might have to be forced to collaborate in putting up dams or irrigation works if the community were to survive: thinly populated Africa could do without it. Thirdly, Mao Zedong aimed to keep his country in a state of permanent revolutionary upheaval. African leaders presided over new and fragile nations liable to be torn apart at any time by social or ethnic conflict. Upheaval was the last thing they wanted. Lastly, these leaders were religious men. Nyerere was a devout Catholic, Kaunda a Methodist lay preacher. They viewed with disquiet a society where there seemed to be no place for God.

The Chinese approached these potential disciples with intelligence and tact. To overcome the initial barrier of unease, they sent out to Africa the most soothing of their evangelists. Foremost among them was Zhou Enlai himself. Zhou was both rational and compellingly persuasive. On his visit to Tanzania he awed the cabinet with a dazzlingly lucid sketch of the world situation. He listed three points, started on 'Point One', discoursed without notes for an hour, then came to 'Point

Two' – long after they had forgotten there was a 'Point Two' to follow. He was unfailingly courteous. He paid the leaders of these small countries a consistent attention unmatched by any other senior foreign statesman. A revealing if fantastic legend circulated among African diplomats in China that Zhou on one occasion offered to express his respect for them by cleaning the shoes of their ambassadors at the Peking Hotel. Above all Zhou came across as a personality. Leadership in China is collective. Zhou for all his gifts was in Chinese eyes a functionary: he came to Africa as the spokesman for the Chinese Communist Party's collective views. But leadership in Africa is personalized. Africans wanted to feel they were dealing with an individual. 'Zhou is *our brother*,' said the slogans on the streets of the Tanzanian capital; 'Tanzania is *his home*.' Zhou's great achievement was to persuade men as different as the austere schoolteacher Nyerere and the prickly visionary Nkrumah to regard him as a personal friend. To some leaders he seemed, ironically, more important than the one Chinese statesman who really did play a decisive personal role – Mao Zedong. Leadership in Africa is visible: the ruler parades among his people with his flywhisk or leopardskin cap. Mao for many years was a presence in the background, and African leaders tended consequently to jump to the conclusion that he must be in decline. Not everyone seems to have grasped that in an Oriental society the greatest power is not necessarily wielded by the most conspicuous figure.

Zhou's efforts were matched at a lower level by an impressive team of ambassadors. By the late fifties the Chinese had begun to form at their Foreign Ministry a corps of specialist 'Africa hands'. The most prominent of these diplomats had worked with Zhou for years, and unlike many of their colleagues were used to dealing with foreigners. He Ying, ambassador to Tanzania, had lived in Malaya, and Huang Hua, ambassador to Ghana, had helped to receive the various deputations which the United States sent to treat with the ascendant Chinese Communist Party during and after the Second World War. They were shrewd, sophisticated, fluent in English, and, most important, they were sociable, ready to mix affably with Africans at cocktail parties and dinners. At traditional African dinners Chinese diplomats found themselves expected on occasion to fall in with some disconcerting customs: to help themselves with their fingers to grain, meat and gravy or submit to the hospitality of hosts who fed them, literally, hand to mouth. Anyone familiar with the fastidious Chinese manipulation of chopsticks and finger-bowls can imagine the inner martyrdom this must have entailed. But the diplomats acquitted themselves stoically – as not all Westerners did.

Lulled by their contact with these agreeable envoys, the first African leaders began coming to Peking. Gently the Chinese offered them an alternative to the liberal social system they had inherited from the West: a collective society of hardworking peasants mobilized in huge rural communes. The permanent exhibition at the model commune of Dazhai flew a red streamer shaped like a map of Africa. African visitors were driven at the start of a day's excursion past a swarm of peasants building up a hillock of earth, then driven back in the evening to observe, to their astonishment, that the earth had already been shifted to the road or dam it was meant for and the hillock was gone.

The visitors were still disturbed by China's totalitarian essence. They were at least as conscious as Westerners that their movements were under surveillance and that ordinary people were kept beyond their reach. But they discovered that the Chinese didn't, after all, have horns and tails; and they made other discoveries which deeply excited them. These leaders were painfully aware that years after independence their countries were only independent in a nominal sense. Their parliamentary procedures were Western; so were the goods in their shops; so were the curricula in their schools. Western companies organized their construction schemes. Western banks lent them money and dunned them for it afterwards. The Chinese however had purged themselves since 1949 of every last trace of the West. They avoided incurring foreign debts. They took no foreign aid and made a virtue of 'self-reliance'. They produced their own goods and even wore clothes of their own distinctive design. They spoke their own language, not a colonial *lingua franca*. They were not moulded by European schooling: as one African remarked wistfully they 'thought in a Chinese way'. There was not a Westerner in sight, and life would to all appearances carry on placidly if the West dropped off the map. In China African leaders found a country which knew what independence was about.

Some at least of the leaders dreamt of improving their people's lives. In China they saw what could be done to transform a peasant country very like their own. In less than twenty years Mao Zedong and his colleagues had succeeded, apparently, in providing a population far larger than all of Africa's with the essentials of food and shelter, clothes and work and medical care. They had not simply dragooned their people

90

to achieve this, but had cooperated with them and drawn on their ideas. One or two leaders, Nyerere in particular, were struck by the attention to agriculture. China had passed up the soft option of racing to industrialization and leaving its peasants to languish.

All too often, in Africa, ambitious development projects were launched only to collapse because both governments and people lacked the will to see them through. In China, however, African rulers were given a picture of a society committed to its goals, willing to sacrifice short-term individual comforts for the common good of all. Corruption, they were told, was sternly punished. Leaders took modest salaries and their wives did the housework. Peking officials owned no cars but went humbly to work on bicycles. China seemed to these Africans a beacon of morality. If Peking could make do with bicycles, why, wondered the ascetic Nyerere, should cars be needed in his capital of Dar es Salaam? Kaunda decided that the Chinese Communists were all good Christians. The remark caused some mirth among his more sardonic associates, but the mirth was not wholly justified. Not altogether unperceptively, African statesmen detected in the air of devotion and newborn purity which hung about so many Chinese in Mao's time a kind of religious faith. China, they felt, was not after all an atheistic country: here too God was present, in an unfamiliar guise.

Quite a few of the leaders finished their Chinese journey rapturous. At the banquets organized in their honour in 1967 Kaunda and his Zambians gave their emotions free rein. Banquets in China as a rule are rather sedate affairs, punctuated by shortish speeches and cheerful but decorous toasting. But the Zambians burst into patriotic songs, and Kaunda on one occasion is said to have startled his Chinese hosts with a euphoric harangue of nearly an hour.

Faced with this enthusiasm the Chinese, however, remained deliberately and skilfully passive. They did not exert themselves, like the old European missionaries, to win African converts to their faith. To do so would have run against the logic of their endeavour. Their object was to help Africa to strengthen its independence by ridding itself of the legacy of alien Western ideas. But by forcing their doctrines on governments they would merely be inviting the continent to exchange one foreign influence for another one – their own. So the Chinese promoted their model; but in a spirit of 'take it or leave it'. They were content to embark, in friendly countries, on a series of original and sometimes spectacular economic aid schemes, and let their achievement speak

91

for itself. Significantly they made no attempt to send advisers to Africa to take the place of the European expatriate civil servants. African leaders could, if they wished, experiment with the Chinese model; but they would have to do it by themselves.

Several regimes did in fact embark on a range of Chinese experiments. Some of them set about training their administrators to combine, as the Chinese did, professional competence with zeal for the country's political goals. Kaunda left a team of Zambians in China to study the relations between the civil service and the Communist Party, and word went forth in Congo-Brazzaville that officials should be, in the Chinese phrase, 'both red and expert'. Some leaders used Chinese techniques to discipline backsliders. A military commander in Congo-Brazzaville made a group of dissidents perform labour in public for the edification of the masses. The commander had been trained in China, at the Nanking Military Academy, and a Chinese diplomat who watched the proceedings judged them highly reminiscent of his own country's methods of shaming political offenders. Shame was the key to punishment in China. Humbled by criticism and public degradation, the wrongdoer would repent, and a wrongdoer who truly repented might start life anew. Still more reminiscent of Chinese custom were the 're-education' sessions organized in Mozambique a few years later for people who had collaborated with the Portuguese colonial forces during the independence war. The delinquents were severely criticized by the president, Samora Machel, and reminded of the futility which had attended the efforts of past traitors like Chiang Kai-shek. They expressed regret for their conduct, and were duly absolved and sent back home as 'trusting, reborn men'.

Some regimes also took steps in the direction of the great self-supporting communes into which Mao had gathered China's peasants. The Tanzanians for instance transplanted their peasants from isolated homesteads scattered through the bush into small cooperative villages. The villages were named after Nyerere's concept of *ujamaa*, African 'familyhood', and were conceived as a blend of Chinese collectivism and African tradition. Tanzanians in pre-colonial times had the habit of working together in simple style, a farmer calling in his neighbours to help him harvest maize or make beer. Nyerere and his associates built on this foundation two concepts of Chinese origin: a collective area on which everyone would gradually be persuaded to work, and a stock of basic equipment like tractors and buses which would be kept for the benefit of the village as a whole.

Finally these apprentice governments did their best to match Mao's great efforts at preventing the emergence of a gulf between the peasant masses and a privileged elite. Education was made more down-to-earth: Tanzanian schools, like Chinese ones, had their own workshops and farms. Chinese school leavers had in principle to work in industry, commerce or agriculture before they could apply for further education, and in Tanzania, correspondingly, it was ordained that no school leaver should have the chance to go to university before he had done two years' national service in a factory or *ujamaa* village. Governments tried to integrate their armies into rural life. Soldiers in China were expected to grow their own food so they would not be a burden on the local peasantry, and were also expected to lend the peasants a hand. Inspired by this example the Nanking-trained commander in Congo-Brazzaville put his men to work rearing pigs and growing vegetables. Years later newly independent Zimbabwe launched an 'Operation Seed' intended to cope in Chinese fashion with the legacy of the recent guerrilla war. Veterans, it was hoped, would make themselves useful on the land rather than polishing their guns in barracks, while the peasants would get used to viewing the soldier as a helpmate rather than a killer. One dedicated leadership even tried to tackle, with a dose of Chinese frugality, the growth of privilege in its own ranks. Days after Zhou Enlai came to Tanzania in 1965 Julius Nyerere was paring down the luxuries enjoyed by his officials. No more hard liquor at receptions, no more flashy cars. In 1967 he subjected them to a formal code of conduct. No more directorships in private companies. No outside incomes, and no extra houses. Other countries followed the example of Tanzania's spartan 'Leadership Code'.

African leaders seldom pushed their experiments very far in practical terms. They had no intention of importing the Chinese system wholesale. Their idea was to tinker eclectically with bits and pieces of Chinese practice that appealed to them, and to hold China up as an occasional example to their subjects of what a disciplined people should be able to achieve. Some of their followers would have liked to go further. Tawia Adamafio, an aide of President Nkrumah of Ghana, voiced noisy dissatisfaction at the number of agreements his master concluded on his first trip to Peking: 'No, we must have more, more, more!' Some young people and intellectuals were not content, as their governments were, to borrow from China eclectically, but dreamt of reordering society on exclusively

Chinese lines. They venerated Mao as a patron saint of independence, and looked on China as a utopia free of the greed and poverty which disfigured their new countries. A few of them went to live in China and spent years translating Mao's scriptures into European or African tongues.

The Chinese, however, handled zealots of this kind with conspicuous caution. They gave some of them a home, and stirred the imagination of others by filling the bookshops of African cities with dashing revolutionary memoirs and political magazines. Otherwise they left them to their own devices. Apart from a solitary history professor who spent six months in Ghana in the early sixties, not a single Chinese lecturer appeared on an African campus to cultivate the young. Now and again it happened that extremist politicians sought Chinese backing against a leader Peking favoured. The Chinese gave them short shrift.

Peking even tried to restrain some regimes which seemed to be carrying their political experiments too far for their own good. In 1964, for instance, Zhou Enlai advised Nkrumah that his new development plan, replete with soaring projects for the industrialization of Ghana, was too ambitious. At approximately the same time, on the other side of the continent, a group of revolutionaries who had seized power on the island of Zanzibar called in Chinese economic planners. They did not get the counsel they expected. The world's foremost socialists urged them not to go in for nationalization. If they must nationalize they should confine their takeovers to one major export and one major import: they should not, at all events, tempt economic collapse by wildly taking control of products which local traders were quite capable of handling by themselves.

Finally, the Chinese discouraged excessive rhetorical claims. African leaders might not want to turn their countries, in practice, into carbon copies of China, but they did sometimes like to maintain that they were following in China's glamorous path. Ahmed Sekou Touré, the Guinean president, told Zhou Enlai grandly in 1964 that China and Guinea were advancing 'under the same banner and in one and the same historical current, determining the nature of universal evolution'. Zhou was politely silent. Present-day China, he indicated, could at best serve as 'a kind of reference' for African countries.

The Chinese had no desire to foster drastic social upheaval in friendly African states. They wished to teach Africans independence, not Communism: Africa, in their view, would not be ready for Communism

94

for many decades to come. African leaders of the present generation were not authentic Communists and could not be hailed as such. There was a hint here that the Chinese reluctance to preach doctrine to Africans was motivated not just by tact but by an assumption of vast superiority. Some African leaders found this galling. But there was also a protective impulse. All China's energies were concentrated on keeping friendly regimes alive. Even in friendly countries China's footing was precarious. The Chinese were close to the leader and his entourage, but their contacts with the army and civil service were poor or negligible. Both these groups were inclined to be more pro-Western than the politicians, and the Chinese were well aware that the army, at least, posed a threat. At home in China politically zealous citizens were mobilized into a 'people's militia' whose function was to keep order and safeguard the Communist Party's control. The Chinese urged their African friends to form similar militias. Recruited among the firebrands of the ruling political party they could act as a counterweight to the army and serve the president as a sort of praetorian guard. Several governments went ahead with the idea: the Chinese trained the militias and supplied them with uniforms and arms. Protective measures of this kind made much more sense, in the Chinese view, than reckless encouragement of premature social change. The watchword had to be delicacy.

The same delicacy was not apparent in China's dealings with the majority of regimes which spurned its mission.

Most of the first generation of African leaders were comfortable with the European legacy. These included some English-speaking leaders like Jomo Kenyatta of Kenya and the great majority of French-speaking ones. They called themselves democrats and constitutionalists, and thought that their countries would be more likely to prosper with a Western liberal economy than a Chinese collective one. These conservative Africans were not happy to hear Zhou Enlai's remark that their continent was 'ripe for revolution'. Word went around that Zhou had been disgusted to find the new leaders of Africa no different in outlook from the Westerners they replaced, that his prophecy of revolution was aimed at them. The authorities in Kenya refused to let Zhou's aircraft refuel on its way home from their southern neighbour, Tanzania. 'It is not clear', they said darkly, 'what type or what form of revolution he has in mind. But the Kenya government wishes it to be known that Kenya intends to avert all revolutions irrespective of their origins.'

Like the European colonists, conservative Africans were deeply afraid of the Chinese. To some extent they inherited colonial fears. One British civil servant in Kenya composed a memorandum on the eve of independence explaining to his successors how 'Communist China is anxious to infiltrate diplomatically, economically and possibly at a later date physically, into the African continent.' But a number of African leaders arrived of their own accord at the bizarre conclusion that they were menaced by a Chinese deluge. Philibert Tsiranana, the first president of independent Madagascar, viewed with the gravest suspicion the Chinese traders who had settled in colonial times on his large and thinly populated island. They were just the advance-guard, he thought. He warned his peasants that if French troops left the country invaders from China would arrive and seize their land. His foreign minister even maintained that the government in Peking claimed Madagascar as a Chinese province. Tsiranana, as it happened, was a patriarch among the rulers of French-speaking Africa, and his phobia spread. Deep in the West African hinterland the president of Upper Volta, Maurice Yaméogo, said dolefully that in view of China's determination to find homes for its surplus millions, 'if we allow Communist Chinese people to enter our country, Upper Volta will no longer be Upper Volta and we would disappear within a few years'.

The Chinese made little attempt to reassure these frightened conservatives. Their conduct suggests they may sometimes have been genuinely oblivious of the fear their presence aroused. They insisted on running large embassies. In many African capitals China retained more diplomats than any other foreign power. Modest in Chinese eyes, an embassy staff of twenty or thirty looked alarming to African rulers, many of whom were nervously trying to keep down the numbers of foreign diplomats on their soil. The Chinese insisted on seclusion. Free and easy and not very secretive, the Kenyans were unsettled to see the Chinese diplomats in their country taking refuge in a building like a fortress. 'The Chinese ambassador here built walls around himself, for what reason we cannot understand.'

Confident, over-confident, the Chinese had little idea of the strength of conservative feeling. They took it for granted, for instance, that everyone in the colonies was anxious to drive out the European rulers, and sometimes they were wrong. In December 1963 the island of Zanzibar celebrated its independence from Britain. He Ying, then ambassador to the mainland republic of Tanganyika, came over for the occasion:

so too did James Mancham, novice politician from the Seychelles, an archipelago to the east of Zanzibar which was still under British rule. It was a chance to spread the gospel. Mancham recalls being buttonholed by this Chinese 'conspirator type'. He Ying ascertained where he came from, voiced satisfaction at the freeing of Zanzibar, then took his arm and moved closer. 'Mr Mancham,' he said, 'if you are interested in getting rid of the British, come and see us in Dar es Salaam after you've been in Nairobi.' The seasoned Chinese diplomat had for once made a blunder. Mancham was a politician so pro-Western he didn't even want independence. He passed the conversation straight back to his British friends.

In the same way the Chinese assumed that all independent African countries must be uniformly in a hurry to free themselves of European influence. Any pro-Western rulers they encountered could be dismissed as stooges of the former colonial masters who would quickly pass from the scene. This misconception can be explained in several ways. The Chinese had few embassies in the more conservative countries, and may not always have been able to form an accurate impression of the mood prevailing there. Some of the embassies they did have may have sent misleading signals: diplomats probably succumbed to the temptation to justify their presence by painting a rosy picture of countries moving swiftly away from the West. Lastly the Chinese were inclined to listen to dissidents. Many of the people who had gone to China in the years before independence had not emerged as leaders when independence came. Elbowed aside by more conservative figures, they had gone into opposition, nursing a mixture of personal resentment, tribal grievances and principled dissatisfaction that so little had changed. But they kept on going to China. In 1964 the Chinese were visited by Oginga Odinga, a politician from Kenya. Odinga had sought their support in the days before independence when his leader, Jomo Kenyatta, languished in a British gaol. Now, with Kenyatta installed as president, Odinga had changed his tune. He addressed the Chinese in flamboyant language and told them that Kenyatta ought to be overthrown.

Given this misconception it is doubtful whether the Chinese cared what conservative leaders thought of them. By 1964 Peking was bypassing these leaders altogether. Kenyan officials grew fretful at the behaviour of Chinese delegations. 'They did not visit the sisal project in Asembo but visited the Hon. Oginga Odinga's house in Kisumu instead.'

The Chinese protest naivety. They failed, they explain, to appreciate in the early days that African governments might be sensitive about their contacts with the political opposition. After all, governments in Europe weren't. In a number of cases, however, they had undoubtedly decided that a regime should not merely be bypassed, but actively opposed. Parts of independent Africa, in their view, were not independent at all. Great events were convulsing the former Belgian Congo. Soon after this territory became independent as Congo-Léopoldville its first premier, the radical Patrice Lumumba, had been deposed and murdered by pro-Western forces backed by European political and business interests. Lumumba's followers had refused to accept the outcome and had risen up against the new regime; discovering, as it were, the truth of the Chinese teaching that the only way to win true freedom was to fight for it. The Chinese, like many Africans, regarded this rising as a war for independence which deserved their support.

Mao Zedong in particular was enthralled by the Congo. Since the failure at the end of the fifties of his colossal attempt at economic take-off known as the Great Leap Forward, Mao had been temporarily shunted by his colleagues into the realm of foreign affairs. He did not know much about Africa, but he had come to regard it as the millenarian battlefield on which the power of the West could be destroyed. Mao also believed that Africa was conductive, that if one place came out unequivocally against the Europeans others would follow suit. Sprawled across the heart of the continent, nine other countries round its borders, Congo-Léopoldville looked like the decisive arena. 'If we can take the Congo,' Mao is said to have remarked, 'we can have all of Africa.'

Buoyed up by these hopes, the Chinese consequently reached out for the bludgeon. New kinds of Chinese missionary appeared on the scene. Prominent among them were the correspondents of the New China News Agency. These were hardbitten and privileged Chinese. They lived apart from the embassy, often working in pairs, a husband and a wife. Their unofficial status as journalists enabled them to roam the back-country and even to venture into neighbouring states where no Chinese embassy was maintained. Not surprisingly, they were the principal arm of Chinese intelligence in Africa. They cultivated discontented Africans, wined them and dined them and sometimes gave them active encouragement: one, in Kenya, was said to have taken part in a radical demonstration and helped to raise money for demonstrators arrested by the police. These journalists were no more, however, than the light auxiliaries of the missionary force. In friendly countries like Nkrumah's Ghana colonels of the Chinese army extended the guerrilla tráining which had been given so effectively to insurgents from white-ruled Africa to dissidents from independent states who had taken up arms.

The Chinese laid siege to the Congo. To the west, in Congo-Brazzaville, the small neighbouring territory formerly ruled by the French, they administered training in three different camps to rebels who had risen up in the name of the martyred Lumumba. To the east they won themselves a foothold in the little state of Burundi by lavishing gifts on the politicians of the dominant Tutsi tribe. The Tutsi obligingly gave the Chinese a free hand to turn their country into a major supply base for the Congolese campaign. Congolese rebels came to call at the embassy China had established in the Burundian capital, on the second floor of a Greek-run establishment called the Paguidas Hotel. The rebels were trained at four camps and were issued with food, funds and arms. Arms supplies were also shipped to the Congolese rebels through Uganda, a little way to the north. A convoy of lorries apparently bound for the Congo, containing seventy-five tons of Chinese weapons, machine-guns and anti-tank guns, rocket launchers and land mines, was detained on its way from Kenya to Uganda in May 1965.

Every step the Chinese took made African fears more acute. Some conservative Africans began to believe that they were prey to a people of superhuman intelligence. The deposed first president of Congo-Brazzaville, an unfrocked *abbé* called Fulbert Youlou, wrote a book entitled *J'Accuse la Chine* (1966) which purported to expose the Chinese machinations in Central Africa. The Chinese of Youlou's book were reminiscent of the Martian invaders of H.G.Wells's *War of the Worlds*. They were all-knowing and all-powerful. They were exploiting the ancient quarrels of the Lulua and Baluba peoples: they had mastered the forest customs and dialects and unlocked the secrets of the tom-tom drums. Through 'a veritable science of subversive war, a mathematical science minutely detailed and implacably applied', Africa, said Youlou, was being subjected to a colonization, coherent, logical and terribly effective, which would in due course turn the entire continent into a gigantic ricefield. The Chinese had naturally never meditated such apocalyptic schemes. What they had done, however, was serious enough. They had broken their own cardinal rule of discretion. By meddling in the internal conflicts of these new and nervous states, they themselves had violated the African independence they claimed to champion. In April 1965 a rebel named Ahmadou Diop tried to assassinate the president of the mid-Saharan republic of Niger. He was found to have been trained by the Chinese. What Diop chose to do with his training may well have been his own affair; but the Chinese could hardly be surprised if the incident triggered a panic in French-speaking West Africa that took years to dispel.

Little more than a year after Zhou Enlai's majestic tour the Chinese mission to independent Africa was veering out of control. The Chinese had certainly been led astray by their basic failure to grasp the strength of African conservatism. But that was only part of the reason. Their conduct was also increasingly affected, from 1964 onwards, by events taking place at home. In 1964 Mao moved to regain control of domestic policy. Prompted by him the more radical elements in the Chinese Communist Party began to campaign, in the name of 'socialist education', against the moderate and pragmatic leaders who had governed the country for the past five years. Some of these radicals began to be posted to Chinese embassies in Africa, to the New China News Agency offices and the military training teams. Monolingual, xenophobic, they had little in common with the sophisticated 'Africa hands' who were their nominal supervisors. They were less concerned to win African trust than to win merit at home for their revolutionary zeal.

The campaign for 'socialist education' was no more than the foretaste of a greater upheaval to come. In 1966 Mao whipped into action against his opponents the frenzied loyalty of the young. Youthful 'Red Guards' began to rampage around the country, chanting Mao's praises and venting their fury on all that he condemned. The rampage went under the name of a 'Cultural Revolution', and the Red Guards initially directed their energies against certain forms of culture they held to be decadent or corrupting: old Chinese temples and classical Chinese literature, Western classical music and Western works of art. But the real targets soon emerged. Veteran politicians, officials and intellectuals, people at odds with Mao or otherwise found wanting in political rectitude, were paraded in dunces' caps, imprisoned and driven to suicide. Violence and disorder were universal, and battles raged in the streets.

Before long the chaos was spreading into the realm of foreign relations. As the campaign grew more feverish China began relapsing into the introverted habits of earlier times. Once more the Chinese exalted their ruler as a sovereign deserving the allegiance of all mankind. African guerrillas training at Nanking were told that their victories should be ascribed not to their own merits but to Mao Zedong's thought; that the publications they issued should exclude references to their own leaders and dwell on Mao alone.

Reason began to depart from China's African embassies. The sophisticated ambassadors were called home, many to denunciation and disgrace, and the lower-level officials, the fanatics and xenophobes, were left in charge. Their sole thought was to spread the campaign. Up and down the continent, unbidden by their leaders, Chinese diplomats and visitors and even passing seamen handed out to all who approached them red badges and paintings bearing Mao's effigy and the *Little Red Book* of selected quotations from Mao's works. Four million copies of the *Little Red Book* are said, for example, to have circulated in Mali. One per head.

The Cultural Revolution laid up still more trouble for the Chinese in Africa. Conservative, pro-Western leaders were still more deeply antagonized. Not content to intrigue with their domestic political rivals, Chinese embassies now appeared to revel in subjecting them to a torrent of public abuse. The future Kenyan president, Daniel arap Moi, observed that he and his colleagues did not appreciate being called 'freaks and monsters'. In many countries, however, the real danger derived from the fact that the Cultural Revolution was only too attractive. Sunk in introversion China ironically made a greater impact on its African admirers than it had ever done before. Young Africans were thrilled by the events in China. Sickened by the corruption in their own societies they felt that China had become a land of liberty where even the most senior leaders could be called to account. They were excited, too, by the notion of *cultural* upheaval, the impulse which had driven the Chinese to rid their country of such alien and pernicious influences as the music of Mozart. In fact China was not permeated by foreign culture, and the Chinese frenzy, as we have seen, was only superficially directed at cultural targets: broader issues were at stake as Mao set out to defend his egalitarian and rural society from the attempts of his opponents to give priority to education, technology and urban-based growth. African intellectuals on the other hand were deeply preoccupied by the continued enslavement of their populace to Western culture and Western consumer fads. Incensed by this phenomenon some young Africans began to agitate in the style of their Chinese contemporaries. Young Tanzanians in green shirts and black trousers, members of the youth wing of the ruling political party, started denouncing Western fripperies, *Playboy* and the Beatles, tight trousers and miniskirts, cosmetics and beauty competitions. President Nyerere seems initially to have been surprised by this campaign. He soon co-opted it. 'You', he told the demonstrators sweetly, 'are our Green Guards.'

African leaders friendly to China were attracted by the way in which Mao had harnessed the energies of the young to serve his own political purposes. Each of them had a ready-made force of militant young people organized in the youth wing of the parties through which they governed: why should they not have cultural revolutions to heighten their authority and rally enthusiasm for their goals? Several of them followed Mao's example and fostered a cult of themselves. The scope of the Tanzanian campaign was widened. Young Tanzanians, like young Chinese, were encouraged to leave their homes and march around the country in support of Nyerere and his economic reforms. Some of them wore badges of both Mao and Nyerere, and the Green Guards were issued with a Little Green Book containing a sample of Nyerere's quotations. In Guinea a whole bouquet of Red, Green and Mixed Guards were directed to assimilate the thoughts of President Sekou Touré, specimens of which, like Mao's quotations in the *People's Daily* of Peking, were emblazoned regularly on the front of the party newspaper. Sekou Touré became, like Mao, the 'Guide' and 'Helmsman' of his country. In neighbouring Mali, where Mao's writings were introduced into the school and college curricula, the more sinister face of the Chinese upheaval revealed itself. The leader browbeat his enemies. The 'cultural revolution' in Mali began with an editorial called 'Great Leap Forward' which appeared in the party paper demanding a purge in the ranks. The followers of the president, Modibo Keita, set up new organs of government, 'committees for the defence of the revolution', intended like the new revolutionary committees of China to bypass a bureaucracy with which the leader had fallen at odds; and members of that bureaucracy, party officials and mayors of towns, were abused for their capitalist lifestyle and forced to resign by the militant young. In some countries the campaigns degenerated into thuggery. The Chinese had no hand in these developments: Africa's cultural revolutions were home-grown. But people were frightened, and the Chinese got the blame.

The result was disaster.

In the 1920s missionaries dispatched by the Soviet Union to promote revolution in south China failed to save the fledgling Chinese Communist Party from a massacre organized by Chiang Kai-shek. The episode has been described as 'Stalin's Failure in China'. What now ensued can be called, with equal justice, 'Mao's Failure in Africa'. For independent

Africa in the mid-sixties was ripe for counter-revolution, and in country after country the Chinese had to watch their mission tumbling down about their ears.

First of all the Chinese lost their friends. Several of the leaders they had worked with most closely fell victim to army insurrections. In Ghana the Chinese seem to have had their ears to the ground. In February 1966 President Nkrumah was due to set out on a trip to Peking. The Chinese *chargé d'affaires* came to his headquarters with an oral message from Zhou Enlai advising him to drop the visit as he 'needed to look after the situation at home'. Nkrumah disregarded it. His regime was overthrown by the army and police while he was still in mid-air. He was received in Peking with full honours, but greeted by Zhou with the reproachful words, 'I told you not to come.' Back in his disordered homeland a team of Chinese technicians, truculent when stopped at a road block, were beaten up by Ghanaian troops. In Mali two years later the army moved to suppress a 'people's militia' that had antagonized rather than counterbalanced it as the Chinese had intended, along with the thuggish young standard-bearers of the local 'cultural revolution'. The deposed foreign minister took refuge, for an embarrassing forty-eight hours, in the Chinese embassy. The *coups d'état* in both Ghana and Mali were provoked by local discontents that had nothing directly to do with China: in a third country, the Central African Republic, fear of China was the force that set the tanks rolling. The president, David Dacko, was judged to be too close to Peking; rumour had it that Chinese soldiers were on their way to the country; the army panicked and stepped in.

Conservative governments rounded on the Chinese in their midst. They broke relations with Peking or froze them for years. In Burundi a pro-Western prime minister was assassinated by a malcontent said to have been in Chinese pay. His successor later exonerated the Chinese, but the incident, in the climate of the time, meant the end of the Chinese embassy. The Chinese embassy was ringed by troops, and four days later its inmates were packed off home. Seven governments expelled the local New China News Agency journalists, and bans were imposed on the wearing of Mao's badges and the reading of Chinese publications. The Chinese had had to learn the hard way that Africans did not necessarily see them as they saw themselves.

A few people kept their heads. China's surviving friends, like Nyerere and Kaunda, earned lasting Chinese gratitude by remaining steadfast,

103

going to Peking at the height of the turmoil. As the African backlash mounted Zhou Enlai tried, through Nyerere, to calm one of the wilder fears. 'You can see', he said, showing the Tanzanian president the back streets of Shanghai, 'that we are not anxious to acquire any more slums that Africa may have.' But the damage was done. The Chinese had suffered a *débâcle*, and beneath a veneer of defiance they felt it deeply. Some careers are likely to have paid for it: at all events their ambassadors to Burundi and the Central African Republic didn't reappear in a diplomatic post till the end of the next decade. The Chinese needed to lick their wounds and rethink their approach to the continent. Probably in the autumn of 1968, a major reassessment took place. Order was to be restored in China's foreign relations. In 1969 the first 'Africa hands' began returning to their posts. They brought with them a new mildness. The Chinese mission to dissidents in independent Africa was rapidly abandoned. The mission to the guerrilla movements in the white-ruled territories was kept up, but there was a new note of caution: Zhou sent word to the movements' backers in Tanzania and Zambia to restrain their activities and avoid provoking reprisals from the white regimes in the south. For reasons which ranged far beyond Africa, China had elected to present itself as a sober member of the world community. The 'Young Chinese Missionary' had become middle-aged.

raffe in Peking. This
nal was presented to the
nese emperor in 1414.
inscription at the top of
painting congratulates
emperor on the arrival
uch an auspicious beast.

(*Right*) An old tomb at Siu on Pate island off the coast of Kenya. The cavities once contained Chinese porcelain bowls.

(*Above*) This figurine was discovered in 1954 by Chinese archaeologists working in the old Tang dynasty capital of Chang'an (modern Xi'an). It was buried in the tomb of a lady who died in AD 850, and is thought to represent an African servant who attended the lady in life.

Pillar-shaped tomb at Mambrui near Malindi, Kenya. Blue white Chinese dishes are still embedded in the side.

lished by Mao Yuanyi in
3, this chart was probably
piled by Chinese
igators in the early fifteenth
tury. The East African
stline runs from left to right
ss the lower part of the
wing. Place names include
Somali port of Brava
the Kenyan ports of
nbasa and Malindi.

The Chinese Columbus.

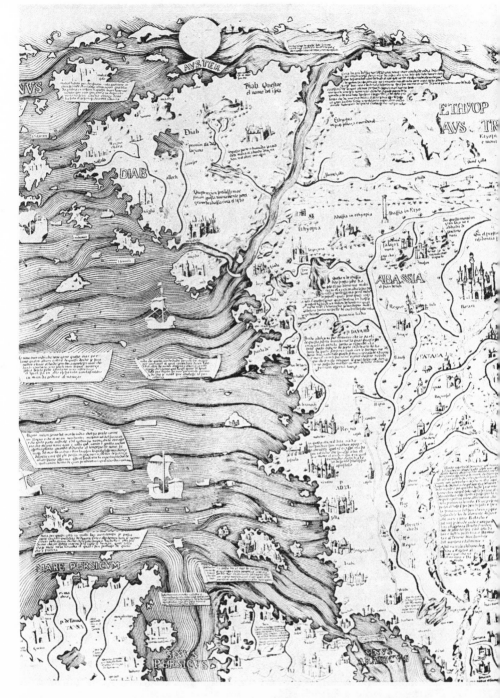

Map prepared for the Portuguese court by the Venetian Fra Mauro in 1459. This section show the east coast of Africa and Madagascar ('Diab'), viewed from the north. A Chinese junk can be seen pressing round the southern tip of the continent, and the inscription on the adjacent coastline records the voyage it made in 'about the year 1420'.

Soldiers from Mozambique guarding the Portuguese governor's palace in Macao. The Portuguese still used African troops in their Chinese colony as late as the 1960s.

Chinese labourers on their way to the South African gold-mines in 1904. Many European settlers were afraid that they would be swept from the continent by an Oriental flood.

Chinese gold-miners in South Africa were confined to guarded compounds to prevent them migrating to the cities and competing for European jobs. The miners in this compound have just been corralled by their European overseers.

Chinese coolies in the French Congo, 1929. Their cheerful appearance is misleading. In fact they resisted every attempt by their French employers to make them work.

ched by his African neighbour, a
ese trader dries sea-slugs outside
ouse in Zanzibar.

ve) Chinese adaptability. This
er settled in the Bajun islands off
coast of Somalia. He wore local
s and adopted a Moslem name,
kh 'Abd al-Adhidhi.

rophet of African nationalism and
disciple. The ninety-three-year-old
k American intellectual W. E. B.
Bois greets Kwame Nkrumah, first
sident of Ghana, at a conference in
2. DuBois told African leaders,
ina is flesh of your flesh and blood
our blood'.

The 'Young Chinese Missionary' (see p. 69).

Ping-pong diplomacy, literally. China's prime minister Zhou Enlai makes friends with President Nkrumah during his great tour of Africa in 1963–4.

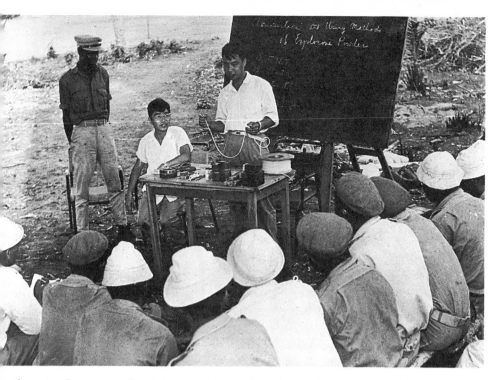

erthrowing European rule. Chinese instructors lecturing on the properties of explosives a class of guerrillas from several different territories at a training camp in rural Ghana.

odesian bomb disposal experts grapple with a Chinese land-mine.

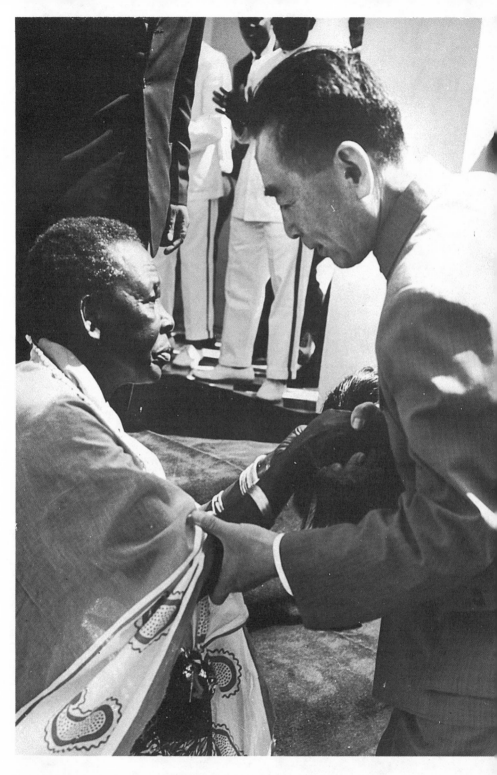

One of the principal reasons for Zhou Enlai's impact on Africa was his matchless courtesy. This photograph shows him greeting the mother of President Nyerere of Tanzania.

(*above*) The Cultural Revolution in Africa. A Chinese official in Mali distributes portraits of Chairman Mao Zedong to members of the public. Many young Africans were enthralled by the Cultural Revolution; but Chinese proselytizing annoyed and frightened their governments.

Fighting the USA. Chinese actors made up to look like Africans perform a drama glorifying the African resistance to US intervention in the Congo-Léopoldville (Zaire).

(*Far right*) China versus Russia: the struggle for influence. This photograp[h] shows President Siad Barr[e] of Somalia addressing a revolutionary rally in 1973[.] The Chinese ambassador has secured himself a plac[e] on the president's left. Th[e] Soviet ambassador has be[en] upstaged.

(*Left*) Peking versus Taiwan[.] Nationalist China's Africa expert, Vice Foreign Minister H. K. Yang, bids for the diplomatic support of President Mobutu of Zaire by awarding him the Special Grand Cordon of the Heavenly Stars. Yang's success was short-lived (se[e] next photograph).

Mobutu in Peking. The grand reconciliation. Mao tells Mobutu: 'I wasted a lo[t] of money and arms trying [to] overthrow you.' Mobutu answers: 'Well, you backe[d] the wrong man.'

(*Right*) Conscious of their fading revolutionary glamour, the Chinese have[e] quietly renewed their commitment to the cause o[f] African freedom. On a visi[t] in August 1986, Bishop Desmond Tutu of South Africa is received by leade[rs] of the Shanghai Communi[st] Church.

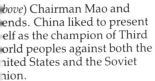

(*above*) Chairman Mao and
friends. China liked to present
itself as the champion of Third
World peoples against both the
United States and the Soviet
Union.

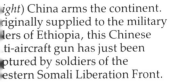

(*right*) China arms the continent.
Originally supplied to the military
rulers of Ethiopia, this Chinese
anti-aircraft gun has just been
captured by soldiers of the
Western Somali Liberation Front.

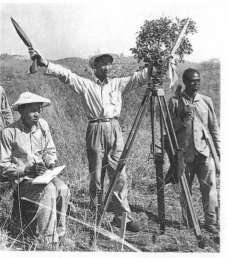

(*Left*) China develops Africa. Engineers from Peking exhibit confident authority as the 'Tan–Zam' railway advances into the bush.

(*Right*) China leaves its marl on the landscape. This bridg was built by Chinese engine at Mange, Sierra Leone.

(*Far right*) Terminus of the Tan–Zam railway at Dar es Salaam, Tanzania. The building is strikingly reminiscent of the railway stations in Peking and Cant

(*Above*) Chinese technicians c the railway made a point of sharing the hardships of thei Tanzanian and Zambian colleagues.

(*Left*) African labourers noted that the Chinese were always smiling, and always polite.

(above) A Chinese clinic in Zanzibar. Chinese medical teams work in the remoter parts of many African countries, and the demand for their services is sometimes overwhelming.

(right) The Chinese commercial challenge. A roadside hoarding in Bamako, Mali advertises Temple of Heaven Essential Balm. This Chinese ointment is popular all over West Africa.

(*Above*) The persisting student problem. African students in China find the environment oppressive and the people unfriendly. This photograph shows students marching down a Peking street during protest demonstration organized in June 1986.

The Chinese as teacher. Late 1986 Peking announced its intention of sending specialist teachers to Africa under a new programme of 'intellectual aid'. Useful and inexpensive, this teaching programme could become an important part of China's activity on the continent in the next few decades.

4

❖❖❖❖

Idealism versus Statecraft

The Chinese then stepped in . . .
We're Communists brothers
to help you build Black Socialism.
Only you must kick out the Russians.

Lenrie Peters, Gambian poet, *Satellites*, 1967

'Guinea may be poor,' President Sekou Touré once declared, 'but we have remained faithful to African ideals.' Many Africans approached independence in an idealistic spirit. After decades of foreign manipulation they yearned to be free of the pressures of the outside world. They did not want to be dragged into alien quarrels like the Cold War, and sometimes they spurned foreign powers that tried to force them to take sides. Unfortunately this was a luxury they could not very often afford. They still needed foreign help to realize their aspirations of building up their countries and delivering their fellow-Africans who were still under European rule. And help and interference went hand in hand, for most foreign powers expected a political return for their assistance. With perhaps one exception: China in its missionary period seemed to the Africans who dealt with it a unique case of a foreign power which did not subject them to pressure. 'At no time', said a Tanzanian diplomat who had served as ambassador to Peking, 'were we reminded or ever made to feel that we represented smaller nations.' China seemed free of ulterior motives. Guerrillas came back from their training convinced that the Chinese were helping them for altruistic reasons. Many Africans felt that China shared their outlook and their goals.

The Chinese took some trouble to foster this impression. When they first appeared in modern Africa at the end of the 1950s they behaved, in one respect, exactly like their Ming dynasty ancestors five and a half centuries before. They used Moslems. As the Ming emperors had sent Zheng He, the Moslem admiral, with his Arabic-speaking interpreters to explain Chinese intentions to the Islamic world of the western Indian Ocean, so the Chinese Communists introduced themselves to Africa

105

by cultivating the adherents of the continent's fastest-growing religion. Members of the small Moslem minorities who lived on the fringe of the new People's China, Uighurs and Kazakhs from the central Asian grasslands, went to Mecca on pilgrimage and from there fanned out into Africa, conversing with the divines and praying in the mosques in the various countries where Islam prevailed, from Somalia in the east to Guinea on the Atlantic coast. African Moslems who came to China were greeted by dignitaries with curious names, half Arabic, half Chinese – Mohammed Ali Zhang Jie, Sheikh Nur Mohammed Da Peisheng – and invited to celebrate the major Islamic festivals in mosques presided over by turbanned Chinese imams. The Chinese were using Islam as a way of conveying to Africans that China was a country fundamentally similar to theirs. At a banquet he gave in the early sixties for a team of trainee guerrillas Mao Zedong made a bolder assertion. China and Africa, he insisted, were one and the same.

The fact was, however, that the Chinese Communists came to Africa with purposes of their own. They were not only missionaries, but also cool strategists. In the foreground they preached the cause of African freedom; in the background they fought a series of duels up and down the continent with the assorted enemies of their new state. But the Chinese were well aware of the idealistic African wish to be free of the pressure of foreign conflicts. They had to avoid affronting African idealism. If possible, they had to enlist it on their side. By insisting that China and Africa were identical, they hoped to persuade Africans that China's enemies were their enemies too.

The Chinese entered Africa locked in combat with the United States. Ever since the Korean War of the early 1950s, when Chinese and American troops fought on opposite sides, the United States had posed a threat to the security of the new Communist China. By the mid-sixties American land and air forces were accumulating uncomfortably close to China's southern border, as they poured in to defend the beleaguered government of South Vietnam. As a principal sponsor of the Vietnamese Communists whom the United States was fighting, China faced the real possibility of an American attack.

But the United States was also active in other quarters. As the European powers pulled out of Africa, the United States had stepped into many of the new African countries as a bringer of economic aid and a defender of Western political interests. It had stepped, most conspicuously, into Congo-Léopoldville. The Central Intelligence Agency (CIA) had

CONGO (L) S. VIET NAM

'The Tropics Are Getting Hotter'. The Chinese viewed Congo-Léopoldville as a 'second South Vietnam' in which the United States could be trapped. Cartoon in *Peking Review*, 21 August 1964.

worked to bring about the downfall and death of the radical premier, Lumumba, and massive American funds had been poured in to bolster the pro-Western regime that replaced him. By 1964 American pilots serving under contract to the Congolese government were flying bombing missions against the rebels who had risen up in the martyred Lumumba's name, and United States transport planes were dropping Belgian paratroops on the rebel stronghold of Stanleyville. The Chinese detected in the Congo the prospect of a 'second South Vietnam'. They observed with satisfaction that America was 'divisible'. United States forces could be pinned down in different parts of Asia and Africa: hard-pressed in one place, they would loosen their grip on others. The Chinese had apparently come to think of Africa in general, and the Congo in particular, as an arena into which American energies could usefully be diverted from their own frontiers.

To embroil the Americans successfully in Africa the Chinese had first to convince its people that they too, like China, faced an American threat. Chinese diplomats began touring the continent and explaining to any Africans who would listen that the United States rather than the vanishing European empires was now their principal enemy. Africans should think twice, in the words of the Chinese proverb, before 'driving out the wolf by the front door to let in the tiger by the back'. They should not be dazzled by American aid. The Americans meant to annex the Congo and gorge themselves on its mineral wealth. Stained with the blood of Lumumba, they would never repent and never 'lay down their butchers' knives'.

Drama made the point handily. In 1965 a drama troupe from the Political Department of the Chinese navy, made up to look like Africans, appeared in Peking in a seven-act play called *Battle-Drums on the Equator*. Visiting Congolese rebels were taken to see the play performed. The plot describes the efforts of a Congolese family to free their country from Western domination. The Congo's former Belgian colonists are represented by a seedy ex-governor named Lubens, but the real villain is an American general called Wayne (John Wayne, presumably) who embraces the Congolese with bogus geniality and sneers at Lubens behind his back. The climax is reached when the hero, Mwanka, misled until now into working for the Americans, balks at a request that he kill Lumumba on their behalf. Grasping at last the true nature of his employers, he turns on them with a valour reminiscent of those other Africans dreamt up by Chinese writers a thousand years earlier – the Kunlun servants of the Tang dynasty stories. He drinks a bottle of unspecified liquor and gives General Wayne 'a tremendous punch. Wayne falls to the ground, the table topples over and a sergeant fires into the air. The GIS who try to tie up Mwanka are knocked over. Mwanka throws back his head and laughs, utterly fearless.'

A subsidiary hero in the play is a black GI named Warren. He changes sides and joins the Congolese. The Chinese were particularly eager to draw the attention of Africans to the hardships experienced by the black population of the United States. In August 1963 Mao made a formal declaration in support of the black American civil rights movement – to an audience of African visitors. America, the Chinese implied, was the enemy of all black people.

Africans were not at first disposed to accept what the Chinese were trying to tell them. The United States was attractive – ironically, for much the same reasons as China was. It had not taken part in the colonial invasion of Africa, and it was felt to be sympathetic to the cause of African freedom. Several guerrilla movements took American funds, and some of the most radical independent governments were impressed by President Kennedy's administration and its apparent desire to aid them.

Kennedy was personally respected in Africa. The Chinese caused much offence by protesting at a tribute paid to the president by an international conference after his assassination in November 1963, and claiming that they did so with the support of African delegates. Zhou Enlai was obliged to make amends for the blunder of his less sensitive colleagues by declaring on his arrival in Africa two weeks later that the assassination had been an 'odious act'.

Episodes of this kind made Africans conscious that a foreign duel, unrelated to their concerns, was raging around them. Some leaders simply wanted to keep it off their soil. The monarch of Burundi, the Mwami, was hoping for American technical aid, and was embarrassed to find that his ministers had permitted the arrival of Chinese diplomats eager to use his country as a base for the rebellion against the American-backed government of the Congo. He sent the would-be Chinese ambassador a note informing him that his credentials would be accepted 'as soon as Chinese and American policies have been harmonized a little'. One or two leaders, however, nursed the grander design of stopping the duel altogether. It was another form of African idealism. On the one hand Africans wished to be left to themselves to pursue their small, local objectives: on the other hand they sought to assert their independence in the wider world, to go out and play a constructive role in the counsels of mankind. President Nkrumah of Ghana, for example, made his last, fatal trip to Peking in a quixotic attempt to settle the conflict which had brought China and America to the brink of open hostilities – the Vietnam War. He persisted with his efforts even after being told that he had just been deposed by his army. It was an intervention the Chinese neither wanted nor expected. The Chinese thought nothing of immersing themselves in the politics of Africa, but it does not seem to have struck them as reasonable that Africans in their turn should wish to take a hand in shaping the course of events in the Far East. In their eyes Nkrumah had plunged into an issue complex beyond his understanding. Zhou Enlai is said to have betrayed some rare signs of exasperation.

In spite of these frictions appreciable numbers of Africans gradually began to share the Chinese point of view. The United States lost its early popularity. This was partly because of the racial troubles in the United States itself, which did Washington's image much harm among African intellectuals influenced by black American leaders like DuBois. The principal reason, however, was America's obsession with fighting

Communism. The United States reacted to China's pinpricks with something close to panic. One American newsman described, for instance, how Africans were being bombarded with political publications mailed from the Peking address of Guoji Shudian. Guoji Shudian, he deduced, was an evil Chinese Moslem. (The name in fact means 'International Bookshop'.) Particular American alarm was occasioned by the revolution which took place in 1964 off the coast of East Africa in Britain's former island colony of Zanzibar, where the African majority rose up against their traditional Arab rulers. Rumours began to spread that the Africans had not acted alone. Sightings were reported of Chinese Communist troops. On closer inspection the Communist troops turned out to be neither troops nor Communists, but the old Chinese gatherers of sea-slugs who had lived harmlessly on the island since the beginning of the century. But that was no comfort when it emerged that the new Zanzibari leadership included a small number of fervent admirers of Mao Zedong. The United States took action. American diplomats hurried to warn the leaders of mainland East Africa that their largest offshore island was drifting into Chinese hands, and the nearest leader, Nyerere, was offered 'anything he wanted' by way of economic aid if he would take the island over. In the end Nyerere and the main Zanzibari leaders decided of their own accord to go ahead with a merger. It was perhaps as well that they did so. Failing a merger an alternative plan was in readiness for British military intervention on the island with American support.

The Americans were prepared to resort to fairly drastic methods to eject the Chinese from Africa. The CIA is said to have supplied bogus documents purporting to prove China's involvement in plans to set up a secret army which were used to justify the overthrow of the government of the Central African Republic in January 1966. CIA operatives in Ghana had a mind to go further. Aware that the army was plotting to topple President Nkrumah, they apparently suggested taking advantage of the confusion of the *coup* to storm the Chinese embassy, kill the inmates and seize the archives.

This anti-Communist manoeuvring was not welcome in Africa. Leaders friendly to China were irritated by American charges that their countries were succumbing to Chinese influence, thereby implying that Africans lacked an independent identity and the wit to preserve it. Africans also sensed that the United States had lost its sympathy with their aspirations, and they were not far wrong. From the mid-sixties onwards

United States interest in African affairs waned rapidly, and in 1969 the Nixon administration formally opted to dismiss independent Africa as inherently hostile territory and to give priority to its ties with the more congenial white regimes of the south. Africans in arms against the white regimes concluded that the Chinese had been right: the United States was their enemy and the supporter of their enemies. Under these circumstances it is easy to see why they came to the further conclusion that the Chinese were helping them without ulterior motives. The Chinese duel with America had become inconspicuous, camouflaged by the fact that China's opponents were now the same as theirs.

Less easily camouflaged was the duel that took place between China – and another set of Chinese. When the Chinese Communists took power in 1949, the defeated Nationalist regime of Chiang Kai-shek had fled over the water to the island of Taiwan. The United States interposed its military power to save the Nationalist regime from extinction, and continued to recognize it as the rightful government of China. Most of Washington's allies in Western Europe, Asia and Latin America fell into line with the United States policy of isolating the new Communist government in Peking by maintaining diplomatic relations with the Taiwan exiles. Supported by the United States and its allies, Taiwan's representatives continued to occupy the Chinese seat at the United Nations in New York. Taiwan threatened the legitimacy of the new People's China. China's Communist leaders faced a predicament a little like that of the Ming emperor Yong'le, uneasy on his throne, troubled by reports that his predecessor survived on the other side of the ocean, seeking the acclaim of distant lands to bolster his prestige.

China was isolated, but as Mao once remarked it was not isolated in Africa. Africa in the sixties was the one major region of the non-Communist world where Peking's diplomats could hope to find a welcome. Africa's new countries insisted on their neutrality: they did not automatically take their cue from the United States. Some African governments in fact made a point of recognizing Peking as a signal that they were free now of Western tutelage and masters in their own house. And African recognition was valuable. African countries were small, but numerous. Each had a seat at the United Nations, and each had the right to cast a vote in the debate which was held year by year to determine whether the Chinese seat belonged to Peking or Taiwan. Each year the victory of the Taiwan delegates became a little more uncertain, as more and more African states took their places in the world organization. Africa, if it wanted, could nibble through the cord with which the West kept China bound.

The Taiwan Chinese saw the danger, and moved to forestall it by persuading African countries to recognize them. In 1960 they organized, with American advice and funding, a project called Operation Vanguard designed to make Taiwan attractive to Africans by filling their continent with Taiwanese news agencies, acrobatic troupes and above all technical aid teams. Like their rivals in Peking they were full of the urge to teach. 'We want to tell Africans about our experience so that our African friends can escape what we have suffered.' Sympathetic African leaders were invited to Taiwan to sip tea with Chiang Kai-shek and learn from the lips of the ageing Generalissimo that they should never, never let Communists get a foothold in their countries. Taiwan's warnings were accompanied by lavish gifts and praise. In West Africa, for example, the Malian leader Modibo Keita was courted unsuccessfully with reproductions of three hundred Chinese paintings from the National Palace Museum, while Félix Houphoüet-Boigny, the president of the Ivory Coast, who came out emphatically for Taiwan, was hailed as the 'leader of leaders'.

Taiwan's campaign was masterminded by a diplomat known as 'Mr Africa', a vice minister of foreign affairs named H.K. Yang. Yang has the distinction of having conducted one of history's more obstinate rearguard actions. Year after year he trudged round the continent, suitcase always packed, ever ready to plead with governments whose loyalty to Taiwan was faltering and ward off the avalanche of adverse African votes which threatened to sweep Taiwan forever from its United Nations seat. When Peking fell foul of a country, Yang would slip in rapidly to solicit recognition, bringing the aggrieved African rulers appropriate condolences and greetings from Chiang Kai-shek. He appeared, for instance, in Ghana after Nkrumah's overthrow in the hope of befriending the new pro-Western military regime, and it was here on one occasion that the normally silent duel flared up into open hostility, when a New China News Agency correspondent ran into Yang at the airport and shouted at him.

Peking reacted with alarm to Taiwan's arrival in Africa. Here, said the official *People's Daily*, was an 'extremely dangerous conspiracy' which 'we deem it necessary to explain further to our African friends'. Peking's diplomats hastened to compete with Taiwan's in the race for recognition. Each country that won independence got warm cables from Zhou Enlai and his colleagues, congratulations and assurances that China recognized *it*. He Ying and his fellow-ambassadors moved round the African map like knights on a chessboard, pressing their suit in countries close to the ones where they were posted. If a government which had previously recognized Chiang Kai-shek agreed to abandon him and embrace Peking instead, the Chinese Communists undertook to take over any technical aid schemes that Taiwan had embarked on. If a government spurned them, on the other hand, they might throw their support to local dissidents. Peking never supported risings against governments willing to deal with it, but it was on occasion prepared, through a little judicious needling, to remind those regimes which refused it recognition that they did so at a price. In February 1964, when Zhou Enlai visited Ethiopia, Emperor Haile Selassie promised to establish regular diplomatic relations with Peking. He failed to keep his promise, and China accordingly spent the next few years training guerrillas who were fighting to free the coastal province of Eritrea from Haile Selassie's rule.

African governments found themselves harangued simultaneously by two shrill bands of mutually hostile Chinese. Many of them were caught unawares by the bitter antagonism between the two Chinese regimes, each of which viewed the other as a threat to its identity. Civil servants in one country innocently sent Zhou Enlai a present in the form of a biography of their leader with old photographs showing the great man on Taiwan being embraced by Chiang Kai-shek. The Foreign Ministry in Peking feared that they would have no alternative but to register their extreme displeasure by sending the volume back. Grave diplomatic embarrassment threatened, but luckily the Ministry felt obliged to inform Zhou Enlai before they rejected the book on his behalf. Zhou with his usual elegance is said to have laughed at the blunder, observing that history was history and he himself had once, in the 1920s, been a member of Chiang Kai-shek's staff.

Even where governments were sensitive to the intra-Chinese feud, they did not entirely see why they should have to take sides, or pay for one party's friendship with the other's. They bridled predictably when one side or the other pressed its case too hard. Twice in 1964 He Ying made the journey from his base in Tanzania to the adjacent British colony of Nyasaland. Nyasaland was about to win its independence as the republic of Malawi, and He Ying hoped to induce the new country's leader, Dr Hastings Banda, to recognize Peking. He offered Banda's government financial assistance: £6m on the first visit, £12m on the second. It was standard Chinese practice, but Banda jibbed violently. He announced that he was an Elder of the Church of Scotland, and was not going to be bribed. He plumped for the rival candidate. By the end of the following year he had arranged for a team of agronomists from Taiwan to instal themselves in the northern town of Karonga, strategically placed to keep an eye on the officers who had been sent by Peking to train guerrillas across the border in the bush camps of southern Tanzania. Set a Chinese to catch a Chinese.

Yet the duel was not wholly unpopular. Unlike the Sino-American conflict it did not overwhelm Africans: they held the whip-hand. Only they could bestow the diplomatic recognition which the Chinese rivals wanted. There was room for exploitation. Leaders could offer their favours to Peking or Taiwan in return for economic largesse, could in fact pressurize *them* with a timely threat to change sides. In an exercise in diplomatic sadism Jean-Bedel Bokassa, tyrant of the Central African Republic, remarked on the eve of a visit to Taiwan that he was ready to establish relations with Peking if it wished. Taiwan was appropriately generous.

More than that, the duel appealed to African chivalry. Many African leaders were moved to compassion by the claims of Peking. People's China, they felt, was a colossal reality, hundreds of millions of human beings: it was no good the United States pretending that it didn't exist. Nyerere quoted Abraham Lincoln: 'God must have loved the common people; otherwise He would not have created so many of them.' Here was the opportunity Africans had longed for to play a decisive role in international affairs. They could lead this great country out of its isolation and into the human community. Only Africans could do it because only Africans occupied the necessary position halfway between China and the West. Nyerere, for instance, was Peking's friend, used to the esoteric style of Chinese political discourse yet used, at the same time, to Westerners and Western ways of thinking. He believed that his small state, Tanzania, could put Peking's case better than the Chinese could or would do themselves, that it could give China a window on the world and interpret China and the West to each other.

Above all Africans saw that they could tip the scales at the United Nations. In the early and middle sixties, when its chances of admission still seemed remote, Peking had railed at the world organization as a cat's-paw of the Americans. This was not a very popular stance in Africa, for Africans increasingly saw the United Nations as *their* organization, a forum in which their little countries could expect to be listened to. At the end of the decade, however, Peking's attitude changed. The new, mild China which appeared on the scene after the disasters of the mid-sixties made it plain that admission to the United Nations was now high on its agenda. The African response was immediate. Friendly governments took the soundings with their neighbours necessary to pave the way for a visit by a Chinese ambassador, the establishment of diplomatic relations and the pledge of a fresh African vote for Peking. At the United Nations General Assembly in 1970 six African states dropped their veto on Peking's entry, and more votes for the first time went to Peking than Taiwan. One year later, in October 1971, the long-awaited avalanche rolled. Peking received 76 votes out of 111, the two-thirds majority necessary to evict Taiwan from its seat. Of those 76 votes a crucial 26 were African. Mali and Algeria were Peking's sponsors, and a former Tanzanian ambassador to Peking led the floor. Africans knew they had made a lasting impact on China's international fortunes. Their delegates exulted. 'Arms swooping above their heads', they 'jumped up and down in their seats as wild applause engulfed the circular chamber'.

The Chinese Communists had won their African duel with Taiwan. Little remained for them to do but consolidate their victory. Quietly, usually in third countries, their envoys made contact with the representatives of those African states that continued to keep their distance, and persuaded them to switch their support from Taiwan to Peking. By the mid-1980s only three countries on the continent still clung to Taiwan's cause: two states in the South African political orbit, Malawi and Swaziland, and South Africa itself.

While idealistic Africans rejoiced in Peking's triumph, the defeated Chinese of Taiwan cut their losses with icy pragmatism. If independent Africa spurned them, they would turn to the white south. Already in the early sixties, when they used their United Nations seat to strike one or two modestly anti-colonial poses, they had themselves explored with the tottering Portuguese empire a scheme for nothing less than colonization. In June 1962 the Central News Agency of Taiwan broadcast the details of a visit which had just been made to the island by the Portuguese director of information and tourism. The official had brought with him a proposal to the effect that five hundred families of Chinese settlers should be transplanted from Taiwan to Portugal's rebellious province of Angola. Others, it was hoped, would follow, and the Portuguese

115

even extended an invitation to refugees from the Chinese mainland, provided they first got screened politically by the authorities in Taiwan. The immigrants were to be encouraged to organize their own communities and schools, and to revive the province's economy with their investment and technical skills. The idea, apparently, was to glue Portugal to Angola with a layer of Chinese ethnic cement.

The scheme was never implemented, but it offered the first intimation of a realignment to come.

In April 1976 H.K. Yang reappeared on the African stage in a new role. 'Mr Africa' had become Taiwan's first ambassador to Pretoria. Taiwan and South Africa, the world's pariahs, were joining forces. Plans were discussed for industrial cooperation, and for Taiwanese investment in the nominally independent 'black homelands' which had been hived off from South Africa, the Transkei and Ciskei. The essence of the new partnership was not, however, economic, but military. Commanders of the Taiwanese armed forces toured South African bases in Namibia, and South African officers were sent to Taiwan to be trained in political warfare. The two partners were combining against a common Chinese enemy. They exchanged information on Peking's weaponry and on its support for the guerrilla movements of southern Africa. South Africa was said to be considering the purchase of Taiwan's Hsien Feng ground-to-ground missiles, and there were ominous signs that the partners were helping each other to manufacture nuclear weapons. The Taiwan Power Company ordered a supply of 4,000 tons of South African uranium to be delivered in the period 1984–90, and scientists from Taiwan were reported in return to be assisting South Africa with research projects intended to bring its uranium to nuclear weapons grade. Such collaboration constituted no great threat to Peking. Even if they did make atomic weapons, the Nationalists on Taiwan would be unlikely to use them against the Chinese motherland. But if Taiwan helped South Africa to acquire a nuclear armoury, the outlook for independent African countries might not be so bright. After the warm professions of friendship which Taiwan had made to independent Africa for so many years it was a somewhat shocking demonstration that for these Chinese, at any rate, Africa's welfare was not a high priority.

China's third and greatest African duel had its roots in the quest for independence. Ironically, the new Communist China which preached

independence to African peoples was not, in the strictest sense, independent itself. Within weeks of their victory in 1949 Mao Zedong and his
colleagues had felt obliged to insure themselves against the danger of
an American attack by forming an alliance with the Soviet Union. In
political, economic and military terms, China became a client of the Soviet
Union, guided by Soviet advisers and sustained by Soviet aid. It was
a role that could not be easily reconciled with the ambition of the Chinese
Communists to restore their country to its traditional majesty. Within
five years the Chinese were growing restive.

The Chinese were not content to be confined to the Soviet camp. They
saw a chance to establish a separate identity in the world of newly independent Asian and African states. In April 1955 these new states gathered
together for the first time in the Indonesian city of Bandung, at a meeting
intended to express their sense of a shared history and common goals.
China, as an Asian country, was invited: the Soviet Union was not.
The Chinese made the most of the occasion. Their spokesman, Zhou
Enlai, captivated the delegates. In a speech unclogged by Marxist ideology, he called on the world's new nations to sink their political differences
and present a common front. The Chinese had found in Asia and Africa
a possible camp of their own.

Five years more, and the Chinese were striking out openly for their
political freedom. China rejected the doctrines expounded by the Soviet
Union and set itself up instead as the pillar of Communist orthodoxy.
In the Communist world as in the Western world, China faced isolation;
and once again the Chinese found themselves looking to Africans for
political support. African sympathy would make it harder for the Soviet
Union to treat the Chinese as outcasts from progressive mankind. The
Chinese accordingly challenged the policies of Khrushchev and his successors with rival doctrines calculated to appeal to Africa in particular.
Chinese spokesmen argued that the 'revisionist' Soviet leadership was
selling Africa short through its emphasis on improving relations with
the West, and insisted that Africans must have the right to rise up violently against their Western masters even if they threatened, by doing
so, to entangle their Communist patrons in an East–West conflict. The
Russians denounced the Chinese as irresponsible, and maintained that
African independence could be won by peaceful means. Both sides
pressed Africans to choose between their conflicting interpretations of
the correct Marxist approach to an assortment of issues ranging from
nuclear disarmament to the Cuban missile crisis. The quarrel raged with

steadily increasing fury at the meetings of a body called the Afro-Asian People's Solidarity Organization (AAPSO), which had sprung up largely under Soviet guidance in the years after the Bandung gathering as a forum for governments and independence movements anxious to hasten the end of colonial rule. By the mid-sixties the conferences of the unfortunate AAPSO began to resemble the synods of the early Christian church, furious bishops exchanging anathemas and wrangling over the nature of the Trinity. Unsuccessful in their attempt to weaken the tightening Soviet grip on the organization, the Chinese by 1967 had elected to boycott it and form rival assemblies under their own aegis.

The Chinese soon discovered that none of the major African independence movements was willing to forfeit Soviet backing by endorsing their doctrines. They switched their support to rival, breakaway groups, where these could be found, and occasionally tried to win over the following of the recalcitrant parent bodies. In Southern Rhodesia, for example, the leader of the ZAPU party, Joshua Nkomo, refused to come out against the Russians. ZAPU, as it happened, had just arranged to send a batch of their recruits to be trained as guerrillas in the Military Academy at Nanking. The training went ahead as planned. The recruits were well treated, and were not penalized for the attitude of their leader: they did find, however, that the Chinese in various subtle ways invited them to question their loyalties. News bulletins containing statements made by their rivals, the breakaway ZANU faction which had taken China's side, were left thoughtfully on their beds or in their common room. On one occasion the recruits were given some fatherly advice by the Chinese foreign minister, Chen Yi. 'Joshua Nkomo', Chen Yi noted, 'is my friend.' But he urged the recruits to remember the history of collaboration between the Chinese Communists and Nationalists in the 1920s. For a while the Communists had had to follow the lead of the Nationalist politicians who were fighting to win control of China: but the Nationalists were not truly revolutionary, and the time came inevitably when the Communists were obliged to turn against them and work for their overthrow. The young Zimbabweans were puzzled, then taken aback when they realized that the parable was aimed at Nkomo. It had not occurred to them to see defects in their leader before.

Africans were unprepared for the deadly conflict between their Chinese and Soviet patrons. At first they refused to believe that the conflict existed. Then, with their usual instinct for reconciliation, they did their best to make peace. President Nkrumah of Ghana offered his services as a mediator, and Angolan guerrillas of the MPLA even brought Chinese and Russians together at a conference in Tanzania. If they couldn't stop the duel, they might at least stop the duellists from depriving the independence movements of badly needed support. Very occasionally someone succeeded in doing this. In 1964 the FRELIMO movement embarked on their rising against the Portuguese rulers of Mozambique. The Chinese invited FRELIMO to condemn the Soviet Union in exchange for training and military supplies. FRELIMO were non-committal, and it looked for a while as though Chinese aid would be squandered on a feeble splinter group called the Mozambique Revolutionary Committee (COREMO) which scarcely fired a shot. But the Chinese did sometimes take African advice. They listened, for example, to Nyerere, respecting him as an incorruptible statesman who told them the truth. And Nyerere was FRELIMO's principal sponsor. The Tanzanian president persuaded the Chinese to keep their assistance flowing to the one movement in Mozambique which really mattered.

Most of the time, however, Africans had no hope of containing the duel. They could not identify with it as they had, to some degree, identified with China's battle against the United States; they could not exploit it as they had exploited Peking's rivalry with Taiwan. It hampered their freedom of movement and distracted them from the sacred duty of rescuing their brothers in the white-ruled south. Above all it was a shock to their idealism. China and the Soviet Union professed to be creating a new and better world; yet here they were engaged in what some Africans suspected was at bottom, underneath all the doctrinal bickering, an old-fashioned and squalid tussle between nation-states. As for the bickering, Africans wanted none of it. They were not receptive to dogma. A Kenyan delegate to one of the Afro-Asian synods had a grumble for both the antagonists:

We are not Marxist–Leninists. Most of us have not read a line of *Das Kapital*, so what interest do you expect us to take in your doctrinal quarrels? I am tired of being asked what I think of the Soviet position when I am eating a sandwich, and what I think of the Chinese position when I am drinking my tea. I would like to be able to eat in peace.

African sentiment reared up in forms that the Chinese hadn't foreseen. In 1964–5 Zhou Enlai and his assistants were working to rally African support for a re-enactment of the triumphant Bandung conference of Afro-Asian countries from which, they hoped, the Soviet Union would once more be excluded. The new meeting was jeopardized by an accident of African politics. Days before it was due to begin, in June 1965, the host, Ahmed Ben Bella, the president of Algeria, was overthrown by a military *coup*. The conference had been a long time in the making, and the Chinese wanted it badly. They hurried to recognize the new Algerian regime, and called impatiently for business as usual. But African leaders were not disposed to behave as though nothing had happened. Military *coups* were still at this time a novelty on the continent, and rulers didn't like to see other rulers being toppled. Many of them were dismayed by the callousness with which China had deserted Ben Bella. Even Peking's closest ally, Nyerere, was distressed that the Chinese should have judged it more important to win a short-term political advantage than to stand by a fallen friend.

If in this case the Chinese gave an impression of indifference to local African concerns, at other times they were inclined to be more African than the Africans. They assumed everyone would applaud their insistence that Africa must fight the West whatever the repercussions in the world at large, and agree with them that the Russians were milksops to fret about the risk of upsetting the global equilibrium. But Africans didn't just care about Africa. They took, as we have seen, a lively interest in the fate of other parts of the planet, and many of them were disturbed by China's apparent indifference to the dangers of nuclear war. There was a broad African humanism that the Chinese had missed.

As usual the Chinese based their plea for African allegiance on the proposition that China and Africa were the same. Physiologically, they observed to a guerrilla from South Africa, Chinese and Africans were as good as identical. 'You're more or less like us: we're not really yellow nor you really black.' But the Russians were different. The Soviet Union, they insisted, was a European power which had no place in the new community of Asian and African nations. And the Russians were white. In territories like South Africa and Rhodesia, where the discrimination practised by the white regimes had tended to make people colour-conscious, this racial argument had some impact. Elsewhere on the continent, however, it fell flat. It was not just that people failed to detect any great physical resemblance between the Chinese and themselves. The truth was that Africans were not particularly given to thinking in racial terms. They were hostile to the European colonists who oppressed

120

them, but they were not, in a crude sense, anti-white. They were stirred by a growing consciousness of their African identity, sympathized readily with the plight of other Africans in different parts of the continent or across the Atlantic; but they were not narrow, not exclusive, not disposed to reject other peoples merely because those peoples were not of their kind. 'Before being Africans,' said Amilcar Cabral, the guerrilla leader from Guiné, 'we are men ... who belong to the whole world.'

Unresponsive though they were to most of Peking's arguments, Africans none the less warmed to the Chinese more than the Russians in these early years. The Soviet Union as well as China gave shelter to freedom fighters, but Soviet support was apt to seem lukewarm by contrast with Chinese enthusiasm. And Mao was more readable than Lenin. To Africans already independent the Soviet Union lacked China's compelling interest as a model for the future. African visitors to Moscow were awed by Soviet industrial progress and the splendid arcades of the Metro; but the Soviet Union, unlike China, seemed in the end too advanced and too complicated to have much to say about the direction their new countries should take. This did not stop the Russians from urging African states to embark on the first steps to socialism which Soviet theory considered appropriate for countries at their stage of development. Africans were not disposed to reject the Russians on racial grounds, but they did feel, in the words of their West Indian prophet, George Padmore, a 'desire to be mentally free from the dictation of Europeans, regardless of their ideology'. The Russians looked to many Africans a little too much like another set of Europeans arriving to give orders. Neither Chinese nor Russians succeeded in monopolizing the personal affections of African leaders, but it is clear that at the very least the Chinese held their own. The radical Kenyan politician Oginga Odinga declared that he felt more relaxed with the Chinese, that the Russians seemed reserved and 'too much like the British'. One of Nkrumah's officials remarked that if a Chinese offered you a drink he would keep his promise: 'the Russians are not like that, they may change their minds'.

At the end of the sixties the great duel took on a new character. In August 1968, in Czechoslovakia, the Soviet Union used troops to stamp out a heresy. Seven months later Russians and Chinese were fighting in the Siberian borderlands. Morbidly fearful of the Chinese millions,

Soviet military theorists began to hint at the possibility of subjecting China to a pre-emptive nuclear strike. The Soviet Union, the Chinese concluded, was no longer simply a doctrinal foe: it had replaced the United States as the major physical threat to their country. The Chinese did not take long to deduce that the time had come for a strategic realignment with the United States and its allies. Their enemy's enemy was their friend.

The Soviet Union was in one respect a more alarming enemy than the United States had ever been. The United States was a distant power which had established a hostile but transient presence on the soil of China's neighbours, Korea and Vietnam. But the Soviet Union was a neighbour itself. It sprawled for thousands of miles along China's northern land border. In addition it was, for the first time, building up a formidable ocean-going navy which could bottle up China's own fleet and strike at the Chinese coast. The Chinese looked on the Soviet naval advance in the Indian Ocean as part of a long-term strategic plan to encircle their country.

Even Africa, in the far west, was a focus of alarm. The Soviet Union was beginning to move into the continent as American interest flagged. The Russians had befriended the government of Somalia, a strategically valuable country which jutted out from East Africa into the western Indian Ocean: Soviet warships docked in the Somali port of Berbera, and from there embarked on sorties which carried them as far as the Equator. This advance was paralleled on the western side of the continent, where the Soviet navy patrolled routinely from 1970 onwards and had begun to win access to the harbours of a series of coastal states. For the first time the Chinese felt themselves threatened in Africa. Each strategic gain that the Soviet Union made there was, in their view, a small step forward in the attempt to throttle them. Soviet progress in Africa had to be halted. 'The monstrous claws of the Soviet Union must be chopped off wherever they stretch.'

It was with these considerations in mind that the Chinese at the end of the sixties cut short their apostolic mission and came back to Africa transformed. They had a new and urgent message. The Soviet Union, not the United States, was the principal enemy against whom Africans must now be on their guard. In the autumn of 1968 events in Nigeria gave the Chinese an early opportunity to signal their change of outlook. In the civil war convulsing that large and vitally important country the Biafran secessionist movement was drawing the bulk of its support from

Western sources. Much influential opinion in the United States was favourable to Biafra, and the likely winner of the impending American presidential election, Richard Nixon, had come out strongly on Biafra's side. But the Soviet Union had emerged as the principal arms supplier to the Nigerian federal government. The Chinese accordingly permitted themselves a public expression of sympathy for the Biafran cause.

Fresh waves of Chinese diplomats were hurried back to the continent to spread the new message. A particular effort was made to concentrate them in the region most troubling to Peking's strategists, the western Indian Ocean and the East African coast. Forty to fifty envoys were assigned to the single island of Mauritius: in the Comoro islands, between Mozambique and Madagascar, Chinese diplomats maintained in the mid-seventies the only embassy of any major power. The task of these Chinese Cassandras was to warn foolhardy governments against the perils of accepting the Soviet embrace. Zhou Enlai, in Peking, greeted Somali diplomats with a gentle caution, 'You must be careful of your friends.'

China's new message was addressed to all African leaders. Never mind if the leaders were emperors, or military dictators: that was a matter for Africans, for China was no longer in the business of crusading against conservative regimes. In keeping with their strategic shift towards the United States, the Chinese were even anxious to make friends with conservative, pro-Western rulers. One promising ally was Mobutu Sese Seko, the American-backed president of the former Congo-Léopoldville, which had now changed its name to Zaïre. Back in the mid-sixties, when they were besieging the Congo, the Chinese had reviled Mobutu as a swindler and puppet, and their cartoons had portrayed him with the head of a dog. In January 1973, however, after months of secret negotiations, Mobutu appeared in Peking. Mao greeted him blandly: 'I wasted a lot of money and arms trying to overthrow you.' Mobutu answered, equally blandly, 'Well, you backed the wrong man.'

The Chinese were not content merely to utter warnings. The Soviet threat was physical and demanded, consequently, a physical response. Within two years Zaïre had become the base for a Chinese attempt to check the Soviet advance in Africa by military means.

South-west of Zaïre, in the colony of Angola, three mutually hostile guerrilla movements were fighting the Portuguese overlords. We have already met China's early clients, the Popular Movement for the Liberation of Angola (MPLA). In the mid-sixties the Chinese had also trained

'Divide and Consume'. By the 1970s the Chinese no longer allowed themselves to discriminate between different African regimes, favouring radical leaders and opposing conservatives. Instead they attacked the Russians for doing precisely that. Cartoon in *Beijing Review*, no. 1, 1979.

the entire leadership of a second faction, the National Union for the Total Independence of Angola (UNITA). A third group, the National Front for the Liberation of Angola (FNLA), had flirted with China, but had never in the past been in a position to take assistance from the Chinese. The FNLA were based in Zaïre: their leader, Holden Roberto, was related to Mobutu by marriage, and the movement was sustained largely by Mobutu's goodwill. And till 1973, Mobutu and China were enemies. Now, however, having made his peace with Mao, Mobutu was anxious to get Chinese help for his kinsman. In December 1973 the Chinese received Holden in Peking, gave him acupuncture treatment for a cyst in his shoulder, and promised what he described as 'very special aid'. Special it certainly was. In August 1974 450 tons of Chinese armaments arrived at Holden's headquarters in Kinkuzu, southern Zaïre. One hundred and twenty Chinese military instructors descended on Kinkuzu to impart their experience to 15,000 of Holden's men. This was not the usual seminar for a team of guerrilla captains. The Chinese were training an army.

But what was the army for? Its obvious function was to contribute to the war effort against the Portuguese. But in April 1974 the government of Portugal had been overthrown by a military junta determined to extricate their country from its colonial wars. By the time the Chinese and their arms arrived at Kinkuzu in August the junta had signalled their clear intention of granting independence to Angola and the other Portuguese colonies. There was no further need to fight Portugal: Portugal was on the way out. Under these changed conditions the training of Holden's forces could only have one realistic purpose: to determine which of the three guerrilla factions would fill the vacuum that the Portuguese had left. The MPLA were best placed to take over, for they held the capital, Luanda. But this, for China, was an ominous prospect, for the MPLA had in recent years become Soviet protégés. By training Holden's army the Chinese could hope to counterbalance the MPLA, save a large and strategic territory from Soviet domination and halt the onrush of Soviet influence into the southern part of the continent.

Early in 1975 the strengthened FNLA marched south in an attempt to seize the capital. The result was civil war and, for the FNLA, a drastic retribution. The Russians were as determined to thwart the Chinese in Africa as the Chinese were to thwart them. Appalled at the possibility that China's surrogates might prevail, they weighed in massively on the side of their clients, fortifying the MPLA with shipments of tanks and missiles, squadrons of fighter bombers and regiments of Cuban auxiliary troops. The Chinese replenished Holden's armoury, and went on training his men. But China could only provide light weapons which were no match for heavy Soviet armaments, and China taught only guerrilla tactics which were no use against an enemy waging conventional warfare with Soviet advice. In November 1975, at a battle known as Death Road, the FNLA guerrillas whom the Chinese had trained for Holden panicked before the blast of Soviet rocket-launchers. They fled leaving behind them stacks of Chinese weapons and stores of Chinese rice. China and the Soviet Union had fought it out vicariously on an African battlefield, and the outcome did not say much for the prospects of Chinese forces in a full-dress war with the Soviet Red Army in the Far East.

The Chinese tried another method of foiling the MPLA, only to find themselves caught up in unforeseen complications. In March 1975 they promised 100 tons of arms to the MPLA's other rival, the UNITA movement. They did so at the suggestion of their old guide and ally, President Nyerere of Tanzania. Nyerere like other African leaders was reluctant at this stage to see the MPLA overwhelm their competitors. Six months later, however, with UNITA sucked into the conflict, the African mood had changed. Most African leaders wanted to stop the bloodshed, and the foreign intervention which was exacerbating it; and some, Nyerere included, were beginning to come round to the view that the best way to stop the bloodshed was to hasten the victory of the strongest group – the MPLA. The Chinese pressed on regardless. They delivered, in August, 93 tons of arms to Tanzania for forwarding to the UNITA troops. They received an unpleasant shock. Nyerere confiscated the weapons. Intent on their anti-Soviet campaign the Chinese had failed to register the change of heart of their closest African friend.

The Chinese even made a brief attempt to mediate on the strength of their old ties with the MPLA. By the latter part of the year, however, Angola was no longer the place for them, even in a mediating role. They were finding themselves in strange and increasingly awkward company. China was not the only outside power trying to thwart the Soviet Union. In September American arms began to arrive for the FNLA and UNITA, and on 23 October South African forces invaded southern Angola in an attempt to rescue those two movements from defeat. The Chinese didn't linger. Four days after the South African invasion China's military instructors were withdrawn from the FNLA camps in Zaïre.

By February 1976 the MPLA had prevailed over all their domestic and foreign opponents and had established themselves as the generally recognized government of Angola. The Chinese had failed in their bid to avert a Soviet strategic gain. It was the end of an episode, but not the end of the veiled Sino-Soviet war. The Chinese fell back on their next line of defence. Flushed with its success in Angola the Soviet Union began to cast an eye over the great central land mass of Zaïre and to foster opposition to President Mobutu's regime. In 1977–8 dissidents based in Angola and armed with Soviet and East European weapons launched two successive incursions into Zaïre's southern province of Shaba. The ironical consequence was that the Chinese came to the rescue of the very regime they had once tried so hard to undermine. Mobutu was immediately sent supplies of small arms, field artillery and anti-aircraft guns; and the Chinese began to consider how they could best protect the long-term security of Zaïre. On the Atlantic coast, at Banana, they embarked in 1980 on the construction of a naval base. Chinese engineers manned the radar equipment, and Peking is said to have tried to win a guarantee from Mobutu that control of the base's communications should be left in Chinese hands. Such an arrangement would have given the Chinese a centre for monitoring Soviet naval activity off the West African coast. At this daring proposal, however, Old Mo, as the Chinese diplomats called the president, apparently balked. The naval project was abandoned, but Chinese military assistance continued in other forms. A General Zhang was dispatched to Zaïre at the head of a team of 130 Chinese officers. By 1982 these officers had trained for Mobutu's benefit a commando brigade specializing in the techniques of counterinsurgency and skilled in the practice of Oriental martial arts.

Angola had taught the Chinese that they couldn't hope to compete with Soviet fire-power. They made no other attempt to tip the military balance, but instead sprinkled modest quantities of arms in countries where they saw the chance to win sympathy by making a symbolic point. Sometimes, as in Zaïre, they could cast themselves as deliverers of regimes exposed to a Soviet threat. Sometimes it happened, too, that a regime which had depended on Soviet military supplies would quarrel with the Russians and discover, in consequence, that its supplies were drying up. The Chinese knew all about that predicament. Back in the fifties they too had been equipped with Soviet weapons: they too had quarrelled with the Soviet Union and had been left abruptly to fend for themselves. They had survived the break by learning to manufacture

127

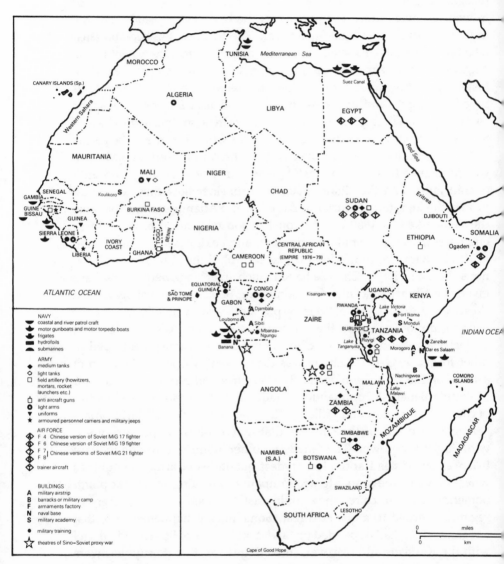

Map 4. Chinese military support for African governments since 1960. (Borders are those of Africa in 1988.)

128

substitute versions of the standard Soviet weapons like MIG fighters and
T-62 tanks, and they were, as a result, in a position to provide forsaken
African governments with the arms and spare parts that they needed.
It was technically appropriate, and a comment on Soviet perfidy. For
some years the Chinese improved the occasion by providing their weapons free of charge, as a way of demonstrating that China, unlike the
Soviet Union, was not an 'arms merchant'. Even the smallest Chinese
donations could be eloquent. The little West African coastal state of
Guiné-Bissau, formerly Portuguese Guiné, was aggrieved in the early
eighties at the inroads which Soviet trawlers were making into its offshore
reserves of fish. China thoughtfully supplied Guiné-Bissau with a couple
of coastal patrol craft.

In countries which steered a course close to the Soviet Union, the
Chinese made a point of being unobtrusive and tactful. Ethiopia was
a typical case. In the mid-seventies this ancient feudal realm had been
swept into a major social revolution by the overthrow of Emperor Haile
Selassie. The Chinese cultivated the military leaders who took over, and
were widely admired by the country's students and university graduates.
At the end of 1977, however, the Russians moved in. The Soviet Union
had initially been allied to the adjoining state of Somalia. But when
Somalia, earlier that year, invaded its Ethiopian neighbour to enforce
a territorial claim to the Ogaden border region, the Russians decided
to change sides. Large and strategically situated at the entrance to the
Red Sea, Ethiopia seemed to them a still more promising ally. They
abandoned Somalia and came to Ethiopia's rescue with tanks and artillery, Cuban infantry and planes. The Chinese commiserated with the
jilted Somalis. After the war was over they replenished Somalia's
defences with jet fighters and light arms. But they did not turn their
backs on Ethiopia. They never endorsed the Somali claim to the Ogaden
region, and never indulged in verbal attacks on the Ethiopian regime.
They inveighed against the outrage of the Soviet intervention, but were
careful not to blame the Ethiopians for permitting a Soviet presence
in their midst. In Mozambique, another fledgling Soviet ally, the Chinese
were equally restrained. They knew better by now than to browbeat
unresponsive governments into following their line. Chinese diplomats
drove home their anti-Soviet message in the most discreet of whispers.
'We think the Russians are dangerous – but you must make up your
own minds.'

But such measures were unlikely in themselves to dislodge the Soviet

129

Union from the continent. The Chinese believed that the Angolan and Ethiopian episodes were the prelude to a Soviet occupation of large parts of Africa. If China lacked the strength to resist it, other powers must be persuaded to do so in China's place. For years the Chinese had devoted their energies to chasing the West from the continent: now they decided that the West had better come back. Chinese leaders began to treat their new-found Western allies to a chilling interpretation of Soviet designs. The Russians, they explained, were driving south. They were trying to secure a series of bases on the East African coast and the islands of the western Indian Ocean – bases which they meant to serve as stepping-stones on their way to the Cape of Good Hope. Once the Cape of Good Hope was in their hands they would be able to wrest control of the sea lanes from the Americans and to threaten the supplies of oil and other raw materials which were shipped to Western countries round the southern tip of the continent. By similar means, and for similar reasons, they were also working their way north towards the Suez Canal. By dominating the coastline of West and North Africa they aimed to turn Europe's southern flank. Finally they were planning to seize Africa round the waist by gaining possession of three great territories, mineral-rich and strategically vital, which spanned the continent from ocean to ocean – Angola, Zaïre and Mozambique. The West, said the Chinese, must act. Why had the British not sent troops to defend Mobutu as the French and Belgians had? Even the American bases in Kenya might not be undesirable. The *New York Times* was sufficiently impressed by Peking's reasoning to print, in June 1978, an article with the euphoric headline *US, China Aims in Africa Coincide*. It is, in fact, unlikely that the Chinese were deeply concerned for the safety of Western mineral resources. They were simply applying their traditional strategic maxim: *Use barbarians to fight barbarians.*

By the late seventies the battle with the Russians took priority in Chinese minds over every other objective. The Chinese had even lost their stomach for African wars of independence. Southern Africa, in their view, had to be stabilized. There must be no more Angolas, no more convulsions which gave the Soviet Union a chance to elbow its way on to the scene. China's task now was to calm the fury of the guerrillas. In the last years of the Rhodesian insurgency Chinese arms deliveries to the ZANU movement dwindled to a trickle, and the Chinese impressed on ZANU's leaders their preference for a negotiated peace. When ZANU triumphed and Rhodesia became Zimbabwe, the Chinese used their

130

influence with Robert Mugabe's government to encourage toleration of the defeated white settlers who continued to stalk the country in their shorts and knee-length socks. The Chinese discovered that they rather liked the former white Rhodesians. These sturdy farmers, they observed, knew how to milk a cow and how to make the grain grow. Under Ian Smith's beleaguered administration they had given the country what China was always urging African regimes to achieve – a self-reliant economy. Their continued presence would help to keep Zimbabwe prosperous and stable, and make Soviet encroachment more difficult. This unexpected solicitude for the whites was displayed still more strikingly when the Chinese turned their attention to South Africa. Chinese leaders insisted that it had never been their policy to drive out the European minority who had lived there for so many centuries. Race war must be avoided at all costs: it would bring the Russians in. The only way forward for South Africa was a peaceful transition to a multiracial government.

The Russians struck back by airing the suggestion that China and South Africa were hand in glove. The Soviet media broadcast repeated charges that the Chinese were collaborating in South Africa's nuclear programme: disingenuous muddling, apparently, of the Peking Chinese with their Taiwan rivals who really were helping South African nuclear research. It was part of a general Soviet counterattack designed to wipe out the advantage China had enjoyed, in the sixties, in the hearts of African guerrillas. The Russians were well aware that China as a poor, non-European country exerted an attraction which the Soviet Union had never been able to match; but they thought they knew how to trump that particular card. The Cuban troops they brought to Angola not only came from a poor country but were also, frequently, black.

In independent Africa, similarly, the Russians were competing with a new vigour for radical support. As the Chinese grew milder, the Russians grew more muscular. The Soviet Union took up the cause of the dissident factions which the Chinese had avoided since they began to cultivate conservative African regimes. Elsewhere on the continent a new generation of radical leaders were proclaiming their allegiance to Marxism, and the Soviet Union offered itself to these leaders as their natural protector and guide. The upshot was that the great duel moved, in the course of the seventies, from the background to the foreground of events. It was no longer an esoteric doctrinal wrangle that bedevilled obscure meetings of guerrilla leaders and maverick politicians, but an

131

open struggle for influence that affected the calculations of every government in Africa. Even an elderly European lady, staying on in independent Zimbabwe, was aware of the rivalry. 'Is it true that Mozambique is the Russian one and we're the Chinese one?'

For Africans the duel was as repellent as ever, but they continued to show a preference for one or the other antagonist. In certain quarters the preference was clearly for the Chinese. Conservative, pro-Western leaders who had dreaded China in the sixties now viewed the Soviet Union as the principal foreign threat to their security. As the Russians pressed for strategic footholds in different parts of the continent they made enemies of several regimes, either by supporting their domestic opponents or by jilting them in favour of rival governments in more powerful neighbouring states. The Russians were still heavy-handed even in dealing with their friends. They were capable of exerting intense pressure on both governments and guerrilla movements to sever their ties with China, and sometimes they overdid it. When Mozambique became independent in 1975 the new Soviet embassy made a bid for precedence over their Chinese rivals. They demanded the right to present their credentials ahead of any other foreign mission. The Mozambique government bristled, and received the Chinese ambassador first.

In much of radical Africa, however, attitudes had changed to China's disadvantage. This time round it was the Russians who had the edge. Africans didn't find it easy to accept the new Chinese message that the Soviet Union was their enemy. They were impressed by Soviet firepower. The Soviet Union, not China, had emerged as the major source of arms for the independence movements. And Soviet arms were more useful. Movements could not win their wars simply by conducting hit-and-run raids with light Chinese weapons in the bush. To clinch their victory they had to be able to seize territory and hold it with the help of sophisticated artillery and anti-aircraft guns; and those sorts of armaments only the Soviet Union was able to provide. Some of China's clients began to grow restive. In 1974 a segment of ZANU's army mutinied out of frustration that their leaders' closeness to China prevented them from getting access to Soviet arms supplies. Radical governments in independent Africa began, in the same way, to turn to the Soviet Union because only the Soviet Union could give them the large-scale military backing they needed to survive. As Soviet military advisers moved in, so China's influence waned. In Burundi a team of Chinese military instructors were reduced to coaching the local basketball and volleyball teams. In Ethiopia the Chinese were tactful, but tact didn't save them. The Ethiopian military regime wanted arms to defeat the Somali invasion. Once they had beaten the Somalis they wanted more arms to suppress a multitude of rebellions launched by the Eritreans and other dissident groups. The Russians were ready and willing to provide the needed weaponry, and the regime judged it prudent to advertise their Soviet loyalties. In September 1978 mass rallies were held all over Ethiopia to condemn China's alleged connivance with the enemies of the Ethiopian state.

But the Chinese were not primarily losing ground because the Russians had more weapons or, for that matter, because the Russians were intrinsically popular. The fault lay in themselves. By giving up their mission they had ceased to frighten Africans; but they had also ceased to attract them. All over the continent China's admirers wavered, because China had subjected their ideals to a new and traumatic shock.

As the Sino-Soviet duel came into the open many Africans found themselves realizing for the first time that China was not, after all, a new type of country motivated by altruism alone. China was a great power like any other. It had come to their continent to achieve strategic objectives of its own, and was pursuing those objectives with a notably unsentimental brand of *Realpolitik*. Dissident intellectuals in independent Africa were dismayed to find China allying itself, in the name of anti-Soviet strategy, with the more unsavoury of their local tyrants. With Nimeiry, the Sudanese dictator who had slaughtered his country's Communists; with Mobutu, a monster of corruption who travelled to Peking with an entourage of 350 to buy silk for his wife. Guerrillas fighting in the white-ruled territories had long since accepted the old Chinese message that the United States was their enemy. They were tongue-tied at the spectacle of Chinese leaders welcoming that same President Nixon who had chosen to throw America's weight behind the white regimes. Radical governments recoiled from China's campaign in Angola. Not because of anything the Chinese had done, but because of their attitude. The Chinese had continued to insist, when South Africa entered the war, that the Soviet Union was the major villain. But for Africans the entry of Pretoria's troops changed everything. The *apartheid* regime was absolute evil, an evil African governments were determined to combat even if they had to sacrifice, in the process, the lives of their citizens and the health of their economies. Anything opposed to South Africa – Russians, Cubans or the devil – could not be entirely blameworthy;

and anything aligned with South Africa, however accidentally, could not entirely escape the taint.

The Soviet Union began to acquire a certain virtue in the eyes of Africans distressed by the ebbing of Chinese enthusiasm for all that they held dear. One PAC guerrilla from South Africa complained that the Chinese could 'do the dirty on you': the Russians were meddlesome, but at least they stuck by the movements they backed. As China subordinated the crusade against European rule to the higher demands of anti-Soviet diplomacy, Africans detected not merely ulterior motives but a chilling self-absorption that was, in its way, as repugnant as any interference would have been. Why, they asked, did China have such a *nationalistic* foreign policy? They began to think the unthinkable. *Did China really care what happened to them?*

Africans did care what happened to China. For years China had fought its duels on their continent with something like impunity, for the Chinese domestic experiment had dazzled them with a lustre which no amount of duelling could dim. China was China, something special and wonderful, a poor country defiantly making its own way forward untouched by the influence of the Western world. Shaken as they were, in the early seventies, by the cold new realism of Chinese diplomacy, African idealists could still take comfort in the knowledge that China's inner nature was unchanged. In the late seventies, however, even that last comfort was taken away from them, as the Chinese began to apply their unsentimental brand of statecraft to the remaking of China itself.

In 1976 the old Chinese leaders died within eight months of each other: first Zhou Enlai, then Mao Zedong. Change followed swiftly. One month after Mao's death his widow, Jiang Qing, and the three other extremist leaders who had stood at his elbow during the Cultural Revolution were arrested. They were held in confinement for four years, then put on public trial for their crimes. Chairman Mao, it was decided, had 'made mistakes'; his Cultural Revolution had been a disaster; and China began to question the whole body of economic and social dogma that had prevailed in Mao's time. For the Chinese, those expounders of dogma, were ultimately pragmatic. They wished to turn China into an advanced and powerful nation, and they were not prepared to carry on being shackled by doctrines that were patently holding it back. Guided by a new leader, Deng Xiaoping, whose motto was that it didn't matter whether a cat was black or white so long as it caught mice, they set about modernizing their economy with a dose of Western-style liberalism. Mao's great rural communes were broken up, and peasants were encouraged to engage in extensive sideline production for their own private profit. Factory hands who had once been expected to work out of sheer enthusiasm for the future Communist society were now offered financial incentives to increase their output. China in Deng's view needed not only Western economic liberalism but Western investment as well. The country which had once taken pride in its 'self-reliance' began to import large quantities of plant and technology from Japanese, American and European firms. The country which had purged itself of foreign debts began to borrow large sums of money from Western banks. It was the economic sequel to the strategic realignment with the West which China had engineered in the first half of the decade.

The Chinese were not abashed by their own change of course. They did not fight shy of their former African disciples but felt, on the contrary, a new urge to instruct them. It was China's duty to discourage friendly African countries from persisting in the attempts at collectivization on which they had embarked under the impact of Mao's ideas. After all, the Chinese reasoned, look at the state they were in. Tanzania and Guinea, for instance, were developing more slowly than any other countries on the continent, and Guinea's economy was even more backward than it had been before independence. Countries like Kenya and the Ivory Coast, which had never shown the least interest in learning from China but had stuck unashamedly to a Western-style, free-market economy, were progressing, by contrast, at a fairly healthy pace. Chinese diplomats hurried to drive these observations home. Their premise still seemed to be that China and Africa were identical: China had 'readjusted' its policies, so Africa must too. African regimes, they declared, should encourage Western investment, not drive it away. They should *not* collectivize their peasants and should *not* disdain the use of financial bonuses to stimulate their workers to perform. As usual the Chinese knew better than to lay down the law. African leaders, they noted, had already discovered these truths for themselves. Even that self-styled socialist, Sekou Touré of Guinea, had acknowledged that there could be a role for Western capital in a developing African economy.

It was a tactful way of putting it, but it didn't soften the blow. African leaders could hardly believe that these diplomats came from the China they had known. African leaders were dazed. They had lost, to begin with, the personal ties which had bound them to the giants of the Chinese revolution, and they felt the loss keenly. President Marien Ngouabi of Congo-Brazzaville had venerated Mao as an elder brother. He mourned Mao's death by staging a memorial ceremony in his home town of Owando. Some of the Chinese who attended the ceremony found it creepy. Here, lingering in the African forest, was the cult of their former leader – a cult to which they themselves had long since ceased to subscribe.

But Africans weaned on the *Little Red Book* could not bring themselves to swallow the new Chinese teaching that 'Chairman Mao made mistakes.' Most of them were instinctively loyal to their own major statesmen, the heroic generation who had led them to independence, and they were shocked to see China rounding on a leader it had followed for so long. They were upset, too, by the treatment of Mao's associates and especially his widow, Jiang Qing. An official in Zimbabwe remarked that the arrest of Jiang Qing had offended against his people's sense of propriety and their respect for family ties. The Chinese, he felt, should not have made a scapegoat out of a woman still 'half dead with anguish and sorrow from the loss of her great husband'. Later on they should have hanged her, if she deserved it, or let her alone: they should not, at all events, have made her into a public spectacle, not tried her in front of the television cameras.

This was not just nostalgia for a few personalities. Africans were not receptive to dogma, but they were receptive to ideas. And once they had absorbed an idea, they held fast to it. They could not bring themselves to discard it, as the Chinese could, pragmatically, unemotionally, because it wasn't working. They had embraced the values of Mao's China, and now they defended them with a stubborn faith. As Deng Xiaoping and his people raced to acquire Western knowhow, and Coca-Cola advertisements appeared on the streets of Peking, African intellectuals continued to argue the merits of self-reliance. Western investment, they conceded, might ensure a rapid growth rate and an abundance of creature comforts; but it was only by learning how to make their own goods and run their own enterprises that Africans could move forward, however slowly, with any kind of confidence and hope. The strange spectacle unfolded of Africans clinging to a China which the Chinese themselves had left behind.

Some African countries still contained 'pro-Chinese' factions, little bands of intellectuals knit together by their worship of Mao. These factions writhed. They could no longer even look to China for stirring political literature: the Chinese had no more to say to them, and all that came nowadays from Peking to Africa were medical journals, children's stories and glossy magazines. They yearned for Chinese revolutionary films, and were offered instead a historical romance called *Miss Rouge*. Some of them plunged into agonized internal debates, mulling over China's recent history, trying to persuade themselves that China had merely grown more outward-looking and had not sold its soul to the West. For others the strain was too great. They condemned Deng Xiaoping and his colleagues as apostates. China, they judged, was no longer China at all but 'part of Wisconsin'.

The anguish of the governments which had followed in China's footsteps was equally poignant, if rather better concealed. For fifteen years these governments had rallied their people with visions of Chinese-type communes and state-run factories: now the Chinese themselves were urging them to turn round and proclaim, in effect, that their visions had been mirages and their policies had been wrong. African regimes were not like the Chinese Communist Party. They did not have an iron grip on their subjects: they could not execute that kind of pirouette without exposing themselves to a devastating loss of prestige. There was little they could do but cling, unhappily, to their long-held beliefs. Leaders like Nyerere who visited Peking began to inquire anxiously if Mao's teachings had been wholly cast to the winds. Officials spoke sadly of China, their lost leader: 'the senior member of the club is no longer one of the club'. There was also, understandably, a touch of exasperation. It was all a bit rich. Here was China coming back, didactic as ever, with a brand new lesson exactly the opposite of the one it had taught before. Breathless from their doctrinal somersault, the Chinese were not yet in a position to teach with authority. 'Why should we listen to them', an African diplomat grumbled, 'when they haven't put their own house in order?'

Some governments looked for a substitute. Disenchanted with China, they still seemed to feel the need to be inspired by an Oriental power. Communist North Korea in the early eighties was a little like the China of fifteen years before. Its envoys came to Africa in bleak grey suits adorned with the badges of their leader, Kim Il-sung. They filled African libraries with copies of Kim's speeches, and borrowed the columns of African newspapers to advertise Kim's ideas. They armed guerrilla factions and fortified regimes, training the party youth wing, the security police and even, on occasion, the leader's bodyguard. There were differences, of course. Kim's volumes were not as digestible as Mao's had been, and were not always used for the purpose their author intended: Zambians were said to carry them over the border with illicit foreign banknotes sandwiched between the leaves. North Koreans, unlike Chinese, did not always give an impression of personal austerity. In Madagascar, for instance, they stayed at the Hilton, and were rumoured to have a fondness for breakfasting on champagne. But African leaders journeyed to the North Korean capital of Pyongyang and marvelled, as they once had in Peking, at their glimpses of streamlined discipline and selfless enthusiasm for advancing the freedom of others. North Korea had two great virtues which present-day China lacked. First, it did not threaten to engulf Africans in the obnoxious Sino-Soviet duel. North Korea took care to steer a political course equidistant between China and the Soviet Union: it was, in effect, a Communist halfway-house, a country which radical African governments could cultivate without drawing down on their heads the wrath of either of the two Communist giants. Soon after Zimbabwe became independent Robert Mugabe's regime considered inviting the Chinese to train the thuggish internal security force which became known as the Fifth Brigade. In the end, however, they settled for the North Koreans as a less controversial choice. Secondly, North Korea seemed to idealistic Africans to have preserved its purity as China had failed to do. It had kept ruggedly independent, free of Western economic and cultural influence. It had not betrayed their hopes.

The Chinese were forced to recognize by the end of the seventies that their duel with the Soviet Union had been a failure. They had not persuaded Africans to share their vision of a worldwide Soviet threat. Worse, they had lost their grip on the African imagination. They could no longer count on arousing sympathy among Africans disillusioned by China's internal policies; and without that basic sympathy it was hard to see how they could fight any more duels in Africa, with the Soviet Union or anyone else. For a while they washed their hands of the continent. Few Chinese leaders even had time to go there. China was busy cultivating new and more powerful allies – the United States, Western Europe and Japan. The Chinese were genuinely frustrated at the apparent African inability to understand their need to move away from the calamitous domestic policies of Mao's last years, and their reaction to African unease

138

was defensive and sometimes brusque. In 1981 a Malian journalist published an article critical of post-Mao China. Local correspondents of the New China News Agency called on him every day for a week to express their displeasure and suggest ideas for a new article retracting his earlier comments. Diplomats, not newsmen, he sighed.

By now, however, Chinese strategists were beginning to think again. The global picture was changing. For the first time in a quarter of a century the Soviet Union was making soothing noises to Peking, and while the Chinese were sceptical of Soviet intentions they no longer felt threatened in every corner of the world. They no longer believed that the Russians could occupy Africa. The Soviet Union, they observed, had made little progress on the continent since its adventures in Angola, Zaïre and Ethiopia half a decade earlier. Its grip on its client states was precarious, and the most it could realistically hope to do was to keep control of a few bases round the coast. Some Chinese leaders were beginning to feel at the same time that their strategic alignment with the West had been carried too far. By 1980 relations had reached the point at which the United States secretary of defence was being welcomed in Peking, and Chinese and American experts were exchanging intelligence on the Soviet military installations in Siberia. China was beginning to be viewed in the West as virtually an unofficial member of NATO. The Chinese had no wish to be drawn into the renewed Cold War between the United States and the Soviet Union, or any worse conflict which might result from that; and they continued to aspire, as strongly as ever, to a position of dignified independence in world affairs. In the interests of both prestige and security the Chinese needed to build themselves a constituency – a separate, neutral group of countries which would sympathize with Peking and give it, when possible, political and moral support. Once more the Chinese found themselves looking towards the club of 'non-aligned' African and Asian states, and Africa in particular. Distant, poor and weak though it was, Africa was, curiously, better suited than Asia to support China's objectives because, unlike Asia, it sometimes behaved as a coherent political bloc. African governments voted together in the United Nations and other international bodies; and their votes could be useful, as Peking had discovered in the course of its duel with Taiwan. Possibly Africa could help the Chinese to win victory in the new diplomatic campaign they were waging – a campaign to preserve the international standing of the regime which had been driven from power in Cambodia by the armies of China's latest enemy, Vietnam.

139

It was time to relaunch the Star Raft.

In 1980 a new prime minister had taken office in Peking. Zhao Ziyang was the nominee of Deng Xiaoping, the driving force in the Communist Party leadership. Deng, not Zhao, held the real power, but the more visible Zhao soon made an impression on African visitors. 'He doesn't say very much, fiddles a lot and what he says is simple, but when you go back home he's the one who seems to be in charge.' Heralded by this reputation, and accompanied by an escort of experienced 'Africa hands', Zhao embarked at the end of 1982 on the first major Chinese tour of Africa since the great journey made by his predecessor, Zhou Enlai, nearly twenty years before.

The tour was an attempt to reassure nostalgic Africans that China had not forgotten them and China had not changed. It was, in the first place, a deliberate re-enactment of Zhou's great expedition. Zhao, like his predecessor, visited a total of eleven countries, and the route he followed was roughly the same: he advanced through the Arab north, moved down into West and Central Africa, and emerged triumphantly on the shores of the Indian Ocean. The tour covered three of the conservative, pro-Western countries which China had befriended in recent years, Kenya, Zaïre and the oil-rich state of Gabon; but more time was spent in the lands ruled by China's old but troubled admirers, in Guinea and Congo-Brazzaville, Zambia, Zimbabwe and Tanzania. It was plainly the Chinese hope, as Zhao embraced old allies like Nyerere and Kaunda, that this new leader would find a way of reconstructing that very special and personal relationship which Zhou had established with them in times gone by. Wrapping himself in Zhou's mantle, Zhao took care not to neglect the other Chinese titan. He vigorously rebutted charges that China was abandoning Mao's legacy. The Chinese had by this time added an important rider to their criticism of Mao. 'Chairman Mao made mistakes – *but no mistakes in relation to Africa.*'

Zhao tried in a number of ways to turn the clock back to the romantic sixties. As he moved round the continent China's unpleasing anti-Soviet message was muted for the first time in years. Once again the United States bore the brunt of Chinese censure. It was, after all, Zhao noted, the Reagan administration which was propping up white South Africa with political and financial support. China was edging back towards its old role as the champion of African freedom. During his stop in Zambia Zhao held talks with the spokesmen of the two main guerrilla movements

140

which were fighting to undermine what was left of white-ruled Africa, SWAPO of Namibia and the South African ANC. Both these movements had been dependent for many years on Soviet military backing. Nervous of offending their Soviet patrons, they had kept their distance from the Chinese. As relations between Peking and Moscow began to thaw, however, new possibilities opened up. Within six months of Zhao's tour both the SWAPO leader, Sam Nujoma, and the ANC leader, Oliver Tambo, had visited Peking and emerged with promises of guerrilla training, ammunition and arms. Chinese ties with the ANC began to grow closer, and two other prominent members of the organization's leadership visited Peking in quick succession in 1986. China's old South African client, the PAC, had fallen into decline, but it too was not neglected. Zhao met the movement's leader on his way through Tanzania, where Chinese instructors were reported to be training 5,000 PAC guerrillas in the old ZANU camps. Fresh Chinese attention was also paid to the independent states which sheltered the guerrillas and were vulnerable to attack from a besieged and vindictive South Africa. Zhao promised Zimbabwe maximum support; and his promise was soon redeemed. From 1983 to 1985 the Chinese strengthened Zimbabwe's defences. Tanks and artillery were supplied to the army, and fighter bombers to the air force, and Chinese officers gave appropriate instruction to Zimbabwean armoured units, pilots and air crews. In early 1987, similarly, a squadron of Chinese jet fighters was delivered to Zambia. The Chinese were not preparing to play the major role in the destruction of white South Africa, but they meant to do enough to ensure that their voice was listened to when the final crisis came.

Zhao's tour, however, was more than just an appeal to nostalgia. It had a new and imaginative quality. For the first time China was not asking Africans to take its side in a duel with another foreign power. The premise was unchanged: China and Africa were identical. But Zhao did not go on to harass Africans with news of a common enemy. His theme was a grander and more positive one. China and Africa were the same, he argued, because both were part of the Third World, the league of the poor.

As early as 1974 Mao had informed Kaunda, 'We are the Third World.' The concept had a strategic beauty, from the Chinese point of view. It placed China and Africa squarely together on the opposite side of the fence to both the United States and the Soviet Union. But its essence was economic, and economic fellowship was an idea which won African

141

hearts. African economies were languishing, and African countries were more and more preoccupied with economic issues. All of them wanted to reverse the growing disparity between the sums they earned for the raw materials they exported to the rich world and the prices they had to pay for the manufactured products they bought in return. Some were beginning to manufacture simple industrial goods, and wanted greater access to the rich world's markets. Many wanted a change in international maritime law which would permit them to extend their rights over their offshore waters and give them a fair share of the resources which more advanced nations were discovering underneath the ocean floor. China, as a poor country, shared their anxieties, and China unlike them was a major power. China began to step forward as their spokesman, an international Robin Hood campaigning on their behalf against the selfishness of the industrialized 'North'. African leaders were rapturous. President Bongo of Gabon called China 'the tabernacle of justice'.

By the time Zhao came to Africa China's willingness to champion Third World causes had already done something to restore its fading glamour. At the United Nations, for instance, in 1981, China alone of the major powers had supported the African and Third World candidate for the post of secretary-general, Salim Salim of Tanzania, against the incumbent, Kurt Waldheim of Austria. African intellectuals who had winced at China's private quarrels viewed with enthusiasm the prospect that the Chinese might one day lead them into an economic showdown with the 'North'. China, said a young Somali proudly, was 'leader of the Third World, master of the Third World'. One Zimbabwean even thought that the Chinese should be prepared if necessary to use their nuclear weapons in defence of Third World interests. Some of the continent's leaders were a little more sober. They were conscious of China's might and they had, by now, learnt something of the workings of Chinese statecraft. China might help the Third World but it might, equally, try to bend the Third World to its will. Relations with China, they felt, could become increasingly awkward in the next few decades as the Chinese developed the ability to maintain a military presence in every part of the globe. Maybe the day would come when the warships of a Chinese superpower would loom up at anchor in uneasy African ports. The Chinese were sensitive to these apprehensions. They carefully avoided claiming the leadership of the developing countries, and Deng Xiaoping assured Africans that even when China became an advanced nation it would still stick firmly in the Third World camp.

What mattered, for the moment, was that the Chinese had at last succeeded in hitting the right note. They had won back a measure of African idealistic faith. Persuaded, no doubt, by their setbacks that the best strategic posture for an outside power in Africa was not to have one, they had given up duelling and had chosen to base their appeal to Africans primarily on China's credentials as an economic ally. It was a natural decision, for China, preoccupied with the tasks of modernization, was increasingly an economic and not a political animal, while African governments were more and more absorbed in the unromantic struggle to feed their people and pay their way. But it was also a shrewd decision, for the economic credentials which the Chinese had accumulated in Africa were strong and unusual ones.

5

The Poor Help the Poor

I am a drop of Yangtze water
Mixed in the swirling Rufiji river.

Sun Shiqi, Chinese doctor,
Rufiji valley, Tanzania, 1975

'China', Mao reflected in 1956, 'ought to have made a greater contribution to humanity.' Full of confidence after seven years in power, the Chinese Communists were determined to reverse the retreat from the outside world which had begun five centuries earlier when their Ming dynasty ancestors put an end to the voyages of Zheng He. They felt a duty to other peoples. Part of their duty was to spread the gospel of independence. Another part, equally important, was the spreading of good works.

This charitable impulse had germinated in the frontier regions of China itself. The western half of China was a vast, empty territory of mountains, grasslands and deserts, peopled, for the most part, by herdsmen of non-Chinese origin, Uighurs and Kazakhs, Kirghiz and Tadjiks, Mongols and Tibetans. One of the first preoccupations of the Chinese Communists when they came to power in 1949 had been to improve the standard of living of these neglected ethnic minorities. The Chinese People's Liberation Army, newly arrived from the east, was put to work growing crops for the herdsmen and irrigating their plains, building them housing and roads and railways and providing them with the benefits of modern medical care. One object certainly was to win the allegiance of these potentially disaffected minority groups to the new regime in Peking, 'to convince them', as Mao put it, 'that they are Chinese'. In the course of their efforts, however, the Chinese discovered a vocation for lifting people of other cultures out of their backwardness. They began to send bands of technicians abroad to carry out similar programmes of public works in neighbouring Asian countries. By the late fifties some 10,000 Chinese were at work in Outer Mongolia, where they reported building

144

190 bridges and 'innumerable miles' of railway track. And by the start of the following decade Peking had taken on its shoulders the task of alleviating the economic miseries of the new African states.

Guinea embarked on its career of independence in a devastated condition. This small French colony in West Africa had rejected the offer of membership in a community of autonomous 'overseas territories' made to it in 1958 by President de Gaulle, and had opted instead for total independence from France. None of France's other colonies had shown such audacity, and de Gaulle was enraged. Guinea had chosen independence: Guinea could fend for itself. French technicians withdrew from the country, dismantling its economy as they went. Some of them even tore out the telephone cables and light fittings. The Chinese were moved to pity for the destitute Guineans, and in 1959–61 they presented the government of Guinea with a gift of just under 30,000 tons of rice. There was a certain bizarreness here. If the Guineans were hungry, the Chinese were starving. These three years of 1959–61 had been marked in China by a series of harvests so disastrous that the peasants in certain provinces were reduced to eating the leaves off the trees. But that made no difference. Chinese assistance to Africa was to be a heroic endeavour. Zhou Enlai summed it up three years later on his great tour of the continent: the poor were helping the poor.

Meagre, backward China had decided not just to give economic aid to African countries, but to aid them on terms more generous than the rich world had ever thought of making available. Zhou proclaimed to his African hosts a set of eight principles on which Chinese aid would be based. These principles reflected China's own experience in the previous sixty years. For most of that time the Chinese had been on the receiving end of foreign aid, and they had not appreciated their client status. They had found themselves continually in debt to foreigners, first the United States and the various powers of Europe, later, after the Communist victory, the Soviet Union. They had had to trim their policies to suit the whims of their foreign creditors, and to take orders from the foreign managers who came to run factories on their soil. Now they were bent on proving that they could do better for Africans than any foreigners had ever done for them. Zhou made it plain that Chinese assistance to Africa was not going to be accompanied by any political demands. Nor were the Chinese going to milk African treasuries. Western loans to Africa carried burdensome rates of interest: even the Soviet Union made a practice of charging $2\frac{1}{2}$ per cent. China would offer African

145

governments loans free, as a general rule, of any interest whatever. Chinese loans, like others, would be used to finance construction projects, and China like other foreign countries would send technicians to Africa to set the projects up. But Chinese technicians would not be permitted to loll in hotel suites and run up expenses as other expatriates did. Instead they would have to content themselves with the same standard of living as the ordinary Africans they worked with – a provision which automatically cut down the debts of the host governments by something like a quarter. And the Chinese would not come pressing for repayment. Long periods were allowed for the governments to discharge their debts to Peking. In practice governments found that they were not called upon to begin repaying their Chinese loans for ten years after the construction projects were finished. The repayments could then be staggered over twenty or even thirty years. No Western bank or ministry was anything like so liberal; but then what could you expect of the rich? One Chinese official made a pointed if unexpected comment about the inability of a camel to go through a needle's eye.

Chinese generosity had other features that Zhou's principles never hinted at. Client governments found that if the costs of a project outran the original estimate the Chinese were prepared to meet the extra expenses themselves. The Chinese didn't confine themselves to making loans. The rice sent to Guinea was just one in a series of outright gifts they dispensed all over the continent, money to balance the budget, blankets and medicines for the victims of earthquake, epidemic and flood.

Africa, in short, had become the object of a philanthropic crusade. The spirit of Zheng He had awoken: huge amounts of money and men began to be mobilized. In the two decades that followed Zhou's proclamation some 6 billion *yuan* were diverted to Africa, a sum corresponding to roughly US$2 billion, or two dollars for every man, woman and child of the present Chinese population. $2 billion was not, of course, an enormous sum by Western standards: in the single decade 1971–81 Britain, for example, disbursed to Africa some $2.5 billion in official bilateral aid funds, the United States $8 billion and France $13 billion. But it was a lot of money for a poor Asian country. Individual sums were earmarked, on Mao's orders, for each African country with which China established diplomatic ties. The average sum was 100 million *yuan* ($30 million), but the amount could vary from five million ($1.5 million) to 1 billion ($300 million) according to the state's size and importance: Zaïre, for example, came at the upper end of the scale.

146

Most of these funds were channelled through a special aid ministry, the Ministry of Foreign Economic Relations, which was established in Peking; but the task of recruiting personnel devolved on the provinces. In each province a foreign aid bureau was set up. If an African state wanted help with maize or sugar production, the ministry in Peking would call on the appropriate maize- or sugar-growing province to recruit a team of experts. In the sphere of medical aid a kind of twinning system was organized. Each province was given the assignment of handling the health care of one or more African country. The northern province of Hebei, for instance, looked after Zaïre; Guangdong, in the south, took care of the Gambia and Equatorial Guinea; Gansu, in the north-west desert, was responsible for Madagascar. The provinces chose teams of doctors to go to their client countries, and paid for them out of their own budgets. The assignment was formidable, but not fantastic, given that the population of most Chinese provinces is considerably larger than that of most independent African states.

Recruits were chosen with care. They were expected to be healthy, morally upright and competent at their jobs. People in Mao's China were accustomed to going where the state directed, and the aid bureaux, consequently, had no lack of technicians to choose from. They could even afford the luxury of exempting a number of unwilling individuals who asked to be excused from the crusade on the grounds that they were needed at home to look after small children or elderly parents. Most of the recruits were keen to go. It was a chance to travel, at a time when ordinary Chinese were forbidden to journey abroad; and there were other, more concrete inducements. Chinese technicians in Africa were maintained with allowances issued to them in the local currency, while their regular salaries continued to be paid to their families at home. This arrangement enabled the families to make some modest savings. When the time came to return from Africa the technicians were also permitted, as a kind of end-of-term treat, to spend any money they had saved from their allowances shopping in the local stores for Western goods like Swiss watches and tape recorders, which they could never have hoped to acquire in their own country. The attractions were sufficiently great that occasional technicians actually concealed their physical ailments in order to 'join up'.

By the early eighties the aid bureaux had sent to Africa a total of 150,000 Chinese technicians. In the first years, when China was still

147

MAURITANIA

Nouakchott
H★TΔⵔ■
Rosso Kiffa Aïoun el Atross
-Y- H+ Néma Timbuktu MALI NIGER
Kaedi Kankossa
Sagata Selibaby
Dakar SENEGAL H+
THE GAMBIA Banjuli ⵔHH HY Markala ▼▼+X Tera Niamey
Θ-Y- Segou TX BURKINA FASO Θ-Y- Saga
▼▼+ Bignona Kudang Kati Bamako Ouagadougou+Θ+Δ
Canchungo Gaoual PCⵔY H+ Koudougou
H+ GUINEA Siguiri TAⵔ Sikasso ⵔY Malanville
GUINÉ BISSAU Kinkon ■ F G Dabola +Θ+F
Fria-Y- B Banfora BENIN
Conakry Mamou-Y-Y Kankan Lama- NIGERIA
ⵔΔCX+◇+ Kindia Faranah ΔKara Garoula +G
Kambia SIERRA LEONE Makeni Y X Macenta Lama- H+
Mange- Mano Magbass IVORY COAST GHANA TOGO ▼■ La
Freetown Bo ▼■ TP Agnibilekrou Y
ΘΔ Kenema Gantal Kumasi Lokossa
Monrovia Ⴄ Abengourou PE Tsevie T Y
LIBERIA Tema Afife Ouidah Lagos Y-Y-Ndoye
Harper CAMEROON
Δ- Yaounde
Malabo +-Mbarmayo
CAPE VERDE (to Equatorial Guinea) ⵔΔ◇ Micomeseng
● ISLANDS Bata EQUATORIAL GUINEA Mongomo
⬤◻ Libreville- Akok BR
◗ Praia SAŎ TOMÉ ● GABON ◖C
Δ & PRINCIPE +
Le
Djambala
ATLANTIC OCEAN Imboulou
A+ Sibi
Loubomo B- Bouel
Pointe Noire H A Madingou
CABINDA
(to Angola)

COMMUNICATIONS
⚬⚬⚬⚬ Railway
— Road
⚓ Bridge
★ Port Construction or Modernization or Shipyard
A Airport Modernization or Construction
◻ Local Small Scale Roadworks
= Canal
⛴ Steamer Service

WATER CONTROL & ELECTRIC POWER
▼ Dam
Θ Well or Bore Hole Drilling
■ Power Station

AGRICULTURE
Y Farming or Milling (Rice,Maize or Vegetables)
ⵔ Tobacco Production
† Tea Production
X Sugar Production
◇ Fishery
◆ Cattle Raising or Abattoir

MEDICAL AID
H Hospital
+ Medical Team

MISCELLANEOUS
● Town Planning
⫯ Broadcasting Station
HW Handicraft Workshop
X Mining

FACTORIES
T Textile Factory or Cotton Production
F Factory or Repair Centre for Farm Tools &
   Other Machinery
S Shoe Factory
C Cigarette or Match Factory
P Pharmaceutical Factory
PE Pencil Factory
∇ Ice Factory
G Groundnut Oil Factory
B Brick or Cement Works or Limestone Crushing
   Plant
TA Tannery
TP Timber Processing
● Ceramics Works
O Printing Works

BUILDINGS
Δ Conference,Cultural or Youth Centre,Assembly
   Hall, Party or Government Headquarters,
   Embassy Buildings
▲ Hotel,Motel or Sportsmen's Hostel
◖ Post and Telegraph Centre
ⵁ Theatre or Cinema
Θ Sports Stadium
☆ School

0   miles   1000
⊢————————————————⊣
0   km   1500

Map 5.   Chinese aid projects in Africa since 1960.

a source of terror to many governments, the technicians had to confine their efforts to some half-a-dozen countries: twenty years later they were at work in all *but* half-a-dozen countries, from the Mediterranean in the north to the Kalahari Desert on the borders of South Africa. These Chinese crusaders launched more than 500 aid projects. China was still predominantly an agricultural country, and many of the projects were modest and rural, six or seven farmers showing local peasants how to cultivate rice or vegetables on a few acres of land. Rice was already a staple food in some parts of the continent: in Guiné-Bissau, as in south China, a person who had not had his helping of rice at dinner time was not considered to have eaten at all. The Chinese took up the cause of this hardy and economical crop, and vastly promoted it. Paddy-fields began to appear in untended river valleys, and rice began to creep into the diets of desert communities who had never touched it before.

But Chinese aid wasn't limited to farming. Even before the Communists came to power in 1949 China already had a network of factories in the cities of the coast and the Yangtze river basin producing a range of light industrial commodities like textiles and paper. Several of the new African governments were hungry for industrialization, partly for prestige reasons but partly also because they wished to avoid wasting precious hard currency on the import of easily manufactured consumer goods. The Chinese were ready to help. They built palm-oil and sugar refineries, factories for producing pencils and matchsticks, shoes and cloth. By the end of the sixties they had carried out approximately half the industrial development of the West African republic of Mali. Knit together by dirt tracks and river ferries, many African countries lacked even the rudiments of a modern transport system. Chinese engineers set to work making good the deficiency. As they did so they began to leave conspicuous marks on the landscape: a road in Rwanda, a port in Mauritania, a bridge across the Blue Nile in the depths of the Sudan.

It was an ironic fulfilment to the dreams of Emin Pasha and the other European colonists who had talked of opening Africa up with the help of Chinese labour. Nearly a century after their time, Chinese had indeed arrived to develop Africa. These Chinese were not, however, the tame coolies the colonists had called for, but confident envoys of a revolutionary state. They did not come to work for the Europeans, but to extinguish European influence. And they had not been in Africa half a decade before they challenged European influence in the most dramatic way possible, by embarking on a venture which the boldest colonists had only dared to imagine.

150

Zambia was scarcely independent in any meaningful sense. In 1964 the British withdrew from this sprawling, landlocked country at the centre of the continent which they had governed till then as the colony called Northern Rhodesia. The new state, however, was no more than an economic satellite of the territories to the south of it which remained under European rule. Much of its investment was provided by South Africa and the white settler stronghold of Southern Rhodesia, and the Europeans also controlled its trade with the outside world. Its principal export, copper, was shipped to the world on two main railway lines, each of which ran through the various white-ruled domains. One line led to the port of Lobito in Portuguese Angola, and the other crossed Southern Rhodesia to reach the sea in South Africa and Portuguese Mozambique. The same lines also carried Zambia's imports from overseas. And so long as Zambia remained an economic satellite, it could hardly expect to be politically free. In 1965 Ian Smith and the settlers in Southern Rhodesia proclaimed a unilateral independence from Britain designed to keep the African majority in subjection and perpetuate white control. Kenneth Kaunda, the Zambian leader, was eager to help his African cousins across the Zambezi River. But there was little help he could give them, for Smith and his allies in South Africa and the Portuguese colonies could throttle Zambia at any time by cutting its trade routes.

For Kaunda this bondage was intolerable. As early as 1961, while the British still ruled his country, he had begun to call for an escape route, a great new railway which would run north-east to the Indian Ocean through the newly independent state of Tanganyika (later Tanzania). Such a railway would enable his people to take control of their future by establishing new and more agreeable trade links with the free African countries to the north. But the enterprise was awesome. The railway would have to be built across half the width of Africa, through nearly 2,000 kilometres of virgin mountain, forest and plain. At the end of the nineteenth century Cecil Rhodes had considered the possibility of constructing a line along this route as part of his grand design for a railway network linking the whole of British-dominated Africa from Cairo to the Cape of Good Hope. But the idea had got no further. The British Colonial Office had revived it briefly in the early 1950s, but had taken no practical steps. Kaunda was able to enlist the enthusiastic support of his neighbour, Julius Nyerere, the Tanzanian president; but neither Tanzania nor Zambia could hope to build the railway by themselves.

The scheme required a huge financial and technical commitment from a major foreign power. Kaunda and Nyerere began to look for backers. First they tried the West, but the West was chilly. The World Bank sent a mission from Washington to take a look at the project, but came to the conclusion that it made no economic sense. Zambia, in their view, already had all the railways it needed. The dominant voices in the World Bank were American and British, and neither the United States nor the British government was in a hurry to help. The Americans were willing to build roads, but had little use for railways; and the Johnson administration disliked what it took to be a Communist initiative calculated to weaken Western influence on the continent. 'Oh God, that political fantasy,' yawned a British diplomat. Languid in the aftermath of empire, the British were also becoming increasingly tight-fisted as their economy decayed. They agreed to contribute just half the cost of a feasibility study. Two years later, in 1966, a consortium of British and Canadian firms carried out a feasibility study and judged that the railway could be built and might even be run at a profit. But the scheme would still require heavy government financing, and the British, American and other Western governments still couldn't make up their minds to come forward with the funds. And while the West deliberated, the Chinese had resolved.

It is unclear at what stage the Chinese first got wind of the project, but it may have been early. In 1961, the year when Kaunda first called for the railway, a journalist named Gao Liang who acted as China's eyes and ears in East Africa wrote an article celebrating Tanganyika's independence and assessing the prospects for relations between his country and this new state. In true Chinese style he drew encouragement from the past. Back at the turn of the century, he noted, the Germans had brought in a thousand labourers from the coast of China to build railways in Tanganyika (German East Africa, as it was called at the time). Quartered in a village which was popularly known as 'Shanghai', these 'hardworking Chinese' had 'cut through high mountains and blazed a trail in the wilderness'. The Chinese do not indulge idly in historical reminiscence, and it is possible Gao was using this obscure colonial episode to advertise the role that his country envisaged playing in the future Tanzania. Peking's choice of an ambassador to the new state may also have been significant. The engaging He Ying had served in the late fifties as ambassador to Outer Mongolia – a post where he had presided over China's earliest foreign construction schemes. By the mid-sixties, at all events, the Chinese were well aware of the forlorn efforts of Tanzania and Zambia to find a sponsor for their railway; and their interest was aroused.

The Chinese saw an outstanding chance to discharge their missionary duty of setting Africa free. Southern Rhodesia's drift towards illegal independence had brought the spread of black rule to a halt on the banks of the Zambezi. But China could turn the tables. By building the railway it could simultaneously deliver Zambia from the threat of economic blackmail and enable the Zambians to offer their territory as a base for exiles who wished to strike a blow for African freedom in Rhodesia and its neighbours. Zambia could be transformed from a hostage country into the southernmost outpost of the African guerrilla advance.

The project was all the more tempting because the West had hung back. The Chinese liked to make a point of shouldering schemes which the West had rejected on narrowly economic grounds, but which were important to African governments for political or psychological reasons. Besides, it was not strictly true, as the World Bank had argued, that the railway would bring with it no important economic benefits. The line would cut through two areas, north-east Zambia and south-west Tanzania, which had been largely neglected in the decades of British administration. Farming could be developed along the route, and iron ore and coal could be mined. Towns could grow up, and factories could be established to produce simple goods like paper and cement. The Chinese also liked to make a point of 'doing something' for districts which the Europeans had been content to leave as backwaters.

Lastly the Chinese looked at the map of Africa, and saw that they could achieve what Rhodes had only dreamt of – that by building this line they could link almost the whole eastern half of the continent, from South Africa to Egypt, by an unbroken band of rail.

By 1964 Tanzanian and Zambian officials were beginning to hint that they might resort to China; but their hints were essentially intended to frighten the Western powers into coming to their aid. No one believed that the Chinese would make an offer. In February 1965, however, when Nyerere went for the first time on a visit to Peking, Zhou Enlai suggested calmly that China might be prepared to take the railway on.

Nyerere's initial reaction was one of bewilderment. Did the Chinese really mean it? Did they understand what the project entailed? Did this poor Asian country have anything like the resources to construct a line halfway across a continent? Rumours began to creep round Tanzania that the Chinese were proposing to build a railway out of bamboo. But the offer was serious. Six months after Nyerere's return from Peking the first dozen Chinese surveyors ventured into the Tanzanian countryside, shielded by local game wardens from the more alarming hazards of the bush. Soon China dissolved in the turmoil of the Cultural Revolution, but the project went ahead. In September 1967, as the Cultural Revolution raged around him, the minister in charge of Peking's aid programme signed a formal commitment to build and finance the line, and in 1970 the commitment began to be fulfilled. Tanzania and Zambia were given a loan, free of interest, for the huge sum of $400 million, and Chinese engineers began laying the first kilometres of track on the outskirts of the Tanzanian capital, the Indian Ocean port of Dar es Salaam. Over the next five years a total of 25,000 Chinese technicians disembarked at Dar es Salaam and headed, in convoys of lorries, into the inland plateau. They built 300 bridges and six miles of tunnels, most of them in the formidable stretch of mountains and torrents between the towns of Mlimba and Makambako in southern Tanzania. (Mountain gorges did not deter the Chinese, but African place names did: the 'Mlimba–Makambako section' was telescoped by the engineers into the single word 'Muma'.) They built 93 railway stations, and shipped in 85 locomotives, 2,100 freight wagons and 100 passenger coaches to begin operations on the completed stretches of the line. Zhou Enlai, in Peking, kept a personal eye on the work. At one point a tussle arose over the braking system to be used on the trains. The Tanzanians wanted air brakes to match the system installed on their domestic railways: the Zambians, for the same reason, wanted vacuum brakes. Zhou pronounced a judgement of Solomon: both systems should be used. Four months before Zhou's death, in September 1975, the line reached the town of Kapiri Mposhi in the heart of Zambia's principal mining region, the 'Copperbelt'. The Chinese had not only finished the railway, all 1,860 kilometres of it, but had finished it, in a final rebuff to the sceptics, two years ahead of the original target date. The 'Tan–Zam' railway dwarfed every other Chinese project on the continent. It was the longest railway in Africa, and the longest railway completed anywhere on the planet since the end of the Second World War.

Like all Chinese doings on the continent, the crusade had two sides. It was part of the missionary drive to rid Africa of the European incubus. At the same time it was also a weapon in the duel against China's private foes. Taiwan was also an aid-giver. Aid teams were sent to more than twenty African countries by this rival Chinese regime. Taiwanese farmers helped local peasants to grow new varieties of rice, fruit and vegetables, and Taiwanese craftsmen trained unemployed Africans to make bamboo furniture for the tourist market. But their projects were small. They lacked the resources to embark on grand enterprises like the Tan–Zam railway, and were also, understandably, reluctant to make large financial investments in countries which might at any time desert their cause for Peking's. Peking accordingly used its aid to trump their modest efforts. African governments could be persuaded fairly easily that they stood to gain by admitting Peking's technicians and showing Taiwan's the door. The Peking Chinese were not only prepared to take over any projects their Taiwan rivals had started, but were also ready to undertake major construction schemes which represented a far more impressive and visible commitment to the future of the country concerned.

But Taiwan was only a secondary target of Peking's crusade. The crusade was meant, first and foremost, to serve as a comment on the failings of China's great adversary, the Soviet Union.

In his search for a foreign power to sponsor the Tan–Zam railway, Nyerere had appealed to the Soviet Union as well as the West. Soviet aid to the continent had been marked, in the early sixties, by conspicuous generosity. All Africa talked of the great Aswan dam which the Russians had built for Egypt. But Khrushchev, the sponsor of Aswan, fell from power two months after Nyerere's appeal was forwarded in August 1964; and the new Soviet triumvirate of Brezhnev, Kosygin and Podgorny lacked their predecessor's appetite for grandiose economic aid projects. The Russians too had turned their backs. The railway was China's rebuke to Soviet stinginess, and China's answer to the Aswan dam. Years after its completion the Chinese were still asking visitors to Africa what they thought of the relative merits of the two rival schemes.

Brezhnev and his colleagues had come to the conclusion that arms deliveries would win them friends in Africa more readily than economic help. By the 1970s they were disbursing twice to three times as much money to African arsenals as they were to African economies. The Chinese could not compete with the Soviet Union in an African arms race; but they could hope to shame the Kremlin by stepping up their charity. The Soviet Union was far richer than China, but China quickly outstripped it in the field of economic aid. More African countries got Chinese than Soviet money, and the sums they got from

China were usually larger than the Russians were willing to provide.

Peking's interventions were often nicely calculated to highlight the contrast between Chinese and Soviet priorities. In the early seventies, for instance, the Russians had supplied the military rulers of Somalia with $132 million worth of arms. They had not entirely neglected the Somali economy, but their aid had been sluggish. For five years Soviet technicians worked on a dam at a place called Fanoole on the Shebelle River in the south of the country. They put up some buildings, but had not yet laid the foundations of the dam or completed more than a fifth of the project when, at the end of 1977, outraged by Moscow's decision to back its enemy, Ethiopia, during the war in the Ogaden desert, the government of Somalia quarrelled with the Soviet Union and drove them out. '"Fanoole"', the Chinese remarked portentously, 'has become a new Somali term meaning failure, a difficult delivery or something impossible to accomplish.' They took the project over and finished it in four years flat.

China's implicit claim to superior virtue was not always warranted. Sometimes the Chinese found it expedient to challenge the Russians at their own game. Not all their projects were innocent of a military purpose. In the mid-seventies, for example, they took it upon themselves to achieve the physical unification of Somalia. Somalia was an awkward structure, pieced together from the merger of a former British and a former Italian colony and shaped like an inverted L. Chinese engineers drove a highway right up the spine of the country, through a harsh semi-desert empty except for anthills and wandering camels. The road benefited the economy in the sense that it enabled grain and fruit to be sent, for the first time, from the agricultural southern region to feed the nomads of the ex-British north; but it also had a double strategic value for the Somali military regime. It enabled the southern-based leaders to tighten their grip on the disaffected nomads, and it ran parallel, for nearly a thousand kilometres, to the frontier with Ethiopia, the historic enemy of the Somali state.

Some Chinese projects seemed calculated less to promote the development of a country's economy than to win for Peking the favour of the regime. Over the years the Chinese became builders of sports stadiums by appointment to half the regimes on the continent. African leaders, like Roman emperors, were fond of amphitheatres in which they could impress their subjects with the splendour of their games and the beneficence of their rule. Chinese technicians in the West African state of Benin were asked to incorporate in their stadium a computerized display system showing the features of President Kérékou and the words of his speeches. The Chinese were quite prepared to embark, when governments asked them, on projects with little or no economic merit of any kind, costly and inessential monuments to the glory of the regime – conference halls and cultural palaces and multi-storey headquarters for the ruling political party. Sometimes they even permitted leaders to appropriate Chinese specialists for their own private use. In Congo-Brazzaville, for instance, President Marien Ngouabi kept a team of Chinese doctors at his home town of Owando to look after his aged mother. The interpreter attached to the team had the run of Ngouabi's villa, and the president's children dropped in casually on the doctors to be welcomed with gifts of fizzy drinks, sugar and Chinese steamed bread. Unobtrusive, trusted, the Chinese specialists were naturally able to glean a certain amount of intelligence on such valuable topics as the current standing of the Soviet Union in the leader's entourage.

Yet the Chinese felt that their band of philanthropy was nobler than that of their great Communist rivals. Every aid-giver sometimes had to do what the leaders wanted. But Moscow, in their opinion, cared only to please the leaders, while Peking was also concerned to better the lives of ordinary folk. At the end of the sixties Russians and Chinese arrived in Equatorial Guinea, a tiny country on the west coast of Africa which had once belonged to Spain. Equatorial Guinea consisted of an island, Fernando Póo, and a rectangular piece of mainland 200 kilometres to the south. Communication between the two parts of the country was effected by dug-out canoe. The Russians tried to improve conditions by inaugurating an air service. The Chinese however noted that this service would benefit only the elite, since most people couldn't afford the cost of a journey by plane. They built a 3,000-ton steamer and presented it to Equatorial Guinea complete with a Cantonese crew.

Care for the people was, in fact, the overriding theme of the Chinese crusade. The Chinese made a point of directing the bulk of their aid at the mass of ordinary Africans, peasants and herdsmen and dwellers in shanty towns. Many of their projects were designed, as one of their diplomats put it, to supply these poor people with goods they could 'eat, wear and use'. This approach had two great advantages. It was an answer to the mounting African charges of Chinese nationalism. By devoting themselves to the welfare of common people whose gratitude could bring Peking no obvious political dividends, the Chinese could hope to demonstrate that they alone among aid-givers had Africa's interests at heart. At the same time it gave them a unique opportunity to expose the limitations of China's opponents, both Western and Soviet. The Chinese intended to prove that they could look after ordinary Africans as no Europeans of any political complexion had ever been able to do.

Actually ordinary Africans viewed the approach of the Chinese with a good deal of misgiving. Some doubted whether the Chinese teams could accomplish anything useful. Nomads in northern Somalia were unenthusiastic when they learnt that hydraulic experts from China had come to drill for water on their barren mountainsides. British technicians had been surveying the region for years. How, they inquired, could the small-eyed people get water where the full-eyed people had failed to find it? There was also some fear. Older inhabitants of Congo-Brazzaville still remembered the riotous conduct of the unruly Chinese labourers whom the French brought to their country in 1929. Would the newcomers behave any better? All over the continent people whispered. Maybe the teams were coming to pocket African diamonds and gold. Maybe they were coming to settle. In one country, Sierra Leone, Peking was obliged to make a formal pledge that its experts would leave for home as soon as their work was done.

Once more, however, the experts prevailed in the face of widespread doubts. Owlish, bespectacled professional men in early middle age, they did not turn out to bear much resemblance to an army of conquering settlers. And they did turn out to be competent. People soon found that the teams had a knack for meeting some of their most basic needs. Ugandans recalled how at a village named Kibimba in the eastern part of their country, Chinese agronomists quietly supplied the local population with rice during the years of chaos and tyranny under Idi Amin. Now and again Amin's troops marched past, but even they had the sense not to destroy the growing crops. In northern Somalia the Chinese did find water, largely because their successive teams built on each other's experience where rival British companies had vitiated each other's efforts by coming forward with endless conflicting plans. They equipped the regional capital, Hargeisa, with a permanent water supply, thereby creating the basis of a settled existence for nomads who had previously moved around after the rain. Malians were thankful to the Chinese for relieving unemployment with the technically simple, labour-intensive factories that they built throughout the land. In Ségou, the second city of Mali, you could hardly find a family which did not have at least one member working at the Chinese textile mill. The Chinese were also remembered for providing entertainment. Their sports stadiums were not appreciated by the leaders alone. Football and other sports were in keen demand among the African young, and the Chinese got credit for helping to alleviate the monotony of daily life.

Greatest of all was the impact of the doctors from the Chinese provinces. These doctors were sent, as a matter of policy, to the poorest parts of the poorest countries. Like the roaming Chinese traders of colonial times, they carried their services deep into the bush, to places where no Europeans apart from a few elderly missionaries were willing to work. In many outlying districts they were the only doctors available other than the village medicine-man. They arrived with the acupuncture needles they used to relieve complaints like lumbago, arthritis and rheumatism, and an assortment of other traditional Chinese medicines: cow bezoar tablets for treating strokes, white powder from Yunnan province for disinfecting wounds, rhizome of the goldthread plant for vomiting and fever. At the same time they alerted Africans to the therapeutic value of local herbs like loquat, eucalyptus and dandelion, and the medicinal properties of tangerine peel.

The patients came flocking. Often the coming of the Chinese caused a dramatic local migration. Usually, in the Third World, people moved from the countryside to the cities in search of a better life. In Senegal, however, on the western tip of the continent, townspeople began to journey into the countryside, for it was in the countryside that the Chinese doctors were encamped. At the Chinese clinics these people got treatment they could not otherwise have hoped to receive; and they were, not surprisingly, grateful. Mothers whose infants' lives had been saved by a Chinese gynaecologist were reported in places to have given the children 'Chinese names': sometimes a name with the meaning 'Chinese', like 'Chinois' in French-speaking territories, sometimes the name of the doctor, Lin or Wang. Africans who had had the chance of comparing Chinese and Western health care often showed a preference for the Chinese brand. Villagers appreciated the Chinese lack of formality. Chinese doctors didn't ask them, as Western ones did, to rack their brains filling out complicated forms: all they had to do was to come to the clinic, sit down on a bench and be treated. Many people found the Chinese herbal remedies reassuringly similar to the drugs of their traditional pharmacopoeia. And acupuncture exerted a unique attraction,

159

especially on the old. Old men of eighty who had never left their towns trekked into the bush in quest of the acupuncture 'miracle' which would cure their aches and pains. Western pills, to their minds, had an ominous character: they disappeared inside you and you couldn't tell what effect they might be having. But the acupuncture needles were visible, on the surface of the skin, and the doctors made a point of explaining the theory behind their use. In several parts of the continent Africans themselves took up the study of acupuncture and started their own private clinics to cater for the steadily growing demand.

African labourers worked in large numbers on many of the projects: 100,000 of them were employed, for example, on the Tan–Zam railway line. The Chinese were determined to treat these workmen with a courtesy few Africans had experienced at European hands. The interpreters who came with the teams were not content to speak to their employees in the language of the former colonial power, English or French or Italian: many had taken the trouble to acquire a fluency in the local African tongue, like Bambara in Mali or Swahili in Tanzania. Ordinary Chinese technicians knew no language but their own, but even they tried to pick up the basic courtesies, to address Africans with the African words for 'hallo', 'goodbye' and 'thank you'. Sometimes the teams overdid it a little. Chinese interpreters on the Tan–Zam railway caused a certain amount of irritation by attempting to correct the Tanzanians' Swahili grammar. But the Chinese were appreciated for making a linguistic effort that few Western aid personnel had so much as considered.

'If any Chinese expert tries throwing his weight around,' Zhou Enlai told the Tanzanians, 'please send him back to us immediately.' Chinese technicians were taught to abide by a golden rule of conduct: 'One, don't beat; two, don't scold' ('*Yi bu da, er bu ma*'). Africans who had served on Western construction sites soon noticed the difference. Labourers employed on a stadium in the West African republic of Benin commented appreciatively that the Chinese, unlike the French, never hit or abused them when they worked slowly because they hadn't eaten enough. Senegalese reported that the Soviet engineers in their country were inclined to be brusque to local workmen: the Chinese, by contrast, were always smiling, and always polite.

The Chinese mucked in. They did not sit on shooting-sticks giving orders, but carried bricks, mixed cement and waded through swamps in the thick of the African workforce. This did not mean they were sociable. They did not chat informally or joke with their African colleagues,

The Chinese aimed to present themselves as helpers, not overseers. Artist's impression of a forge in one of the Tan–Zam railway workshops, Peking, 1975.

and their failure to do so proved to be a major shortcoming. But they were modest and unassuming, and that counted for much. Africans were astonished to observe how even the most senior Chinese personnel rolled up their sleeves. Often, they remarked, you could not tell who was a supervisor and who was an ordinary engineer. When night fell the French or Americans withdrew to the comfort of their verandahs, but the Chinese stayed where they were, in their camp at the village work-site. Labourers in the Sudan declared that the Chinese were the only foreigners who never gave them an impression of superiority.

Teams also tried to raise the morale of their labourers. For decades Africans had been accustomed to working under European direction, and many were still inhibited by the timid notion that what the Europeans had failed to do could not be done at all. The Chinese made it their business to prove this notion false. Europeans had declared that tobacco could never be grown in Somalia, or sugar in Mali. The Chinese came and grew both. Europeans had scoffed at the idea of the Tan–Zam railway: the Chinese came and built it. By toiling at their projects for fourteen hours a day, and at night when occasion demanded, the teams hoped to prove that there was no limit to the results which dedicated effort could achieve. China once more was striving to galvanize Africa with its soaring confidence.

The response was a little mixed. Africans tended to find these exertions slightly unnatural. Maybe, they conjectured, the technicians were really convicts serving long-term penal sentences. Few felt like working at the Chinese pace, and some contrived ingenious ways to avoid it. Young Tanzanians on the railway found that they could keep their Chinese colleagues happy if they sat down under a tree engrossed, to all appearances, in a conspicuous volume of Mao. At the same time the labourers couldn't help feeling a certain admiration for these strangers who were working so hard to develop countries thousands of miles from their own. Quite a number felt shamed into making a special effort, and many seem to have absorbed at least some vestiges of the Chinese confidence. One group of Tanzanians who travelled to Peking in the year of the railway's completion praised the Chinese for teaching them to 'do away with the retrogressive attitude of considering some things to be too difficult to tackle or impossible'.

The trouble was that the confidence the Chinese gave with one hand, they took away with the other.

Confidence could only be instilled with any lasting effectiveness if Africans could be trained to run the projects by themselves. In theory this was exactly what the aid teams came to ensure. It was one of Zhou Enlai's principles that the experts sent to Africa should pass on their knowledge by training the people they came to help. The Chinese had a proverb which they spread throughout the continent: give a man a fish and he'll eat for a day; give him a fishing-rod and you've fed him for life. As time went on, however, it became increasingly evident that the teams were not, in practice, training their clients adequately and the fishing-rod was not changing hands.

The Chinese talked of training without fully anticipating what training was going to mean. They blithely imagined, in the early sixties, that they could walk into an African country and start factories and railways with no greater difficulty than they were accustomed to meeting at home. In fact they faced frightening problems. There was a real language barrier. Teams found themselves surrounded by a sea of African workmen who outnumbered them, sometimes, by a factor of ten to one. One or two fluent interpreters were seldom enough to cope with these numbers, and the ability of the average technician to say 'thank you' in Swahili was not very helpful when it came to imparting knowledge. There was widespread illiteracy and ignorance. Many of the Tanzanians and Zambians recruited by their governments to work on the Tan–Zam project knew nothing about railways and had never even seen one. Some African workmen had received a little basic schooling, others had no education of any kind. Often the teams were reduced, as an engineer remembers, to 'telling the ones who understand to teach the ones who don't'.

The result was that most teams spent little time on formal classroom instruction. They preferred to teach without words. A technician would assemble and dismantle a piece of machinery and encourage his African apprentices to follow suit until they got the procedure right. Many observers were impressed by this emphasis on practical demonstration. But it wasn't entirely a substitute for classroom work. The apprentices had not received the conceptual grounding they needed to deal, for example, with an unforeseen technical breakdown. At a couple of factories they built in Tanzania the teams introduced a number of simple management systems which the future African staff were intended to copy. They held regular planning meetings and used ledgers for recording the daily and weekly output of the plants. But it wasn't enough, necessarily, to institute a practice if the reason for the practice had not sunk

163

in. Some of the systems were retained after the Chinese had departed, but others struck the Tanzanians as 'monotonous' and fell into disuse.

If on the other hand teams did organize formal training courses, they could never be certain that the projects would benefit. Sometimes the trouble was lack of application on the part of the pupils. 'They're not very fond of studying,' the Chinese sighed. More often the difficulty was that trained African workmen refused to stay put. In the years that the Tan–Zam line was being built the Chinese ran technical and managerial courses for 1,200 Tanzanians and Zambians who were intended to take up positions in the newly established Tanzania–Zambia Railway Authority (TAZARA). But TAZARA was a semi-official body funded out of the slender resources of the Tanzanian and Zambian governments, and the freshly qualified Africans soon found that they could earn higher salaries working for private companies. They abandoned the railway, and took their skills elsewhere.

Faced with these kinds of difficulties, even the Chinese were inclined to give up. They had other priorities, and training conflicted with these. Doctors were overwhelmed by the floods of patients who came to their clinics for treatment. They explained that they had no time to give classes to local orderlies, and no translated textbooks to teach them from. Speed was a trademark of the construction teams, and training slowed them down. Semi-skilled African labourers might break the machinery. It was, they observed, more efficient and more economical to do the work themselves. There was force in these arguments. But by doing the work themselves, the Chinese forfeited any chance they might have had to transfer the technology.

The truth was that the Chinese preferred, as a general rule, to rely on their own people. Their entire aid programme was flawed by a deep-seated tendency to go it alone. They were not always anxious, for instance, to keep their clients abreast of the detailed planning of their schemes. They came to help Africans, but not necessarily to consult them. 'Why do you want the costs?' they asked the Somali highway authorities. 'You want a road.' Blueprints were apt to be in Chinese only, and as soon as the projects were completed the technicians took them home. This caused dismay in Freetown, the capital of Sierra Leone, where the Chinese had built one of their innumerable stadiums. The electricity broke down, and so did the plumbing, but no one knew how to repair them, as the Chinese had left with the plans.

The Chinese relied not only on their own people, but also, to a bizarre extent, on their own construction materials. Chinese marble was used in the conference halls, Chinese bitumen on the highways and Chinese cement in the stadiums. Rumour even had it, on some projects, that the Chinese had used their own sand. (This habit was often a source of frustration to African businessmen who had hoped to earn money supplying projects with local tarmac or stone.) And what the technicians assembled with these materials were, without exception, buildings they were accustomed to constructing at home. One team endowed Somalia with a national theatre so minutely faithful to Chinese design that visiting ballet troupes from China could cable in advance their requests for lighting and scenery without even needing to look at the inside. In Dar es Salaam, the eastern terminus of the Tan–Zam railway was a perfect replica of the majestic railway stations in Peking and Canton. The same grand staircase swept up from the centre of the concourse to the same broad landing, lined with pillars, which gave on to the platforms. Over the landing hung a 'bird's eye view' of the railway, with the principal stations neatly labelled in Chinese. China was remodelling Africa in its own image.

Pressing ahead by themselves, the aid teams showed little interest in slotting their projects into the rest of a country's economy. Projects were apt to be superbly and bafflingly self-contained. The Tan–Zam railway came to its western end in the middle of nowhere. The Chinese had made no attempt to link it up to the old Zambian Railways network, and passengers wishing to change from the new railway to the old one had to get out and haul their luggage for a mile in the broiling sun. Part of the problem was that other roads and railways were usually the work of Europeans or Americans, and the Chinese were reluctant to coordinate their efforts with other foreign powers. Sometimes, in the early years, they exhibited active hostility to other aid personnel. In 1970, for example, a team of American engineers were building a road between Tanzania and Zambia on a route approximately parallel to the one the Chinese had earmarked for their railway line. A party of Chinese surveyors had staked out with their red flags a tract of land in south-west Tanzania which the Americans wished to enter. The Americans asked the Chinese to remove the flags. The Chinese refused. They surrounded the Americans, chanted slogans at them for five hours and threatened them with their steel-tipped survey rods. In the end the Tanzanian police were called in, and several Chinese were deported.

To understand why the teams behaved in this oddly self-centred

165

fashion, we have to remember the spirit in which the aid programme was conceived. It was to be a heroic endeavour. To collaborate with others meant diluting China's glory; and this the Chinese leaders could not afford to do. Mao and his colleagues could not count on getting unanimous domestic support for their crusade. The Chinese Communist Party was not monolithic: there were critics in the ranks who might well start asking why so much money and skill was being diverted to a distant continent. To carry these critics with them it was important for the leaders to prove that their philanthropic adventure was worthwhile.

Mao and his colleagues devoted considerable effort to 'selling' the crusade. It was an effort of which Africans were largely unaware. Nyerere even praised the Chinese leaders for the modesty with which they abstained from making propaganda out of their triumphant performance on the Tan–Zam railway scheme. Nyerere was right in the sense that the Chinese tactfully avoided inflicting propaganda on *Africans*. But they did try by every means in their power to convince their own followers that the crusade was a national epic of which China could justly be proud.

In the first place they stressed that the aid projects were winning friends for China. A volume of poems recording the achievements of the workers on the Tan–Zam railway project was issued in Peking under the title *Rainbow of Friendship*. Tanzanians and Zambians referred to the project as the *Uhuru* (Freedom) railway, but the Chinese, in their own publications, called it the Friendship Line. The Chinese liked calling their projects 'Friendship', and African governments were usually happy to let them have their way. Friendship roads, Friendship ports and Friendship buildings sprang up all over the continent, wherever the aid teams went. Once the Chinese tried to bestow a more ambitious name. It is one of the oddities of the Cultural Revolution that nothing in China got named after Mao. The Chinese, unlike the Russians, were reluctant to tamper with traditional place names. In Africa, virgin terri-tory, they felt no such inhibition. Late in the sixties one of the aid teams built a textile mill on the outskirts of Dar es Salaam. The Chinese sug-gested calling it the Mao Zedong Textile Factory. The Tanzanians were unwilling to jeopardize their political neutrality by making such an expli-cit declaration of allegiance to Peking, and the Chinese were too tactful to insist. They settled instead for Urafiki, the Swahili word for Friendship, and embroidered the theme by fashioning a pair of clasped Chinese and African hands in the ironwork of the gate.

African villagers help a Chinese technician on the Tan–Zam railway. A Chinese artist's glimpse of the 'Rainbow of Friendship', Peking, 1975.

The leaders were fond of drawing attention to the physical impact which China had made, through its projects, on far-flung tropical states. In West Africa, for example, in the republic of Cameroon, Chinese technicians lopped off the top of a small mountain which overlooked the capital, Yaoundé, and set in its place a palace of green and white marble. A visiting Chinese journalist proclaimed to his readers at home,

> The Cultural Palace our country is building is one of the largest edifices in Yaoundé, and is called the Flower of Friendship by our Cameroonian friends. It sits like a white crane on the top of Tsinga hill, and can be seen from every corner of the city.

Finally the Chinese leaders presented the crusade to their people as a gallant sacrifice. China was offering up the very lives of its citizens on the altar of African aid. 'Don't ask for any favours,' Zhou Enlai told the technicians he sent to Africa. 'If you die there just make sure that they cremate your body.' Over the years 145 Chinese technicians did in fact die in various parts of the continent, from disease, traffic accidents and injuries sustained on the job. The Chinese called them 'martyrs', and honoured their memory. At Ilala, a suburb of Dar es Salaam, a visitor will notice two obelisks standing under the palm trees a little way back from the dusty road. They bear inscriptions recording, in Chinese and Swahili, the 'martyrdoms' of engineer Zhang Mincai, stung to death by bees in 1967, and technician Li Shunqing, who died of malaria in 1970. Up and down the continent, in the same way, small plots of land were reserved to enshrine the remains of the Chinese 'martyrs', and each year, when it is spring in China, Peking's diplomats perform a traditional springtime duty by making a pilgrimage to sweep the graves of the dead.

The assumption was that a call to national glory and sacrifice would make more sense to the average Chinese citizen than a summons to help foreigners on the other side of the world. So far as the aid teams were concerned the assumption was probably right. The technicians were buoyed up principally by a sense that they were leaving their footprints in regions where no Chinese had ever trod before. They worked and if necessary died in the service of unknown Africans; but there is little evidence to suggest that they felt the personal calling which prompted occasional Europeans like Livingstone and Schweitzer to give their lives to the peoples of this strange continent. They did what they did for China, and in the name of Norman Bethune. Norman Bethune was the patron saint of the Chinese aid teams. A Canadian doctor of Communist sympathies, he made his way to the Chinese interior in 1938 to contribute to the war effort against Japan, and devoted himself to tending the wounded of Mao's Red Army till his death from blood poisoning at the end of the following year. Mao held him up as a model of internationalism from whom all Chinese should learn. But internationalism was still an unfamiliar concept to a people who had always viewed themselves as the core of the human race. It is, perhaps, significant that the hero selected by Mao to inspire his followers to make a greater contribution to humanity should have been not a Chinese who served foreigners, but a foreigner who served Chinese.

Like Zheng He's voyages the crusade was always precarious. It was the brainchild of unusual leaders willing to override the ethnocentric instincts of much of their own population; and it could only be sure of surviving as long as the leaders did. In Peking in 1974 President Nyerere of Tanzania met Zhou Enlai for the last time. The Chinese prime minister lay mortally ill with cancer. He observed to Nyerere that he had been able, over the years, to do a certain amount for Tanzania: he had told his successors to continue the work, but he couldn't guarantee what would happen after he was gone. Nyerere said simply that he had already done a great deal. Within four years of that meeting the leadership of China had passed into the hands of men who were very much less inclined to distribute charity to backward countries halfway around the world. Deng Xiaoping and his colleagues were dismayed by their own country's backwardness. China, they noted, was desperately short of professional skills. The principal cause of this shortage was the Cultural Revolution. For ten years Mao's zealots had played havoc with the educational system: book-learning had been vilified, and young people driven from their schools to herd pigs on the rural communes. But it was not just the Cultural Revolution. Ever since the early sixties China's limited reserves of skilled manpower had been depleted by the constant outflow of technicians to projects in far-off African states – a brain drain that had been sharply accelerated after 1970 by the demands of the Tan–Zam railway. Medicines were running short, not least because so much medicine had been poured into the African countries with which Chinese provinces were 'twinned'. Two decades of philanthropy had cost China dear.

By turning their aid programme into an epic of national heroism, the Chinese government had pinned their country's reputation, as no Western donors ever did, to the success of the projects they built. The result was that they felt deeply humiliated, as no Westerners would ever have dreamt of feeling, when the projects began to go wrong. By the late seventies the flaws were showing through. The great Tan–Zam railway had not lived up to its promise. In July 1976 Mao's engineers went home, leaving the line in the hands of the TAZARA organization. They had hardly turned their backs before a series of troubles arose. There were defects in Chinese technology. Some of the railway embankments the Chinese had constructed turned out to be too narrow and got washed away by the rains. The 'East is Red' locomotives which the teams had brought with them proved too feeble in traction power to haul their trains up the escarpments of southern Tanzania, and TAZARA was driven eventually, to Chinese mortification, to replace them with West German machines. But the most serious problem was TAZARA itself. It soon became painfully obvious that the team had not left behind them a competent African staff. Peking's equipment was faulty, but TAZARA's technicians made it worse. 'They don't have the habit of repairing,' lamented the Chinese. Tanzanian and Zambian railwaymen were failing to perform the all-important work of preventive maintenance, and the failure was soon apparent. Five years after the completion of the railway only thirty of the original eighty-five Chinese locomotives remained in regular service: the rest had been belatedly consigned to the workshops, or written off. Officials in TAZARA showed little gift for management. Wagons were delayed at either end of the line, and Zambian goods piled up in the congested port of Dar es Salaam. In October 1978 the frustrated Zambians began once again to send their copper exports southwards through white-ruled Rhodesia, defeating the political purpose for which the Tan–Zam line had been built. These failings couldn't be blamed entirely on TAZARA. It looked very much as though the weaknesses in Chinese training were finally taking their toll. The Chinese, however, felt that their African clients had let them down. Tanzanian visitors to China were greeted with reproachful questions: Was it true that the Tanzanians had failed to run the railway the Chinese had built for them?

Africans had once been afraid that the crusaders from Peking would overstay their welcome. Now they were only worried that the teams would leave too soon. Already in 1976 TAZARA had asked the Chinese to leave behind a nucleus of advisers who could carry on training and help with the operation of the line. It was a request that would not have startled a European aid team. Europeans were used to lingering in their former colonies to make up for the shortage of local skills. But the Chinese had never envisaged 'staying on'. They thought they could simply finish a project, hand it over and go. They were anxious to hurry their specialists back home where their skills were so badly needed. They now began to discover that it was easier to get into Africa than to get out again. They agreed, reluctantly, to leave a contingent of a thousand to serve as advisers for a couple of years. Two years elapsed; but TAZARA still needed help. The advisers were slowly reduced in numbers, but never eliminated, and every two years a new 'extension period' had to be agreed. On project after project the story was the same. Africans took over the management, but Chinese technicians were asked to stay and advise. It was not a happy arrangement. The Africans were diffident enough to feel that they still needed Chinese advice, but they were often too proud to take it. The Chinese for their part felt that once they had yielded control of a scheme it was wrong of them to interfere with African decisions: all they could decently do was to 'express their opinion'. The upshot was that the performance of many projects continued to decline.

Staying on was bad enough: coming back was worse. In some parts of the continent the Chinese had succeeded in making a clean break. Malians finally took over the factories the Chinese had built in the sixties. 'We're going to have to work really hard,' they said apprehensively, 'now that the Chinese are leaving.' They soon found they couldn't cope. Their workmen proved unable to repair equipment with the machine tools the Chinese had left them and were obliged, consequently, to bombard Peking with incessant demands for spare parts. But the factories in China had been updated since the sixties, and no longer necessarily produced the components the Malians required. Some of the Malian factories began to grind to a halt. To prevent a total breakdown the factory managers had no choice but to ask the Chinese to return and start their projects all over again. For the Chinese this was traumatic. It was tantamount to asking them to confess to the world that their original work had not been properly done.

These concerns of the government were heartily shared by the Chinese man in the street. As China under Deng's guidance began to liberalize its economy, ordinary citizens were encouraged to aspire, for the first time in a generation, to a higher standard of living. They were not impressed by the spectacle of their government building palaces in exotic African cities. In their view China had been filling the pockets of venal African politicians with money which would have been better spent on its own development needs. Shoppers in Chinese cities were still obliged to queue for vegetables in the small hours of the morning. In Tibet and the minority areas of the south-western mountains, cloth was still a luxury and trousers and dresses were scarce. China, they felt, was a poor country and ought to behave like one.

Chinese technicians in Africa were especially disenchanted, for reasons of their own. The technicians shared their compatriots' hopes for a better life. They did not see why they should continue to be 'martyrs' while the peasants at home got rich. They started complaining. For years they had been obliged to put up with extreme physical hardship. On the desert highway in Somalia they had camped in tents in the dust and their steamed bread had got sand in it. In Benin their eyes had been weakened and their black hair bleached by the sun. Doctors had been crowded, twenty at a time, into houses without running water, electricity or air conditioning, houses whose walls were sometimes literally collapsing about their ears.

They had too little money. It was all very well, they grumbled, to say that Chinese specialists should make do with the same living standards as their local colleagues: the idea had been carried too far when a qualified Chinese doctor was expected to subsist on the same wages as a junior West African nurse. In some African cities the cost of living was as high as anywhere in the world. Teams found that their allowances weren't being adjusted to keep pace with the galloping inflation. In 1980 an unprecedented incident occurred. An aid team stationed in Mauritania, on the north-west coast of the continent, decided that their living conditions were no longer tolerable and went on strike.

There was excruciating boredom. All over the continent technicians struggled to find ways of beguiling their limited leisure hours. Engineers on the Tan–Zam railway kept song-birds in cages, and went to stare at the cameras, radios and tape recorders in the windows of a Dar es Salaam establishment called Dusara's Music Shop. Doctors in Congo-Brazzaville occupied themselves with a range of artistic pursuits. They made presents for their families, boxes and *mahjong* tiles carved from the local ebony. One gynaecologist took to sketching the plaits of Congolese women: by the end of his stay in the Congo he had amassed a collection of 183 different hairstyles. Most teams, however, were reduced

172

to gazing listlessly under the stars at stale films provided by the local Chinese embassy. In the claustrophobic world of the work-sites, friction, not surprisingly, was apt to develop between Chinese and Chinese. Teams from northern and southern China were thrown together and squabbled. Engineers in Zaïre commented wryly that the doctors enjoyed the patronage of President Mobutu, and consequently had access to comforts like a swimming pool which were not available to them.

Most teams were homesick, with a homesickness which grew chronic as African governments required them to stay at their postings on and on and on. In theory the tour of duty was two years – one year more, as the teams claimed enviously, than the stint usually demanded of Western aid personnel. In practice many team members stayed a good deal longer. Interpreters unlucky enough to have acquired a knowledge of Somali or Swahili found themselves sent back to Africa repeatedly, and it was not uncommon for construction workers to be retained on a project for five or six years. Almost none of the technicians had their wives with them, and some observed darkly that 'things happened in families' when separations were as long as that. One Tanzanian journalist wrote a cheerful account of the Chinese crop growers who had been installed at a rice farm in the south-west of his country. 'They fell in love with the place,' he reported. 'A year after their arrival they decided to stay there permanently.' That was not quite how the crop growers saw it. There they still were, in 1981, fifteen lonely Chinese lingering in the shadow of the Great Rift Valley five years after their project was supposed to have been finished. They had hoped to leave that year, but hadn't been allowed to. One day, perhaps, the Tanzanians would at last be able to run the farm by themselves – 'and then', they said pathetically, 'we can go home'.

Lastly the teams were unable to conceal a degree of frustration with their clients. There were basic conflicts of temperament. Chinese technicians were sticklers for punctuality. If a team had fixed a meeting with an African official they would arrive six minutes early, identify the rendezvous, vanish and reappear at the precise appointed time. Africans seemed content to turn up within twenty-four hours. Kinder and more patient than many Europeans in dealing with their employees, the Chinese didn't find it entirely easy to accustom themselves to the tropical pace of life. Granted that it was necessary for the Moslem Mauritanians to stop work five times a day and say their prayers, did they really need, on top of that, to slip off for an hour three times a day to drink tea? Sometimes the technicians felt they were adrift in a sea of boundless indiscipline. At their textile factory in Mali they discovered that the African workers were stealing strips of cloth at the end of the day. Embarrassed to intervene directly, they arranged for Malian policemen to supervise the plant. The police also stole strips of cloth. *Quis custodiet ipsos custodes?*

The Chinese authorities made no attempt to suppress the murmurs of their aid teams: on the contrary, they drew attention to them. The policy now was to make African governments conscious of the terrible burden China had borne for so long. By 1978 Deng Xiaoping and his colleagues were making it bleakly clear that China could no longer afford to distribute large-scale charity. The time had come to cut costs.

From 1978 onwards new African appeals for help were greeted with wariness, and sometimes fended off. In 1981 President Mobutu came calling in search of largesse. The Chinese leaders pointedly bewailed their country's poverty, and the potentate from Zaïre was too embarrassed to press his demands. He was dispatched on a sightseeing tour.

Grants turned into loans, and loans became scarcer. In many countries, the pace of construction was slowed down to one new project a year. 'One mouthful at a time,' said the Chinese grimly. Their schemes from now on were going to be simple, ricefields rather than railways; and they were not going to cater any longer for African *folie de grandeur*. The Kenyans, for example, wanted them to build a sports stadium in Nairobi with 100,000 seats. The Chinese said this was too much. Nairobi didn't even have a million inhabitants. Peking, they observed, managed comfortably with a 100,000-seat stadium, and Peking had a population eight times the size. The Kenyans had to settle for a modest amphitheatre, 60,000 seats and no more.

China was no longer prepared to act as a kind of free maintenance centre for struggling African projects. If the Malians, or the Tanzanians, wanted spare parts to revitalize an old Chinese factory they would, in future, have to pay for them. And when China agreed to send out aid teams the host governments would, from now on, have to foot part of the bill. Governments found themselves expected to meet, for the first time, the living expenses of the Chinese doctors, their return air fares and part of the cost of the medicines and instruments they used. The Chinese were willing to be flexible, and a really poor country might still be asked to pay little more than a token contribution. But the change was fundamental. China had uncovered a new layer of meaning in its doctrine that the poor should help the poor. In an assessment of China's new policies published in 1982, a newspaper in Madagascar put it philosophically: 'We help the Chinese to help us.'

Ten years before, at the height of the Tan–Zam railway project, Chinese funds had been flowing into Africa at the rate of some $800 million a year. By the early eighties the flow had been reduced, by these various measures, to no more than $200 million.

All the signs were that the great crusade of charity was drawing to a close. The strains were too great, and the benefits not obvious. Even the political attractions were fading, as the duel with the Soviet Union grew slowly less intense. The overwhelming instinct of the Chinese leaders and the Chinese people in general was to pull back from Africa, like Zheng He's retreating squadrons, and concentrate on building up their own neglected land. By the early eighties the country which had once lavished aid on suppliant Africans was looking for aid itself. Deng Xiaoping and his government were approaching bodies like the World Bank and the International Monetary Fund for the foreign currency which would enable them to buy the Western technology they needed for their modernization plans. But this hunger for foreign currency had another, unexpected consequence. The Chinese did not, after all, pull back from Africa. Africa was suddenly interesting in a new way.

For years, under Mao's rule, the Chinese trading instinct had slumbered. The Chinese Communists had not been interested in doing large amounts of business with the outside world. There was a huge domestic market for Chinese produce. China needed relatively few raw materials from abroad, and was determined to prove that it could survive without making heavy imports of foreign industrial plant. As late as the middle of the 1970s the total foreign trade of this enormous country was rather less than that of the Canary islands.

Trade with Africa was an especially low priority. The Chinese needed almost nothing from Africa apart from one or two strategic minerals which they bought from the great mining countries of Zambia and Zaïre, copper for their electric power transmission and electronics industries, cobalt for hardening the steel in machine tools and for producing the gamma rays required in nuclear weapons research. At the same time they were anxious to demonstrate to their new-found African friends that they were not motivated, like Westerners, by sordid thoughts of profit. Such business as they did was benevolent, and the purpose of

175

it was to 'look after African countries'. The Chinese helped Africans by buying surplus produce which no one else was prepared to take, or by selling them goods on the cheap. In the early sixties, for instance, they traded with Kenya according to a kind of barter system. China would supply, say, manufactured items worth $100 on the world market, but the Kenyans would only be expected to provide $50 worth of their produce in return. The deal in effect saved Kenya $50 worth of hard currency, and the Chinese had contented themselves with making a handsome loss. Peking was even willing to teach African governments how to do without Chinese goods. Ever since the late eighteenth century Chinese green tea had been finding its way into the markets of north-western Africa, where people drank it flavoured with mint. It was one of the main imports of the republic of Mali, and every year cost the Malian government precious foreign exchange. The Chinese, however, sent technicians who showed the Malians how to produce a substitute brand of their own. The new tea was labelled '4960', a name combining the dates of the Communist victory in China in 1949 and the independence of Mali in 1960; and the episode became celebrated throughout Africa as a parable of Chinese commercial selflessness.

Where the Chinese did push their exports the idea was not to make a profit but to drive out the Europeans. The building of the Tan–Zam railway was accompanied by the supply to Tanzania and Zambia of huge quantities of Chinese consumer goods. These goods, in the short term, cost the African governments nothing. They were provided as part of the thirty-year loan for the railway, and were sold within Tanzania and Zambia by state trading bodies set up for the purpose: the earnings made in local currency were used to pay for the upkeep of the aid team and for any local construction materials that might be used on the line. The beauty of it was that these free Chinese imports could be used to replace a wide range of goods which Tanzania and Zambia had previously bought from Britain. The Chinese were freeing these countries from their economic dependence on the former colonial power.

The process was not quite as smooth as the Chinese might have expected. Africans were as stubborn in clinging to European brand names as they were, on occasion, in clinging to European friends, and they were not in a hurry to swap their Raleigh bicycles for Chinese 'Flying Pigeons'. Dark suspicions were entertained about the chemical formula of Chinese Maxam toothpaste. By 1971 the Chinese had none the less succeeded, through this uncommercial strategy, in ejecting Britain from its place as Tanzania's principal trading partner. Three million Chinese umbrellas, recalled a British expatriate gloomily: 'enough to last us the rest of our lives'. It was a hint of what Chinese business acumen might achieve in Africa if it ever got unleashed.

After Mao's death in 1976 the moment at last arrived. Deng Xiaoping and his colleagues were in search of foreign currency, and the obvious way to obtain foreign currency was to export more. China's state trading companies were prodded into action. They began to launch their products with a new vigour into every accessible foreign market. The markets of the West were attractive, but not always accessible. China was an exporter primarily of cheap garments and simple household wares, and Western countries tended to restrict the influx of Chinese products that threatened to undercut their own domestic industries. Money could be made more readily in those Third World countries which had not yet begun to produce such goods on a large scale themselves, and which at the same time were anxious to avoid having to import them at exorbitant prices from the West. Right on their doorstep the Chinese had a major market in the populous developing countries of South-east Asia. But there was also promise elsewhere. Not all African countries were as poor as all that. On the West African coast, for instance, several states had found oil and had oil money to spend. Foremost among them was Nigeria, that huge territory which contained within its borders a quarter of the continent's people. In earlier years Peking's trading companies had been content to ride into Nigeria and other West African states on the shoulders of veteran British merchants who were willing, in return for a commission, to introduce local wholesalers to the merits of Chinese wares. Now they began to dispense with these European middlemen and do their business direct.

Like the Celestial traders who crept round the countryside of the old European colonies, the state trading corporations of People's China made it their speciality to sell Africans cheap goods. Their exports were, quite simply, cheaper than anyone else's. They seldom represented a large proportion of an African government's import bill, but what they lacked in value they made up for in sheer volume. By the early eighties the colourful market-places which adorned the poorer quarters of most African towns were brimful of Chinese articles: Flying Eagle safety razors and White Elephant batteries, hurricane lamps and thermos flasks, padlocks and keyrings, penknives and sandals and incense-burning coils for driving mosquitoes away. Fifty per cent of the goods in some markets

177

were manufactured in China, and some rather unlikely products caught on with impressive effect. Markets in Nigeria had their 'grinding corners', where Chinese motorized grinders were used to grind pepper. All over West Africa Moslems performed their devotions on Chinese-made prayer mats, and hawkers paraded with trays filled with little round boxes of Temple of Heaven Essential Balm. Essential Balm was a kind of ointment rubbed on to the forehead and body and used to alleviate colds and headaches, mosquito bites and fatigue. It was China's outstanding trademark in that part of the continent. Senegalese traditionally relieved their complaints by rubbing their foreheads with the leaves of selected herbs, and they reckoned that this Chinese ointment had virtue of a similar kind. Malians liked it so much that they sometimes even put it in their coffee, or their '4960' tea.

The results were spectacular. In the four years after Mao's death, 1976 to 1980, Chinese exports to Nigeria soared from $128 million to $378 million, and the country became China's eighth largest trading partner. The same pattern repeated itself in the less populous markets of the continent. By 1980 Peking's trade with Africa had risen by 70 per cent, to a total value of $1.1 billion: $600 million of that figure consisted of Chinese exports. Chinese advertisements started to fill the pages of local magazines, and to appear on hoardings by the side of city streets. The Chinese were discovering that they had, after all, a reason for staying in Africa. Africa could help to pay for China's modernization.

Money could be made out of Africa in more ways than one. Even the relatively few goods which the Chinese imported from the continent could be pressed into service in the great battle to earn foreign exchange. Virtually no one in China drank coffee or ate chocolate. But the Chinese bought coffee and cocoa from countries like Guinea and Ghana and earned money by re-exporting them to other parts of the world. They bought raw cotton from the Sudan, processed it in their factories and earned export revenue by selling the finished cloth. In a pleasing echo of mediaeval practice they bought frankincense from the Somali coast. The frankincense was used as an additive in medicines – which the Chinese sold to Somalia.

Many of these were long-established Chinese commercial tactics. In 1978, however, a new and exciting road to profit was discovered by purest accident. A Chinese aid team was working, in that year, on a routine construction project in Nigeria. The Nigerian government happened at the time to be looking for foreign engineers to help them build

178

a few kilometres of motorway on the edge of their capital, Lagos. No Western company was likely to be interested in such a tiny scheme, and the Nigerians asked if the Chinese technicians would be willing to take it on. Money was no object, for the Nigerians had plenty: they merely wanted the technical help and were ready to pay for it. It dawned on the Chinese that they possessed a precious asset in the reputation their aid teams had won in earlier years for swift and competent work. Now was the chance to cash in on that reputation by offering their services to Africa as cut-price engineering contractors. Aid, they realized, could be turned into business. At the end of the Rainbow of Friendship they discerned a crock of gold.

There were various possibilities. Chinese contractors could be paid by the client African government, if the government had the resources: otherwise they could collect their money from whatever syndicate of Western or Arab banks was willing to finance the job. They could work on their own, or team up with a third party. In Nigeria, for instance, they could join forces with their cousins from Hong Kong. Hong Kong industrialists had been active there ever since the fifties running enamelware and textile plants. The attraction was that they understood, as Communist Chinese did not, the Western-style methods of enterprise management which were prevalent in the country, and knew how to make their way through the morass of back-handers which constituted a Nigerian business deal. Alternatively the Chinese could send skilled labourers to Africa to work in partnership with a Western contracting firm. The labourers could simultaneously earn hard currency and pick up sophisticated Western technology to introduce at home. As the idea caught on Chinese technicians began to reappear, like entrepreneurial ghosts, on the sites of their former aid schemes. Back in the seventies the desert highway in Somalia had been built by a team of engineers from the south-western province of Sichuan. In 1983 the Somalis wanted help with a new road. The same team from Sichuan came forward and offered to tackle it. The difference this time was that the team were not offering aid but were bidding commercially against Western companies for the contract to do the job. Somalia remembered with gratitude their earlier efforts, and advised the World Bank, which was putting up the money, to award the contract to them.

The Chinese could, finally, invest side by side with Africans in a profit-making joint venture. One simple example was a Chinese restaurant chain. The African partner could provide the buildings and the noodles,

China the sauces and the cooks. Chinese cuisine made good sense for impoverished African countries, since the Chinese were experts at making a limited quantity of foodstuffs go a long way.

Increasingly the business of China was business. In early 1982 the old aid ministry in Peking, the Ministry of Foreign Economic Relations, was amalgamated with the Ministry of Foreign Trade. It began to look as though Chinese aid would soon be replaced entirely by new-fangled money-making activities. The trouble was that Africans weren't ready for such a transition. Few of their governments had the funds to pay Chinese contractors, or to pool with Chinese investors. Plagued by domestic unemployment, they had no wish to welcome an Oriental labour force. They were taken aback by the tightening of Peking's purse-strings, and deeply nostalgic for the charity of the past. One Tanzanian official remarked soulfully that he was sure the Chinese would not wish to try anything new on a country for which they had already done so much for so many years.

Aid was a source of goodwill, and the Chinese couldn't ignore it. It continued to bring them political benefits at a time when their old revolutionary magic had largely ceased to charm. In West Africa, for example, the government of Guiné-Bissau had not approved when China in 1979 went to war with its neighbour, Vietnam. They admired Vietnam no less than China, for Vietnam had for years resisted the military might of the West. But China had provided half the doctors in the whole of Guiné-Bissau, and the government felt unable to deny their gratitude. They refrained from taking sides.

Trade, on the other hand, had sometimes brought Peking into political disrepute. Did the Chinese trade with South Africa? For years Africans had been distressed by rumours of a surreptitious business conducted between Peking and Pretoria through middlemen based in Hong Kong. In 1963–5 the Chinese were accused of having purchased maize from South Africa to make up for their domestic shortage of food. The Chinese protested heatedly that they had had no trading contacts with South Africa since 1960, and ascribed such rumours to hostile sources such as the Soviet Union. Twenty years later the alleged trade seemed to be going the other way. In March 1985 the general manager of the South African Maize Board claimed that China's newly prosperous exporters of cereals had supplied his country, by a roundabout route, with 20,000 tons of grain. Even if such a transaction had taken place it would not be very meaningful. Under the conditions of the world market a seller operating through an entrepot like Hong Kong is unlikely to know, let alone designate, the ultimate purchaser of his produce. No solid evidence ever emerged to indicate the existence of a direct or purposeful trading link between Peking and Pretoria. But no amount of Chinese protestation could quite lay the gossip to rest.

The Chinese were forced to recognize that the pill of business would have to be sweetened with the sugar of continued alms.

At the end of 1982 Zhao Ziyang arrived on the continent with a thoughtful compromise. Zhou Enlai had proclaimed eight principles for aiding Africa: his successor, perhaps in keeping with the new Chinese thriftiness, confined himself to four. The gist of his message was that Chinese aid must from now on be varied in form and bring practical advantages to donor and recipient alike. Zhao was serving notice to Africa that the new, commercially oriented projects had come to stay. He coupled this message, however, with an unexpected return to the old generosity. Over the years many African countries had helped themselves lavishly to Chinese long-term loans and had, in consequence, run up enormous debts to China which they showed little sign of ever being able to repay. Zhao now made it clear that his government was willing to treat the debtors with some indulgence. Zaïre, for example, owed $100 million. Zhao agreed that $10 million of this debt could be written off. (The Zaïre national radio announced hopefully that the entire $100 million had been cancelled, but this was pushing their luck.) The sole, ingenious condition was that the cancelled $10 million should be invested in China's cherished joint venture schemes. The debt for the Tan–Zam railway now stood at a horrendous $500 million, and repayment was due to begin. Zhao listened to the financial woes of Nyerere and Kaunda, and the outcome, seven months later, was a protocol which excused Tanzania and Zambia from starting their repayments for another decade.

The Chinese agreed for good measure to send out a new batch of 250 advisers to help restore the performance of the floundering railway line. This was a major concession. The Chinese were accepting, in practice, that they couldn't afford to let their crusade collapse in ruin. They had to go back to the work-sites and rescue the projects they had helped to build. There was one condition, however. If the Chinese came to the rescue they expected to have a free hand. Advisers who returned to the Tan–Zam railway and other struggling projects could no longer be limited to 'expressing their opinion' from the wings. They must be

181

given proper titles, chief engineer, chief accountant and even general manager, and must have the right to participate in all decisions on the running of a scheme. And there could be no more Chinese asceticism. African governments must pay the advisers proper salaries graded in proportion to the importance of their work. The medicine was harsh, but it seemed to be effective. One of the first acts of the advisers sent back to the Tan–Zam railway was to purge the TAZARA organization of incompetent managers. In 1984 TAZARA reported a profit for the first time in years.

The obvious hazard was that projects would revert to the construction stage. Once more the Chinese would be in command, working by themselves and not passing on their knowledge to the people they came to help. But Peking had learnt from its errors. By the time Zhao came to Africa the Chinese were exhibiting a new awareness of the importance of training. In China itself a programme of seminars had been launched under the sponsorship of the United Nations. Twice a year, in Shanghai and the eastern province of Shandong, seventy-odd Africans attended courses of two or three months designed to instruct them in China's experience of rural medicine. They learnt about maternity care in the countryside and about the elimination of disease-bearing creatures such as mosquitoes and field-mice and the snails that spread schistosomiasis in irrigated rice paddies. A similar effort was being made to pass on agricultural techniques. Visiting African farmers were taught how peasants in China used methane derived from the human and animal dung with which they fertilized their fields as a source of energy. In May 1986 a special workshop on food production was held for the benefit of Africans in the city of Canton. The Chinese explained how they managed to support 22 per cent of the world's population through devices like the new 'rural townships' in which surplus labour was put to work repairing farm machinery and farmers increased their income by processing agricultural produce. In these modest exercises there seemed to exist the prospect of a serious and lasting transfer of ideas.

The Canton workshop formed part of China's response to the terrible African drought of 1984–5. The Chinese effort was unsung in the West but it was, none the less, spirited. In 1984 the Chinese government distributed to Ethiopia, the Sudan and the stricken countries on the fringe of the Sahara a total of 120,000 tons of maize. China could afford it, that year. Thanks to the liberalizing policies introduced by Deng Xiaoping, the countryside was thriving, and China was producing more grain than it needed to feed its own people. 1985, by contrast, was a year of natural disasters, but still the Chinese gave – 170,000 tons, this time. Peking's aid was, as always, a state-run operation: there was no Chinese Oxfam. But in charity, as in other spheres, Western ideas were gaining fashion, and the Chinese media reported their country's contribution in surprisingly individualistic terms. They spoke of a schoolgirl with a collection box raising money for African children at the Peking railway station; of a police squad in the north-east that had given $600 for the famine victims; of a Buddhist monk who had sent his life's savings from his temple on the Yellow River. At the end of 1985 Bob Geldof was sufficiently encouraged to make overtures inviting China to take part in his latest fund-raising project, Sports Aid. The idea of a sponsored marathon was strange to Chinese thinking. The commonsensical Chinese knew what to do with people collecting money. You sat them down, poured them a cup of tea and gave them what they asked for. But why should they *run* for it? Possibly for this reason the Chinese didn't take part in the worldwide charity marathon of May 1986. But they digested the example of Sports Aid and organized, two months later, a special event of their own. Charity performances were staged in Peking by singers, dancers and acrobats from all over China to raise money for the African famine. College students were encouraged to take up the fund-raising effort, and 7 September, the first Sunday of the autumn term, was officially designated the day of Chinese Live Aid.

While aid regained its momentum, business in the meantime pressed quietly ahead. There was less scope now for some of the simpler Chinese exports. Several African countries were beginning to make their own shoes and textiles, and were imposing quota restrictions to keep out Chinese goods which threatened to suffocate their infant industries. But the Chinese were moving up-market. In January 1986 the China National Electronics Import and Export Corporation joined forces in Madagascar with descendants of the old Chinese traders of colonial times. The plan was to build a factory for making radios and cassette recorders. These products would be sold not only in Madagascar but in the various neighbouring countries of the Indian Ocean and the East African coast. Chinese radios and cassette recorders were still by and large too primitive, in design and finish, to find favour with Western consumers: poor Africans, however, were not so fussy. There was, perhaps, a hint here of China's ultimate commercial ambitions. Fifty years earlier, between the two world wars, Japan had begun its career as a global trading power by selling crude manufactured goods, which Western countries wouldn't take, to the undemanding inhabitants of colonial South-east Asia. Gradually, in this market, the Japanese had refined their products until they were ready, in the sixties and seventies, to bombard the West with a hail of sophisticated gadgetry. Africa, in the same way, could provide the Chinese with a kind of testing-ground in which to prepare their future entry into the showrooms and gift shops of the industrialized world. What sold in Africa today would sell, in a more advanced form, in America and Europe tomorrow.

Many of the major powers were beginning, by the mid-eighties, to distance themselves from Africa. Western countries like the United States and Britain looked on the continent increasingly as a whirlpool of hopeless chaos: governments intent on recouping loans to insolvent debtor nations were cutting back their aid or maintaining it at a minimum level, and companies tended to confine their operations to a few isolated areas of relative calm. The Soviet Union was busy retrieving its own economy from the long neglect caused by its obsession with military spending. But the poor were still helping the poor. Chinese technicians were working on more than a hundred aid schemes all over Africa, and new interest-free loans worth millions of dollars were announced at frequent intervals for projects such as fisheries development in Somalia or road-building in Cape Verde. In the more prosperous states of the continent teams of Chinese engineering contractors were vying with each other for the chance to build roads and dams, ports and airports, railways, water-supply systems and even abattoirs. China's investment in the continent was still small compared with that of the developed Western countries, but the odds were that Chinese activity, in one form or another, would grow in the coming decades. The Chinese were not immune to the frustrations of Africa, but they were, in the end, better suited than richer peoples to ride them out year by year. The African struggle for subsistence was nothing new to them. They were readier than Europeans or Americans to judge the continent's travails from a long-term perspective, less disposed to give way to impatience or despair. One young African wrote appreciatively to a Peking magazine, 'While the Western news media are always pessimistic about developments in the Third World, you are of the view that in spite of this there is room for improvement.' The Chinese could no longer give Africa's needs priority over their own, but they could, instead, hitch Africa's progress to China's through their new, judicious mixture of philanthropy and commerce. On the eve of Zhao's tour of the continent the head of the newly merged Ministry of Foreign Economic Relations and Trade spelt out her country's policy. 'China', she said, 'should be spending less money *but doing more.*'

6

Bridging the Chasm

I'll love you dear, I'll love you
Till China and Africa meet
And the river jumps over the mountain
And the salmon sing in the street. . . .

W. H. Auden, 'As I walked out one evening'

L ike Zheng He's voyages the Star Raft of modern China has been
the object of careful planning. A nucleus of sophisticated Chinese
leaders thought hard, from the earliest years, about their
country's approach to Africa. Sometimes, to begin with, they failed to
understand certain African sensitivities. But they went home, assessed
their mistakes and returned with new policies better attuned to the continent's aspirations and needs. As a result of their efforts China has often
been more successful, in its collective political and economic dealings
with Africa, than the various European adversaries with which it has vied.

But not all dealings are collective, and not all dealings can be planned.
Any large-scale meeting of peoples is bound to involve some episodes
of a spontaneous, personal kind. And not everyone is sophisticated.
The shrewd and resourceful men and women who staged the encounter
with Africa brought in their train large numbers of ordinary Chinese
citizens who were appreciably less well prepared for that encounter than
they were. The evidence suggests that where dealings have been casual
– where there hasn't been a script – the Chinese performance has fallen
short of that of the Europeans. Ordinary Chinese have got on less easily
with Africans, on an informal basis, than the Europeans have done.
And the Chinese leaders have needed to devote a fair part of their
ingenuity to averting possible mishaps in human relations and to redress-
ing such mishaps as have from time to time come to light.

There is nothing especially dramatic about this. It would be surprising
if it were otherwise. Down through the centuries the mass of the Chinese
population have been unused to contact with foreigners of any kind.

186

Living, as they have imagined, at the centre of the world, exalted over all other peoples by a unique and glorious culture, they have viewed the few 'barbarians' who crossed their path through a haze of bewilderment. In the early nineteenth century, for instance, it was believed quite widely in China that Europeans had no knee-joints. They could easily be defeated in battle, because once you knocked them down they would not be able to get up again. Africans were even more puzzling apparitions. Down in the south people sometimes noticed the African servants who toiled in the European households at Macao, and identified them, correctly, with the Kunlun slaves brought to China in earlier dynasties. Other parts of the country had never so much as seen an African face. In 1801 two slaves, Caetano and Mariano, arrived involuntarily in the Chinese interior. They came from a Portuguese ship which had been hijacked by mutineers: the mutineers put them ashore on the Korean island of Cheju-dō and the Koreans, vassals of China, forwarded them to Peking. Peking was baffled. The Manchu court couldn't decide where they belonged. They wrote left to right in the Western fashion, but were black and recognized pictures of a rhinoceros. They spoke of Macao as their place of origin, but described themselves as a southern people. In the end the court resorted to the unimaginative solution of sending them back to their most recent starting-point, the island of Cheju-dō.

Now and again, in the nineteenth and early twentieth centuries, the Celestial traders who had settled in the European colonies on the island fringes of Africa brought home their native wives and children for a dose of Chinese culture. The results were not very happy. In 1889 a contingent of Creole women and children were taken to southern China by traders returning from the island of Mauritius. The traders' families refused to accept these strangers, and they were left destitute in Hong Kong. One unfortunate woman who was carried to China from Madagascar at the beginning of this century is said to have excited such ridicule that she had to be repatriated at the expense of the French colonial government.

This resistance on the part of families in China to the unexpected arrival of foreign relatives can be easily understood. Sometimes, however, Africans appeared to provoke displays of hostility of a more random nature. In 1922, for example, riots broke out in Macao after one of the Mozambican soldiers who were used to garrison the colony accidentally knocked over a child in the Chinese quarter. Thirty years later, just after the founding of the Communist state on the mainland, a border clash took place. One of the African guards who had been assigned to police the colony's border with the new People's Republic received fatal injuries from a grenade tossed by one of his opposite numbers on the Chinese side. A week of skirmishing followed. The colonial government of Macao eventually judged it advisable to phase out the African border guards and use Portuguese instead.

Ordinary Chinese tended to react rather strongly to the physical characteristics of the various 'barbarians' from overseas. Europeans, for example, were hairy and had big noses. In the case of Africans the conspicuous feature was generally the colour of the skin. Prophets of African nationalism like DuBois and Marcus Garvey called for a unity of the darker races of mankind – a category in which they included the Chinese. But the Chinese didn't consider themselves to be one of the darker races. The Chinese thought they were white. In their eyes, white was beautiful. The lighter a girl's skin, the more attractive she was reckoned to be. Peasants, by contrast, were 'black' from working in the fields under the sun. So too were the swarthy inhabitants of Canton and the southern provinces. And no one with pretensions to aesthetic sensitivity wanted to look like them.

Given this aesthetic outlook it is not very difficult to imagine the response which an isolated African guardsman was likely to arouse. In a book called *The Great Harmony*, drafted in 1884–5 and completed in 1902, the political theorist Kang Youwei (1858–1927) attempted to outline a utopian world government of the future. Kang had reflected on the pretensions of Europeans who asserted that they were white and the Chinese merely yellow. His response was to divide the world into a more powerful 'silver' race and a wiser 'gold' one. In the long run, he proposed, the aim should be to abolish this distinction by 'smelting together' the 'gold' and 'silver' races through intermarriage. By and large, Kang's doctrine of fusion compares favourably with the narrow insistence on racial segregation which was preached by so many Europeans in his day. When it came to black people, however, his aversion was painfully clear. They were not physically pleasing, and in consequence 'promoting mixed marriages with them is next to impossible'. His answer, a preposterous one, was a change of habitat. He found promise in the tundra. 'The only solution is to remove them wholesale to Canada, Sweden and Norway, to occupy the empty lands there.' Between them the cooler temperatures and gradual intermarriage with the brown-skinned races would make black people brown themselves after two or three centuries, and in seven hundred to a thousand years even the blackest Africans would have become part of the uniform future race into which the gold and silver peoples would already have merged. For Chinese, as for Westerners, the colour black was infused with a number of negative connotations. In traditional Chinese opera, vagabonds had black faces, and so did the King of Hell. As English-speakers talked of 'black magic' and 'blackmail', so the Chinese used 'black' in phrases laden with overtones of deviousness or villainy. Members of 'black societies', gangs or mafias, talked to each other in 'black speech', a sort of thieves' argot, and smuggled criminals or contraband in 'black ships'. In the Communist society created after 1949, drop-outs who drifted round the country without the household registration documents needed to certify their civil status were referred to as 'blacks with black households'. Any black person stepping into the thick of Chinese society had a formidable number of preconceptions to overcome.

Yet the prejudice was by no means entirely home-grown. Many Chinese were infected, through no fault of their own, by the contemptuous attitudes which were carried round the planet by the conquering Europeans. From the mid-nineteenth to the mid-twentieth centuries the bulk of the information they acquired about Africa was supplied to them through the medium of the Western traders and missionaries who arrived on the China coast. The influence of these informants can readily be detected in the first substantial Chinese account of Africa to be published since the time of Zheng He's voyages. The geographer Xu Jiyu, an official who held appointments in the south-eastern province of Fujian, published in 1848 a description of the world based, in large measure, on the oral reports and writings of Western missionaries. His section on Africa reproduces the familiar Western picture of a continent lacking a history or culture of its own:

> Its atmosphere is heavy and murky; its people are stupid. Consequently, even though since the beginning of the world there have already passed thousands and ten thousands of years, the people are simple and sorrowful, appearing as if they were living in the most ancient times. They were unable to develop a civilization by themselves.

In China, like the West, this myth took root with depressing rapidity. Kang Youwei, for example, gained his initial knowledge of the outside world by reading Xu's book; and Kang follows Xu in making the unquestioning assumption that Africans are dense. The idea was initially con-

189

fined to a handful of intellectuals. Most Chinese people would barely have heard of Africa, if at all. By the mid-twentieth century, however, the stereotype had seeped into the public consciousness. A Canadian journalist who lived in China in the sixties sauntered on one occasion around an island in the West Lake in the scenic city of Hangzhou. In front were three young Englishmen who had beached their boat and gone for a stroll, leaving their shoes behind. The Canadian overheard an old Chinese couple engaged in an anxious discussion. 'Yes,' said the old man, 'they *are* walking barefoot, but they don't look like Africans to me.'

These notions were no different to the racial fantasies harboured in other parts of the world. They were the product of ignorance and unfamiliarity. They did not survive close contact. Mixed marriages weren't impossible, whatever Kang might say. In the early days of the Portuguese settlement at Macao, observers remarked how a number of the Chinese townsfolk married African maidservants and had children by them. In the European colonies in Africa, as we have seen already, mixed marriages were relatively common. Even Kang noted that Chinese who had lived among the dark-skinned peoples soon gave up the idea of their unattractiveness.

Far from deploring Africa's imagined lack of culture, some of the Chinese traders who settled on the continent went to considerable lengths to adopt the culture of their neighbours. Sheikh 'Abd al-Adhidhi, for instance, was a Chinese gatherer of sea-slugs who set up house on Chovayi Island off the coast of Somalia and died there in about 1963. He took a local name, wore local dress and is said to have undergone circumcision at an advanced age to win the acceptance of the Moslem villagers. Chinese in the colonies were less inclined than their cousins at home to make disparaging comments about African 'backwardness'. After all, they were exposed to the haughtiness of European rulers who regarded them, too, as an inferior species – and they continued to suffer that indignity well after China proper had shaken off the last vestiges of foreign domination. In South Africa, for example, Chinese traders like Africans were condemned by the doctrine of *apartheid* to the status of non-whites. (Visiting Japanese businessmen were accounted to be white – but the Japanese had money.) Some of the emigrants tried to climb to the European level, and many kept a low profile; but a few identified vigorously with the African cause. Fay Chung belonged to the third generation of a Cantonese family which had made its home in Southern Rhodesia. Enrolled in the early sixties as the first Asian student at the University of Rhodesia and Nyasaland, she was sensitive to the rising tide of African unrest. Revolution was imminent, and it forced her to a choice. Was she merely going to be a Chinese expatriate, or was she going to be part of the country where she had always lived? She chose the second option. When the uprising started she joined the ZANU movement, gave classes to the guerrillas and flitted between their bases in Tanzania, Zambia and Mozambique. The Smith regime denounced her as 'Mugabe's Chinese secretary'. After Zimbabwe became independent in 1980 she was rewarded with a senior post in the Ministry of Education, and in 1988 she became a cabinet minister with responsibility for the country's primary and secondary schooling. Africans had no hesitation in accepting those who accepted *them*.

But emigrants in the colonies were untypical of the mass of the Chinese population. It was these ordinary people from the deep interior, unused to foreigners, unused to foreign countries, whom Mao and his colleagues mobilized in their great endeavour to set Africa on its feet – whom they propelled into the continent as apostles of independence and bearers of philanthropic aid.

One of the most striking features of the Chinese sent to Africa by the Communist government was their almost total failure to mingle in any casual way. Like Zheng He's squadrons, the Star Raft of modern China came, did its business and left. Its pioneers dealt courteously with the Africans they encountered, but they virtually never tried to know them as individuals. Right from the earliest years of Peking's arrival in Africa, informal contact was shunned. Chinese embassies lived in an airtight world of their own. Not even the chauffeurs or the cleaners were recruited from the local populace. Some of the Chinese who worked on the aid teams spoke African languages with formidable skill. But they did not learn the languages from Africans: they taught each other. At the Foreign Languages Institute in Peking, Chinese instructors trained Chinese interpreters in Hausa and Swahili. The interpreters went to Africa, and gave basic tuition to the doctors and engineers. Doctors who had come to the end of their tour of duty gave crash courses to their replacements. Africans, generally, were never involved.

Aid teams lived in the villages and shared the local hardships. But they had little social contact with their African assistants. Chatting on the job was discouraged, and there was no fraternizing in the evenings.

191

When the day's work was done the teams parted company with the labourers and trooped off to their camps. With Africans not employed on the aid schemes there was no contact at all. Market traders in Bamako, the capital of Mali, called the Chinese 'the dumb people'. They strolled round the market in twos and threes, picked up the goods and examined them, and never addressed the traders by so much as a word.

During Mao's time the seclusion was easy to understand. It was politically essential. Peking needed to reassure nervous governments that its envoys had not come to Africa to subvert the population. And Peking also needed to prevent its envoys from getting subverted themselves by the material temptations of a non-Communist society. In Africa, as in all parts of the world where Chinese were sent at this period, casual dealings with foreigners were accordingly taboo. A diplomat who struck up a friendship with an African risked being denounced by his colleagues and sent home in disgrace. After Mao's death, however, these constraints should have disappeared. The climate in China had mellowed. It was all right to talk to foreigners. But somehow the Chinese in Africa still didn't really unbend. A Tanzanian factory manager reported that a Chinese technician would now, for the first time, accept an invitation to dinner, but solely, as it were, on behalf of his government. He wasn't personally interested in going to have dinner. And when he arrived he would be as grave as a minister. You had to show him that you too were serious and try not to joke so much. Now the Chinese, fully relaxed, have a lively sense of humour. It began to look as though the technicians found it difficult to relax in this company. The evidence seemed to suggest that the Chinese had not merely refrained from social mixing because their government forbade it: they had never even *wanted* to mix.

To understand the reason we must try to look at the continent through the eyes of the average Chinese. Most of the diplomats and technicians transplanted to the continent were in a state of culture shock. They had difficulty adjusting to some of the most basic features of African life. They couldn't bear the food. In theory the Chinese with their low standard of living might have been expected to take more readily to the simple local meals than an American reared on hamburgers and ice-cream. But the Chinese are fussy about their diet. Western cuisine, in their view, is discouraging enough, with its uncooked salads and its foul-smelling cheeses. Not surprisingly they shrank from African dishes. One diplomat who served in Congo-Brazzaville had unpleasant recollections of yams:

192

Congolese soaked potatoes in smelly water. When these had fermented they pounded them to a flour, mixed them with more water and kneaded them into cakes, wrapped them in bamboo leaves and steamed them. These yams had a sour flavour, and very few of the embassy people dared to eat them.

Food in other parts of the continent was no great improvement. The Chinese are averse to large chunks of meat: they abominate steaks. They are partial to pork, duck and chicken, but find lamb and goat meat unacceptably pungent. Yet in rural Somalia the staple fare is goat meat, great hunks of roast kid washed down with goat meat soup. No wonder, under these circumstances, that in most countries the Chinese weren't interested in going to have dinner. Some of the more sophisticated 'Africa hands' performed gallantly, as we have seen, at formal banquets. But most of the diplomats and technicians retreated into a reassuring world of their own. They brought their own cooks to prepare familiar Chinese specialities. They grew vegetables in the privacy of their compounds, and waited for shipments of canned Chinese foodstuffs that were sent to them by steamer twice a year. It was an opportunity wasted. African villagers are delighted if a foreigner shares their meals, and the Chinese might have won many hearts over a dish of cassava or plantain. But they couldn't quite bring themselves to leap the cultural gap.

Drinking was an important part of African social life. African villagers loved to sit, like southern Europeans in their cafés, whiling the hours away with a beaker of maize beer or palm wine. But the Chinese are not great drinkers. They drink alcohol only at banquets, and little enough of it then. Technicians posted to Africa couldn't bear to tipple with the locals. They stuck to their jobs, and surveyed the carefree village life with a sort of resigned indulgence. Let them drink, said a farmer from Shanxi province as he contemplated his labourers in south-west Tanzania. They could still help with the bricklaying – as long as they turned up.

Now and again the aid teams went to watch the communal dancing which took place in the villages on festive occasions. The peasants invited them to join in, but they firmly declined. 'They know we don't do that.' Dancing, to the puritanical Chinese, was suggestive of sex. Like Du Huan twelve centuries earlier, they tended to suspect that Africans were a shade easy-going in their love lives. They were shocked by the prostitution which was a feature of some of the larger African cities. Some of the aid teams felt that their virtue was under siege. Engineers who had worked on the stadium project in Benin told how the local women were forever trying to seduce them. Luckily they were 'disciplined', and had resisted the snares of the flesh. The few women experts who travelled out with the aid teams seem to have lived in constant fear of African Romeos. One Tanzanian official employed on the Tan–Zam railway scheme recalled how if Chinese women interpreters came to call at his office they were almost always chaperoned by male compatriots. If by any chance one came on her own – to collect a Swahili document, say, for translation into Chinese – she would stay no more than two or three minutes before fleeing back to the safety of her barracks. Sometimes, perhaps, the women were taken aback by African affability, and thought they were the object of advances where none were meant.

One or two people did succeed in bridging the cultural chasm. In Mogadishu, in Somalia, an interpreter from the Chinese embassy studied at the local university and was celebrated for his knowledge of the Somali language and culture. He was even known affectionately by a Somali name, 'Farah'. Doctors were forced into contact with Africans by the nature of their work, and some at least appear to have come home impressed by the broad sense of human brotherhood which the influence of the great universal religions has created in African minds. A doctor who had worked in Equatorial Guinea recalled how he had been addressed by one of his patients. '*Médico*, some people despise us for the colour of our skins, think it's black and ugly. But don't look at that. Our blood is all red. We are all part of the world's people.'

But these were exceptional cases. Most Chinese felt themselves to be strangers in a very strange land. Coming from a country where relative social equality was the norm, they were shaken by the sharp contrast between rich and poor which was characteristic of many African cities, and by the crime which that contrast engendered. Several technicians reported having their luggage stolen at the airport and their purses snatched in the market-place. Even if they had been able to face the food, the drink and the dancing, many of them were probably too frightened to venture into African social life.

Africans tended to find this a perplexing and faintly distressing phenomenon. The Chinese, they noted, came and discharged their duties with unfailing competence. But what was the point of coming if they didn't mix with the people? Africans were gregarious, and personal contact, in their eyes, was the essence of an encounter. Some of them felt that they preferred the rough-and-tumble of their dealings with Westerners to the impenetrable Chinese reserve. The Europeans had abused and bullied them as no Chinese would ever do. But they had also laughed with them. Many young aid volunteers from Europe and America had made a genuine effort to appreciate African culture, to join in African parties and sample African food. The Chinese by contrast seemed to be missing the opportunity providence had given them for a rewarding human exchange. One scholar in Cameroon felt that they were 'not doing justice to history'. They reminded him, in their polite seclusion, of a shy girl of sixteen. 'Very pleased to meet you,' they seemed to be simpering, 'but please don't come too close.'

In the eyes of many Africans their visitors scarcely even seemed to possess distinct personalities. African clothes were always colourful, always individualistic. The Chinese all looked the same, in their drab regulation trousers and white cotton shirts. And their conduct was equally uniform. 'When they wave goodbye to you,' a Somali observed, 'they all do it together.'

Up to a point this discipline was highly admirable. No one could fail to be impressed, for example, by the aid teams' chastity. Twenty-five thousand Chinese, almost all male, worked for five years on the Tan–Zam railway without becoming entangled in a single adventure with local women. Like Zheng He's crews, they left no children behind them. 'We have yet', said Kaunda of Zambia, 'to see a Chinese-coloured baby since they came here.' When a team from Italy had been stationed in northern Tanzania local men had complained that the foreigners were stealing their girlfriends; and African officials were pleased to be spared a recurrence of that kind of trouble. But not everyone was gratified by this display of virtue. One section of the public was distinctly aggrieved. Cheated, as they perceived it, of valuable custom, a bevy of Dar es Salaam prostitutes chased a squad of Chinese engineers down a street casting aspersions on their lack of virility. More detached onlookers viewed the Chinese restraint with bewilderment: *how did the aid teams manage?* And now and again the bewilderment shaded off into something like unease. It was another case of aloofness, of a rejection, polite but definite, of shared humanity.

Baffled by the lack of contact, Africans could only speculate and try to comprehend. Was the politeness, perhaps, just a mask imposed on Chinese ethnocentrism by a unique act of collective discipline? Kindly

195

but perceptively, one Tanzanian put his finger on at least a part of the truth. Here, he observed, were ordinary citizens plucked up from the depths of the Chinese hinterland and set down abruptly among 'people who must seem very barbarian to them'.

It is possible, in the light of this general reluctance to mingle, that the teams were not kept in seclusion for political reasons alone – that their leaders were equally anxious to head off the risk of a conflict of cultures. If so they were successful. Very few clashes were ever reported from the Chinese construction sites. Social relations were slight but they were, at least, harmonious. More complex problems were created by the leadership's decision to bring Africans to China as part of its missionary work.

From the late fifties onwards, as the Communist leadership developed its ties with the continent, Africans started to take up residence in the principal Chinese cities. There were diplomats, political exiles and trainee guerrillas. Above all there were students. The leaders in Peking had extended their mission to the classroom. In their drive to purge the continent of European influence they began in 1960 to offer young Africans a higher education free of charge. Scholarships were dispensed through the agency of friendly governments and radical groups. By 1961–2 a total of 118 students from eleven different countries had been accommodated at the Languages Institute in Peking. The idea was that they would spend two years at the Institute acquiring the essentials of spoken and written Chinese before moving on to take specialist courses in practical subjects such as medicine, metallurgy and textile engineering.

This time it was the Africans who suffered the culture shock. The students had jumped at the chance of a scholarship to China. But few of them had ever left their homelands before, and fewer still had any clear picture of what to expect. Unlike their presidents and prime ministers they did not sweep through China for a fortnight in a triumphal motorcade, but were consigned to the humdrum reality of Chinese daily life for periods of up to seven years. (One is reminded of the contrasting receptions accorded, in Song dynasty China, to the honoured African envoy, Zengjiani, and the doleful Kunlun.) They shivered in the bitter Peking winters and succumbed to the peculiarly vicious Chinese colds – germs unknown to the outside world which lie in wait for the unwary foreign visitor. They were also taken aback by the physical squalor. Far from being 'backward', as the Chinese often imagined under the influence of Western racial mythology, many of the students were used to a distinctly higher standard of comfort and hygiene than they found in

Peking. They were dismayed by their cramped living quarters and un-kempt lecture halls, repelled by the general addiction to noisy spitting and by the all too public spectacle of peasants 'patriotically fertilizing the land'. The harshness of the environment was not mitigated by the meagre student grants. At 80 *yuan* a month (about $25), the young Africans felt that their grants were inadequate to meet their need for nourishing food and warm clothing, let alone for amenities like drinks and cigarettes. Nor was there much consolation to be found in the content of their studies. African leaders who came to Peking were treated with circum-spection, and their hosts tactfully avoided telling them what to think. But the students were taught Chinese out of the standard Maoist text-books. 'The people's communes,' they were informed, 'like a newly risen sun, light up the path of progress for the Chinese people.' The students thought they were being force-fed with propaganda. Their instinct was to laugh. Even if they went on to complete their specialist courses, the prospect that awaited them was to go back to their countries uttering Chinese technical terms which nobody understood, and brandishing Chinese diplomas which nobody recognized.

But these were peripheral grievances. The core of the problem was, once again, the distressing lack of informal human contact. The students wished to make friends. Obviously they had the company of their African classmates, but friendship with other Africans was not enough. They were in China now and they wanted, consequently, to make friends with the Chinese. But Chinese society, in Mao's time, had no place for casual friendships with foreigners. The students found they were allowed to share rooms only with their fellow-Africans. They could not get to know young Chinese except on the most superficial basis, and often their Chinese acquaintances turned out to be agents assigned by the authorities to report on their activities and their political ideas.

Nearly all the students were male, and like any other young men set down in a new environment, they looked around them for girlfriends. This was even more unthinkable. The students ran up against a wall of puritanism. They were allowed to organize dances, but no Chinese could come. Some of the bolder spirits pressed on regardless. They met a few girls surreptitiously and walked with them in the parks. The girls ended up being questioned by the security police. African diplomats look back ruefully on the experience of their young people. 'The boys went mad. . . .'

The students felt unwelcome. Their sense of isolation was made still

197

harder to bear by the attitude of the Chinese populace. Students became aware that they were objects of incredulity to the citizens of Peking. Girls in the street turned round to find Africans at their elbows, and fell off their bicycles. Classmates and passers-by marvelled at the students' long fingers and frizzy hair, asked them if their black skin had not been painted, or charred by the sun. 'Hallo, uncle black man,' they called. The students didn't like it. Some of them believed that *hei ren*, the Chinese term for 'black man', was an abusive expression. Actually *hei ren* is no more pejorative, in itself, than 'black man' in English. But the word *hei* was undoubtedly sometimes used in an abusive context. On one occasion a young African walking down a Peking street heard a couple of citizens muttering that he was 'as black as a lump of coal'. He rounded on them indignantly. 'You may think I'm black,' he expostulated, 'but Chairman Mao doesn't think I'm black!'

Many of the students came to the conclusion, however, that the blame for their predicament lay precisely with the authorities. They began to protest. 'We threw all pretence and caution to the winds,' one remembered, 'and spoke exactly as we thought.' But Chinese do not 'speak exactly as they think', and this blunt outspokenness grated on their sense of decorum. These foreigners seemed to have no manners. The nature of the protest also irked the authorities. Spearheaded by the large Somali contingent, the students were clamouring for an increase in their grants. But the Chinese reckoned, with some justification, that they had already gone to considerable lengths to provide these young people with schooling at a time of extreme domestic hardship. The Africans were already receiving grants twice to eight times as large as the stipends accorded to the Chinese teachers and students. Why should they now want more? In the end, however, the authorities consented to raise the allowances of the Africans by 20 *yuan* ($6) a month. The director of the Languages Institute announced the concession in a bitter little speech. 'You can thank the Somalis,' he said.

Friction between the students and their hosts grew steadily more acute. Some of the students claimed that they were the victims of discrimination; that people from other continents were served in the hotel shops that catered for foreigners, but they got turned away. On 20 March 1962 matters came to a head. A student from Zanzibar named Ali went that evening to the shop in the Peace Hotel and asked to buy a carton of cigarettes. He was given a single packet and told that was all there were. The response seems harmless enough, but the students were plainly keyed up to a level of sensitivity at which even a mild rebuttal could be construed as a racial provocation. Ali promptly lost his temper. He pushed his way behind the counter and started to hunt for the missing carton. Chinese self-control does not snap easily, but when it does snap the consequences are drastic. A group of the hotel attendants set upon Ali and beat him up. For the students this was the last straw. They staged sit-ins and hunger strikes and demanded their return air fares. 'Send me back to Mother Africa!' cried a Zanzibari girl. The upshot was a simultaneous exodus of twenty-two Zanzibaris. But the student programme had already begun to disintegrate before that, as growing numbers of Africans dropped out of their courses. By April 1962, 96 out of the original 118 had left prematurely for home.

The episode found its chronicler in a Ghanaian student named Emmanuel John Hevi. The conduct of this Ghanaian is a little obscure. According to one of his former African classmates he began his spell in Peking as something of a toady, eager to win the favour of the Institute authorities, but was soured by his inability to find a girlfriend. The classmate believes that he came home spoiling for revenge, and that his rancour was exploited by American officials eager for a chance to dent China's image on the continent. The following year, at all events, he published in London an account of his experiences entitled *An African Student in China*. The book was savagely polemical. It found no merit either in the student programme, or in any aspect of Communist Chinese life. In places it was singularly lacking in internal logic. It was hardly fair to complain, as Hevi did, about the discomfort of foreign students, and then to attack the Chinese for granting foreigners special privileges at the expense of their own people. But the book none the less offered a disturbing contrast to the glowing accounts of China which so many short-term African visitors were bringing home in those years. Its appearance rang down the curtain on a brief and catastrophic experiment.

For some years the Peking leaders gave up their attempt to school young Africans. The results had been too embarrassing, and with the onset of the Cultural Revolution conditions were unsuitable for any student exchange. In the early seventies, however, they felt impelled to try again. African engineers had to be trained for work on the Tan–Zam railway. Above all the leaders needed to keep pace with their Soviet rivals, who were teaching large numbers of Africans at centres like the Lumumba University in Moscow. So the programme was revived. But the new batches of students soon turned out to be little happier than their predecessors a decade before. In 1972 three of the Zambians sent out to train for work on the railway wrecked their hotel rooms and smashed Mao's portraits in a desperate attempt to get expelled. They succeeded in their objective. Dawn two years later revealed to an astonished public the sight of China's first streaker – a naked and inebriated Tanzanian who had fled by bicycle half-way to Peking airport.

Mao's death in 1976 brought a certain improvement. As the leadership in Peking grew less dogmatic in its outlook propaganda began to disappear from the textbooks, and students no longer believed that their teachers were bent on turning them into docile instruments of the Chinese state. 'We love our courses,' a Ugandan declared. But China was still a Communist country, and some of the teaching it offered remained woefully ill-suited to African conditions. In 1979 two mournful undergraduates from the Central African Empire found themselves trapped in the ultimate Catch-22. Sent out to learn economics, they had embarked on their courses only to discover that 'economics' consisted solely of Marxism–Leninism, which they had no wish to study. But they had to go on studying it, or return home; in which case, they lamented, *having* studied Marxism–Leninism, they would be shot.

Some relaxation certainly took place in the social atmosphere. After Mao's death the ban on casual contact between Chinese citizens and foreigners was unobtrusively lifted. The students could now, for instance, have Chinese room-mates. They could, on occasion, get away with dating Chinese girls. They could even marry them. There was no legal bar to marriage, though the process of getting permission was often an arduous one. And some Chinese women were willing to take African husbands in the belief that life in Guinea or Mali would be brighter than at home. Several students from Mali returned home with Chinese wives.

But this relaxation didn't always result in greater harmony. Ordinary Chinese did indeed feel freer than they had done in Mao's time. Freer to mix with Africans; and freer to resent them. Some of the Chinese students were openly envious. Africans not only got grants several times larger than they did, but were allowed the relative luxury of sharing a room with a single companion: most Chinese students had to squeeze into dormitories of four or five. Besides, the Chinese had been brought up to believe that Africans were 'backward'. Yet here were affluent young Nigerians stepping in from Hong Kong with sophisticated playthings Chinese students could only dream of, video recorders and Sony Walkman sets. Unable to imagine that Africans could afford such gadgets themselves, the Chinese could only conclude that their government was pampering these strangers with comforts it was denying to its own young people. Conscious of their superior wealth, some of the Nigerians and other West Africans tended to treat their Chinese contemporaries with a certain haughtiness which did nothing to ease the strains.

African students who tried to make friends with local women were increasingly apt to provoke a violent reaction both from their Chinese classmates and from the local petty officials. A student from Sierra Leone was reported in 1980 to have been beaten up by police for having a Chinese girl in his room. Marriage caused other problems. Some of the Chinese brides who went off to countries like Mali came back complaining loudly that they couldn't stand the food and that their husbands had turned out to have several wives already. The Chinese public were outraged. All the old myths of African licentiousness – myths which had sunk, in the West, into a well-deserved oblivion – were given a new airing. By the mid-eighties rumours were even running round Peking that the students from Africa were carriers of AIDS.

The result was a vicious circle. Spurned, as they felt, by local society the lonely Africans vented their frustration in a boisterousness that alienated the locals even more. They took taxis and ran off at the destination without paying the fare. And they spent their leisure hours in a desperate search for fun. Life on the campus had changed since the disorders of the Cultural Revolution. Academic pressures were formidable, and Chinese undergraduates worked day and night. But the Africans found this boring. They rebelled at the monotony. In the mornings they skipped classes: in the evenings they sipped beer, held parties, and worst of all played loud music which made quiet study impossible. The industrious Chinese were, understandably, enraged.

The authorities had endeavoured to reduce the strain on Peking by scattering the Africans to provincial centres of learning. It only enlarged the problem. In city after city conflicts began to break out. In July 1979 the campus of the Shanghai Textile Engineering Institute was ravaged by three days of ugly rioting after a group of African students ignored a request to turn their radio down. Twenty-four Chinese were injured, students, teachers and police, and nineteen Africans. One of the Chinese was knifed, and one of the Africans sustained a serious eye injury. The following year demonstrations took place at Nanking. Chinese students put up posters denouncing their government for lavishing food and clothing on African visitors. Finally, in 1986, after an interlude of relative calm, the culminating upheaval shook China's third largest city, Tianjin. It was 24 May, the eve of the anniversary of the founding of the Organization of African Unity, the greatest day in the African calendar. Glad of an opportunity to enliven their existence, the African students of Tianjin University decided to celebrate with a dance. Unfortunately it was also the eve of a Chinese examination. At midnight a deputation of Chinese students came to the dining-hall where the dance was being held to protest about the noise. The Africans responded angrily. Seven of the Chinese came back reporting that they had been assaulted. Matters were not improved by the fact that three Chinese girls had been taking part in the festivities. The examinees struck back, with a vengeance. For the next five hours the twenty-five dancers were subjected to an onslaught reminiscent of the siege of the foreign legations in Peking by the Boxer rising of 1900. Four hundred Chinese students ringed the dining-hall and bombarded it with a hail of bricks and stones. The dancers took shelter behind the bar, surrounded by broken bottles and the remains of a shattered chandelier. At five o'clock – a trifle belatedly – the police arrived to lift the siege and escort the Africans off the campus. The object was to confine them in the relative safety of a local hotel. But the Africans no longer felt safe anywhere in Tianjin. Chinese students were on the march demanding that the *hei ren* be punished. On the night of 30 May a band of Africans fled the city and set out on foot for Peking. They had walked through the night for six hours and had covered some eighteen miles of the eighty-five-mile journey before the authorities caught up with them. After a halt in a nearby guest house they were allowed to complete the exodus the following day by train. Then it was the Africans' turn to stage a demonstration. On 6 June two hundred Africans marched through the streets of Peking to the State Education Commission, with banners painstakingly inscribed in Chinese. One of the banners inquired if the Chinese had forgotten the great occasion when Africa helped China gain its rightful place in the councils of the world. *Do you still remember the United Nations in 1971?* Another banner asked simply, *What is this so-called friendship?* For the Chinese friendship was, as it had always been, something collective and abstract. But the Africans were looking for friendship of a personal kind, and it had not been accorded to them.

Seen in perspective the woes of the African students were nothing unique. Similar troubles were encountered by other foreigners living in China. European as well as African students who went to China in Mao's time complained of the difficulty of making local friends. Even in the last ten years, when China has officially been 'opening up', foreigners of all nationalities have continued to encounter occasional displays of antipathy and suspicion from a people to whom the outside world is still extremely strange. Japanese as well as Africans have excited envy by parading imported luxury goods in front of their Chinese classmates. Americans as well as Africans have aroused resentment by getting drunk and chasing Chinese girls.

Similar troubles were encountered by Africans living in other parts of the world. Clashes with local citizens were reported quite commonly from the Soviet Union and Eastern Europe. And in early 1987 black students were reported to have been subjected to a series of racial attacks in the enlightened universities of New England. The difference was that in Western countries, at any rate, the problems of black communities had become in the last generation a matter of public concern. People discussed the problems: governments were making an attempt to remedy them. In China, by contrast, most citizens were unwilling to believe that a problem even existed.

The Chinese had not taken part in the European enslavement and conquest of Africa, and they were, in consequence, unburdened by the modern Western feeling of atavistic guilt. They had no idea that they harboured any racial stereotypes. In the summer of 1982 a play about Zheng He's voyages was presented in Peking. When the Grand Eunuch arrived, in the climactic scene, off the Somali port of Mogadishu, a Chinese actor appeared made up as a 'black man of Africa', naked to the waist and clad in a grass skirt. 'Mogadishu! Mogadishu!' he roared delightedly, bounding about the stage. A sophisticated Western public would have squirmed in their seats at such a caricature. But the Chinese saw no harm in it. One or two of the audience even guffawed. It was shocking; but also naive.

And if Africans misbehaved, the Chinese felt free to say so. They had no hesitation in blaming the incidents in their cities on the lawless and inconsiderate behaviour of the African visitors. They observed, with justification, that the behaviour of the Tianjin dancers in denying sleep to the Chinese examination candidates had been selfish in the extreme. Few of them were ready to concede that the attitudes adopted by their fellow-citizens might have been part of the trouble. After all, their government taught them that China was the only country on earth which was free of racial prejudice.

But something had to be done. Bitter tales were filtering back to the continent and undoing all the goodwill which China had been earning through its championship of Third World causes and its philanthropic aid. The imaginative and enlightened policies which the Chinese leadership had crafted for Africa were being undermined by the raw ignorance of their domestic population. One option might have been to wind up the student programme for good. But that was out of the question. The student programme had itself become an important piece of philanthropy. The irony was that in spite of their misadventures, Africans went on needing the Chinese scholarships. As the West grew stingier university places in the United States and Britain were increasingly hard to come by, and even the Soviet Union was less accessible than it once had been. Sometimes, after a disagreeable incident, African governments stopped sending their young people for a period – but they always started again. By the end of 1982 there were over four hundred African students in China, and 'pro-Western' countries like Kenya and Liberia were joining the programme for the first time. By 1986, when the Tianjin campus erupted, the numbers had reached a record level of 1,600. The Chinese had set in motion an educational carousel, and to stop it now would be to make a confession of failure in human relations that did not bear thinking of.

An alternative might have been to dismiss the tales as evidence of student immaturity. But that, too, was impossible. The students were not the only unhappy Africans in Peking. African diplomats, too, were having a difficult time of it. In Mao's day, when China had few foreign friends, they had been treated to euphoric cocktail parties, and the Chinese had actually subsidized the upkeep of their embassies. By the late seventies, however, as Deng Xiaoping and his colleagues cultivated new partnerships with the West and Japan, the welcome was cooling fast. The subsidies were ended: embassy rents went up, and so did the price of meat. Diplomats from some impoverished countries were virtually reduced to living off such food as they could scrounge at other diplomats' receptions. They felt ignored at Chinese official functions, and treated in general with less respect than they deserved. Some also reported meeting hostility in the form of petty victimization. Minor misdemeanours were visited with penalties of bizarre severity. A Nigerian whose car knocked down and bruised a Chinese pedestrian is said to have been informed by the police that all the citizen's bones had been broken and required to pay an indemnity of 10,000 *yuan* (about $3,000). Diplomatic blandness was wearing thin. The Chinese might persuade African governments to laugh off the gripes of the undergraduates: they could not expect them to disregard the vicissitudes of their own embassy staff.

The sole practical course was to lend an ear to African grievances. In October 1980 the Foreign Ministry fielded the subtlest of their 'African hands', the veteran charmer He Ying. He Ying took the entire African diplomatic corps on an outing to the Fragrant Hills, west of Peking, and listened to their sorrows. From then onwards the diplomats found they were treated with greater respect. An ambassador from Uganda was pleased to note that when the time came for him to go home shortly afterwards, he was given a farewell reception not at the Peking Hotel, as was ordinarily the custom, but in the more prestigious surroundings of the Number Eighteen Guest House, which was usually reserved for heads of state.

With the diplomats partially mollified, the authorities were ready to turn their attention to the more intractable problem of student discontent. In early 1982 an internal circular was issued by the Central Committee of the Chinese Communist Party. The circular is said to have urged greater understanding towards African students in the interests of China's image abroad. At the end of the year, as Premier Zhao Ziyang prepared to set out on his tour of the continent, the Peking media treated the students to an unexpected paean of praise. For years the students had grumbled that their Chinese instructors regarded their brains as 'porridge'. Now the New China News Agency reported that the Africans were 'diligent and usually the best in the class'. It was not entirely flattery. Several African languages such as Hausa and Kikuyu are spoken, like Chinese, in a range of different tones, and partly for this reason African students often learnt to speak Chinese faster and better than their Western counterparts. Some of the students, the news agency added, had also made striking progress with their specialist technical work. A high-power radio transmitter, for instance, had been designed in Nanking by an Equatorial Guinean who had never so much as learnt geometry.

Such praise was gratifying, but did not in itself redress the basic African complaint of local hostility. In 1979, after the riot at Shanghai, there had been a move in that direction. It was announced that young Chinese at the Textile Engineering Institute and other Shanghai academies were to be educated in 'internationalism' and 'discipline'. The rules which governed the conduct of Chinese technicians in Africa were evidently to be applied at home. But the Chinese leaders could not bring themselves to condemn their compatriots in more explicit terms. The ultimate blame for the riot, they declared, lay with certain foreign students who 'provoked incidents after getting drunk, in violation of school discipline and Chinese law'. Four years later, however, the official attitude underwent a dramatic change. In October 1983 there took place in Peking an almost exact repetition of the notorious Ali incident of twenty years before. A student from Burundi named Claver went at midnight to a counter at the Friendship Hotel to ask for some beer. The staff were uncooperative. There was a quarrel, and two of the attendants attacked Claver and injured him. For the first time the authorities made no attempt to disclaim responsibility. Claver's assailants were arrested and punished; and to compound their disgrace, in a country where appearances are all-important, their names were disclosed in the Chinese press. Several times in the past two years, the media reported, young waiters had been cold or rude to African students, had served them grudgingly or not at all. This was bad behaviour, which had wounded the students' pride and undermined their friendship for China. At long last the Chinese leadership were coming to grips with the problem. They were acknowledging that their people were no freer of original sin than the Europeans or Americans – that they had to make an effort, as the West had done before them, to catch up with the realities of a racially integrated world.

A harder task was to bridge the chasm of strangeness. In the first place the Chinese had to rid themselves of the notion that Africa had no culture. Implanted, as we have seen, by Western missionaries and traders in colonial times, this notion had undoubtedly done a good deal of damage. Culture was always more important to the Chinese than any concept of colour or race. Black American students in Peking, for example, were said to be treated by local officials with more consideration than their African counterparts on the grounds that they came from the West. Chinese could respect the West because the West had science, technology and other useful knowledge for them to learn. But what could they learn from Africa? Asked what ideas they had picked up in their postings on the continent, Chinese technicians and diplomats were apt to look a little agonized. They wanted to think of something, but the answers wouldn't come. One engineer who had worked in Benin racked his brains for some minutes before hazarding the suggestion that the craftsmen of that country were good at making floor tiles.

Africans were sometimes vexed by the Chinese air of cultural superiority. Why, they demanded, was it never thought reasonable that *Chinese* students should come to *Africa* to be trained? Why in all the thirty years of comings and goings had it never once been suggested that *Africa* might give *China* aid? A Somali academic who visited Peking found his hosts politely impervious to his opinions. 'They are very arrogant', he reflected, 'in a deep passive way.'

Conscious of these murmurs Zhao Ziyang made a point of stressing, when he set out for the continent in 1982, that one purpose of his visit was to draw on local experience. Groups of technicians were sent to learn the methods used to extract diamonds in Zaïre and Botswana, and trainees were dispatched to Kenya to study wildlife conservation and the tourist industry. At the same time a nucleus of Chinese scholars were beginning to pay Africa the compliment of serious research. Research was pursued in the capital at an Institute of West Asian and African Studies and an Asia and Africa Institute attached to Peking University. Other Africa specialists could be found at Xiangtan University in the south-central province of Hunan and in the geography faculty of the University of Nanking. In 1980 the scholars at Nanking launched an Association for African Studies to bring together some two hundred full-time and part-time Africanists from all over China. Conferences of the Association began to be held every other year. The scholars relied heavily on translated Western material, and were usually short of funds; but a few of them were beginning to make field trips to Nigeria, Ethiopia and other important states.

In the course of these activities the Chinese began to show signs of making the vital discovery that Africa was not, after all, a cultural wilderness. Granted, the continent might not have a wealth of modern technology to offer Peking. It might not be likely to compete, in the near future, with China or the West in the production of eminent scientists. But it did have a literature. Back in the early sixties, as a gesture of political sympathy, the Chinese had started to translate African writing, novels from Senegal and Ethiopia and poems from Mozambique. Now, twenty years later, they began to study it. The Foreign Literature Publishing House translated in 1980 a two-volume Soviet analysis of modern African works. The fact was that for the past three decades African turbulence had been a far more fertile breeding-ground for literature than Chinese

207

regimentation. Fiction in China was expected to glorify Communist Party policy. In the years since Deng took over, the Party controls had relaxed a little, and young Chinese writers were venturing into previously forbidden topics like the tyranny of petty officials and the joys of romantic love. But their work was still constrained by the need to conform to the current political guidelines. Nothing of world quality had come out of China since the thirties – certainly nothing to match the spontaneity and freshness of the best African poetry and prose. And the Chinese, tacitly, admitted it. In July 1986 the Peking *People's Daily* printed an article deploring the fact that no African or Chinese author had ever won the Nobel Prize for Literature. In giving the precedence to Africa over China, the *People's Daily* was not just being polite. The Chinese knew very well that African works stood the better chance of world recognition. Three months after the appearance of the *People's Daily* article Wole Soyinka of Nigeria was awarded the Nobel Prize.

This discovery of African literature was scarcely going to make a profound impression on the mass of the Chinese public. But it was still a step forward. Culture, for the Chinese, was inseparably connected with the idea of writing. Even their word for culture, *wenhua*, embodied the notion of letters. One of the major features of their civilization, as we saw at the beginning, was the existence of a continuous body of written records stretching well back into the first millennium BC. And Africa by contrast seemed mute. Few people knew about the chronicles of the Swahili cities or the great Moslem libraries in the dunes of Mauritania. But now that modern African writing was gaining international favour it would not be quite so easy to dismiss the continent as an unlettered portion of the globe.

Some years ago a Western diplomat was transferred to Peking from a posting in Zaïre. He adorned the walls of his apartment with a collection of Kasai masks. 'Ugly,' said his Chinese visitors. The Chinese had not had the benefit of painters like Picasso who opened the eyes of Westerners to the merits of traditional African art. But in visual arts, as in literature, the conventional attitudes were beginning to disappear. In May 1987 an exhibition of African art was organized in Peking. The exhibition received a visit from Ji Pengfei, a veteran member of the Chinese leadership. Some of the new generation of *avant-garde* Chinese artists were also beginning to show encouraging signs of interest in Africa's heritage. By the mid-eighties one of them, Liang Quan of Hangzhou, was producing works inspired by photographs he had seen of African rock paintings.

Progress could also be made if the Chinese could only discover that Africans were not so very different from themselves. 'The two most different peoples in the world,' a Tanzanian once sighed, and many Chinese concurred. Yet there were points of resemblance, and one or two perceptive observers were beginning to notice them. African societies rested on a bedrock of peasant values which the industrial West had lost. Africans who made a success of life were morally bound, for example, to spend time and money helping out their 'extended family' of siblings and in-laws, cousins and nephews and members of their tribe. And the Chinese understood this. In China, too, till the Communists came to power, the older members of a family had reached out a hand to the younger, and a man's first loyalty had been to his clan. The Communists had tried in various ways to break down Chinese clannishness. Mao had endeavoured to replace family ties with the claims of the rural commune: Deng hoped to trim families down to a nucleus of a father and mother and one single child. But in China, like Africa, pre-industrial values were difficult to uproot. Many an unfortunate citizen of Hong Kong or Singapore, coming back to visit the village of his forefathers in one of the southern provinces, found, as the entire village claimed kinship with him and clamoured for gifts of televisions and washing machines, that the Chinese 'extended family' was still far from dead.

Personal ties in Africa were more important than the formal machinery of the state. People in African countries mostly sought to achieve their objectives by exploiting a friendship with official x who knew official y. The Chinese did the same, and called it 'having connections' or 'going through the back door'. Peasants in the Sudan had a distaste for litigation. If a dispute arose within a family, or between one family and another, they would rather resolve it by private mediation than refer it to the courts. In China, ruled though it was by a vast and complex bureaucracy, an identical instinct prevailed. Business contracts with foreign firms stipulated that in the event of a difference formal arbitration should only be resorted to as a last extremity in cases where friendly discussion had failed to yield results.

Africans honoured their ancestors. When President Mobutu of Zaïre visited China in 1974 the *Peking Review* reported a curious little ceremony which took place at his welcoming banquet. 'Allow me', said the president, 'to propose a toast in the manner of Zaïrois authenticity, that is to say, to pour a little drink in the ashtrays in memory of our respective ancestors, so that they may protect us and enlarge our friendship.' One's first reaction is to suppose that the fastidious Chinese were repelled.

209

Pouring drink in the ashtrays? But China too had a deep-seated tradition of piety. Tablets representing a family's ancestors were kept at the Chinese hearth, and newly wedded couples were brought before the bridegroom's family tablets to pay their respects. And at springtime Chinese families visited the graves of their ancestors to burn incense and sprinkle wine. In theory such practices were obsolete in the scientifically oriented Chinese Communist state. But in giving publicity to the incident of the ashtrays the Chinese were probably signalling that Mobutu's quaint libation had struck a chord with them.

Lastly, as part of the same pious outlook, Africans respected the old. Young men and women valued the wisdom of their elders. Parents were taken care of, and old people rarely left alone. Chinese, in the same way, were brought up to observe the Confucian rules of filial piety. Those who knew the West were profoundly shocked at the cavalier manner in which young Europeans and Americans moved out of the family home and left their parents to fend for themselves in old age. Some of them noted in the contrasting African conduct a mark of the human feelings which alone constituted a truly civilized man. Westerners might have more to offer them in terms of technology, but Africans, not Westerners, shared their most fundamental ethics.

This was of course an insight which only the most sophisticated Chinese intellectuals were likely to attain. But a handful of ordinary citizens were also beginning, in small ways, to modify their ideas. Ordinary Chinese were travelling in growing numbers to Western countries, to study and to work. And in countries such as Britain, France and the United States, they found themselves unexpectedly confronted by an abundance of black people. Their initial reaction was to gasp. How could these Western countries cope with such an influx of *hei ren*? But then second thoughts began to occur to them. They noticed that, contrary to all they had been led to suppose, Africans in the West were on the whole better assimilated than they had been back in Peking. Some of them even worked up an unaccustomed sympathy for the African point of view. Strangers themselves to the fast-moving Western cities, they saw that these black people shared their sense of alienation. One student from Peking who had visited New York spoke out quite warmly on behalf of the population of Harlem. It was wrong, she declared, to condemn the *hei ren* for laziness. Their historical background was different from that of the West. Naturally they found it hard to adjust to the discipline and long working hours imposed by Western industrial society. And it was wrong to criticize them, as some people did, for thronging together in ghettos. She could well understand their need to live in poor areas: she was poor herself.

On a less rational level ordinary people were beginning to be knit together invisibly by the ties of popular culture. By the early eighties the best-known Chinese in Africa was not Mao, but Bruce Lee. All over the continent cinemas celebrated the exploits of this deceased Hong Kong film star and exponent of martial arts. Pictures and posters of the 'king of *kung-fu*' were on sale in the shops, and young African city-dwellers walked the streets in Bruce Lee T-shirts. In a rather similar fashion, young Chinese were absorbing the various forms of music bequeathed to the world by the African diaspora in the West Indies and the United States. Not all the youth of China were bent grimly over their textbooks. In September 1986 policemen outside Mao's birthplace in the village of Shaoshan were seen relaxing to the strains of the Caribbean rock group Boney M. And young people slipped in to listen to the veteran Chinese jazz band which played nightly at the Peace Hotel in Shanghai.

Little by little the underlying challenge of human relations was being overcome. In November 1986, six months after the Tianjin violence, the Chinese leaders, ever resourceful, were trying a new idea. Two groups of officials from the State Education Commission were sent off to tour a series of West African countries, and a third was due to visit East Africa in the New Year. The plan was to set up a number of training centres in different parts of the continent to instruct young Africans in the Chinese language. Teachers proficient in other fields would also be dispatched to provide African countries with 'intellectual aid'.

It was a stroke of minor genius. By shifting the focus of the educational programme from China to Africa the Chinese could at last hope to settle the problem of student unrest. Africans would be studying in their own relaxed environment, far from the tensions of Peking. At the same time the shift would once more enable the Chinese to extend their didactic influence deep into the continent. The 'intellectual assistants' could awaken fresh interest in China, and encourage a new generation of Africans to deal with the oncoming wave of Chinese entrepreneurs. And the language teachers could hammer a further nail in the coffin of European rule. Given the desire felt by many African intellectuals to escape the grip of the European *lingua franca*, and the facility shown by many African students in mastering spoken Mandarin, it was by no means

211

unimaginable that Chinese might gain ground, in some areas, as an alternative second language.

But would these new benefactors be able to build on the slow growth of human understanding? Would they be able to grasp, what Africans took for granted, that personal contact mattered, that good works were valuable but not enough? Could they adapt to their surroundings? Could they make friends? If they failed, the chances were that the Chinese impact would be, once again, ephemeral. Like Zheng He's ships they would sail away into the sunrise, stately, inviolate and leaving no more than a memory to suggest they had ever been. But perhaps a few might learn, like the old Celestial traders, to walk and talk with Africans and to make a second home in African lands. In that case there was a hope that the talent and drive of the Chinese people would leave a more lasting mark on the continent's future – that the Star Raft might, for the first time, have come to stay.

◆◆◆◆

Bibliography

This bibliography is divided into three sections, covering the contacts between China and Africa in pre-colonial, colonial and contemporary times. Readers of Chapter 1 should consult the pre-colonial section; of Chapter 2, the colonial section; and of Chapters 3, 4 and 5, the contemporary section. Chapter 6 draws on sources contained in all three sections.

Historical contacts up to 1500 (Chapter 1)

PRIMARY SOURCES

Du Huan, *Jing xing ji* (*Record of My Travels*), preserved in Du You, *Tong dian* (*Encyclopaedia*), AD 812
Duan Chengshi, *Yuyang za zu* (*Assorted Dishes from Yuyang*), c. AD 850
Fa Xian, *Fo guo ji* (*Records of the Buddhist Lands*), AD 399–414, trans. H.A.Giles, *The Travels of Fa-hsien*, London and Shanghai, 1877, new edition, Routledge and Kegan Paul, London, 1956
Fei Xin, *Xing cha sheng lan* (*Triumphant Tour of the Star Raft*), 1436, ed. Feng Chengjun, China Bookshop (Zhonghua Shuju), Peking, 1954
Kosmas Indikopleustes (Cosmas Indicopleustes), *Universal Christian Topography*, AD 545, trans. J.W.McCrindle, 1897
Luo Moudeng, *San Bao taijian xi yang ji* (*Expedition to the Western Ocean*), 1597
Ma Huan, *Triumphant Tour of the Ocean's Shores* (*Ying yai sheng lan*), c. 1433, trans. and ed. J.V.G.Mills, for Hakluyt Society, Cambridge University Press, 1970
Ming History (*Ming shi*), 1733
Polo, Marco, *The Travels*, trans. Ronald Latham, Penguin Books, London, 1965
Suleiman the Merchant, *Memoirs*, AD 851, trans. into French Gabriel Ferrand, Paris, 1922
Tang dynasty short stories: in *Taiping Miscellany* (Song period), People's Literature Publishing House, Peking, 1959

Tale of 'Kunlun' Mo	*Taiping Miscellany*	Ch. 192
Tale of Lu Xu	*ibid.*	Ch. 340
Tale of Tao Xian	*ibid.*	Ch. 420
Tale of Yan Jingli	*ibid.*	Ch. 339
Tale of Zhang Lao	*ibid.*	Ch. 16
Tale of Zhou Han	*ibid.*	Ch. 422
The Kunlun Slave	*ibid.*	Ch. 194

Theal, George McCall (ed.), *Records of South-Eastern Africa*, printed for Government of the Cape Colony, 1898, from *Asia Portuguesa* by Manuel de Faria e Sousa, Lisbon, 1666–74, 9 vols
Veritable Records of the Ming Dynasty, early seventeenth century
Wang Dayuan, *Dao yi zhi lüe* (*Description of the Island Barbarians*), 1349, ed. with commentary by Su Jiqing, China Bookshop, Peking, May 1981
Zhao Rugua, *Zhu fan zhi* (*Gazetteer of Foreigners*), 1225
Zhou Qufei, *Ling wai daida* (*Information from Beyond the Mountains*), 1178
Zhu Yu, *Pingzhou ketan* (*Topics from Pingzhou*), 1119

Relevant excerpts from the Chinese works cited above, with the exception of those by Luo Moudeng and Ma Huan, may be found in:

Zhang Xinglang (Chang Hsing-lang), *Zhong xi jiaotong shiliao huipian* (*Collected Historical Materials on Sino-Western Contact*), vol. 3, *Gudai Zhongguo yu Feizhou zhi jiaotong* (*Early contacts between China and Africa*), Peking (Peip'ing), 1930
For Zhao Rugua see Hirth, Friedrich and Rockhill, W. W., *Chau Ju-kua: His Work on the Chinese and Arab Trade in the 12th and 13th Centuries, entitled Chu-fan-chi*, St Petersburg, 1911

SECONDARY SOURCES

Allen, J. de V., and Wilson, Thomas H. (eds), *From Zinj to Zanzibar, Studies in History, Trade and Society on the Eastern Coast of Africa*, Paideuma, no. 28, Franz Steiner Verlag, Wiesbaden, 1982
Allen, J. de V., 'Swahilization Past, Present and Future', paper presented to seminar on Swahili language and society, School of Oriental and African Studies, London, April 1982
Annual Report of The Antiquities Department, National Museum, Dar es Salaam, Tanzania, 1964–75
Azania, British Institute in Eastern Africa, Nairobi, 1966–80
Belrose-Huyghes, Vincent, 'La Cartographie de Madagascar à travers les ages', in *Cartes anciennes et cartographie moderne*, Musée d'Art et d'Archéologie, Antananarivo, Madagascar, July 1981
Caton-Thompson, Gertrude, *The Zimbabwe Culture – Ruins and Excavations*, Oxford, 1931
Chang Kuei-sheng, 'Africa and the Indian Ocean in Chinese Maps of the Fourteenth and Fifteenth Centuries', in *Imago Mundi*, vol. 24, 1970, pp. 21–30
Chen Gongyuan, 'Zheng He xia "Xi Yang" yu Zhong-Fei youyi' ('Zheng He's Journey to the Western Ocean and Sino-African Friendship'), in *Hai jiao shi yanjiu* (*Research into the History of Maritime Communications*), pub. by Research Institute of the History of Chinese Maritime Communications, Social Sciences Research Institute, Fujian province, and Museum of the History of Maritime Communications, Quanzhou, Fujian province, no. 3, 1981
Chin, Elizabeth Yee Yin, 'Geographical Aspects of Chinese Contacts with East Africa during the Mediaeval Period', thesis, School of Oriental and African Studies, London, 1978

Chittick, Neville, *Kilwa – An Islamic Trading City on the East African Coast*, 2 vols, British Institute in Eastern Africa, Nairobi, 1974

Chittick, Neville, 'The "Shirazi" Colonization of East Africa', in *Journal of African History*, VII, 3, 1965

Davidson, Basil, *Black Mother*, Gollancz, London, 1961 (Pelican edition, 1980)

Davidson, Basil, *Discovering Africa's Past*, Longmans, London, 1978

Davidson, Basil, *Old Africa Rediscovered*, Gollancz, London, 1959 (new edition Longmans, London, 1970)

Duyvendak, J.J.L., *China's Discovery of Africa*, Arthur Probsthain, London, 1949

Duyvendak, J.J.L., 'The True Dates of the Chinese Maritime Expeditions in the Early Fifteenth Century', in *T'oung Pao*, XXXIV, Leiden, 1938

Elliot, J.A.G., 'A Visit to the Bajun Islands', in *Journal of African Studies*, XXV, London, 1926

Elvin, Mark, *The Pattern of the Chinese Past*, Eyre Methuen, London, 1973

Fage, J.D., *A History of Africa*, Hutchinson, London, 1978

Filesi, Teobaldo, *China and Africa in the Middle Ages*, trans. David L. Morison, Cass/Central Asian Research Centre, London, 1972

Freeman-Grenville, Greville, 'East African Coin Finds and their Historical Significance', in *Journal of African History*, I, 1 (1960), Cambridge University Press, pp. 31–43

Fripp, Constance, 'A Note on Mediaeval Chinese–African Trade', in *Native Affairs Department Annual*, vol. 17, Southern Rhodesia, 1940, pp. 88–96

Fripp, Constance, 'Chinese Mediaeval Trade with Africa', in *Native Affairs Department Annual*, vol. 18, Southern Rhodesia, 1941, pp. 12–22

Garlake, Peter, *Great Zimbabwe*, Thames and Hudson, London, 1973

Grandidier, A. and G., *Collection des Ouvrages anciens concernant Madagascar*, tome 1, Comité de Madagascar, Paris, 1903

Grottanelli, Vinigi L., *Pescatori dell'Oceano Indiano*, Cremonese, Rome, 1955

Huang Shengzhang, 'The Traditional Friendly Relations between China and Somalia', Geographical Research Institute, Chinese Academy of Sciences, 1980

Institute of West Asian and African Studies, Peking, *Feizhou Gaikuang (African Survey)*, World Knowledge Publishing House, Peking, 1981

Kirkman, James, *Fort Jesus: A Portuguese Fortress on the East African Coast*, Clarendon Press, Oxford, 1974

Kirkman, James, *The Arab City of Gedi*, Oxford University Press, 1954

Li Changxing, 'Ancient Friendship Blooms Again', in *Renmin Ribao (People's Daily)*, Peking, 30 December 1982

Lin Mingyang, 'The Giraffe and Sino–African Friendship', in *Renmin Ribao (People's Daily)*, Peking, 16 January 1983

Mathew, Gervase, 'Chinese Porcelain in East Africa and on the Coast of South Arabia', in *Oriental Art*, new series vol. II, 2, 1956, pp. 50–5

Needham, Joseph, *A History of Science and Civilization in China*, vol. IV, part 3, Cambridge University Press, 1971

Radimilahy, Marie de Chantal, 'Archéologie de l'Androy', thesis, University of Madagascar, 1980

215

Sassoon, Caroline, *Chinese Porcelain in Fort Jesus*, National Museums of Kenya, Mombasa, 1975

Shen Fuwei, 'Du Huan's Journey to Molin in the Tang Period', in *Shijie lishi (World History)*, no. 6, Peking, 1980

Shen Fuwei, 'Zheng He's Treasure Fleet and its Voyages to the East African Coast', in *Zheng He xia Xi Yang lun wen ji (Collected Essays on Zheng He's Journey to the Western Ocean)*, Association of Chinese Maritime History, People's Communications Publishing House, Peking, 1985

Swanson, Bruce, *Eighth Voyage of the Dragon*, Naval Institute Press, Annapolis, 1982

Tanganyika Notes and Records, Dar es Salaam, 1936–59

Wheatley, Paul, 'Analecta Sino–Africana Recensa', in *East Africa and the Orient: Cultural Syntheses in Pre-Colonial Times*, ed. Neville Chittick and R.I.Rotberg, Africana Publishing House, Nairobi, 1975

Wheatley, Paul, 'The Land of Zanj: Exegetical Notes on Chinese Knowledge of East Africa Prior to AD 1500', in Robert W.Steel and R.Mansell Prothero, *Geographers and the Tropics: Liverpool Essays*, Longmans, London, 1964

Wilding, Richard, 'The Ceramics of the Lamu Archipelago', thesis, University of Nairobi, 1977

Zhang Tiesheng, *Zhong-Fei jiaotong chu tan (Initial Inquiry into the History of Sino–African Contacts)*, New China Bookshop, Peking, 1973

Contacts during the colonial period, 1500–1945 (Chapter 2)

PRIMARY SOURCES

Documents relevant to the presence during the colonial period of Chinese labourers and traders in Africa, and of African labourers in China, may be found in the Kenya National Archives; Royal Commonwealth Society, London; Historical Archives, Macao; National Archives, Antananarivo, Madagascar; Mauritius Archives; Archives of the Chinese Chamber of Commerce, Mauritius; National Archives, Dar es Salaam, Tanzania, and the Zimbabwe National Archives.

Published materials

Baron, Capitaine, 'L'immigration chinoise à Madagascar', in *La Grande Ile militaire*, no. 20, Madagascar, November 1954, pp. 6–7

Beaton, Rev. Patrick, *Creoles and Coolies; or Five Years in Mauritius*, James Nisbet & Co., London, 1859

Billiard, A., *Voyages aux colonies orientales, ou lettres écrites des Isles de France et de Bourbon pendant les années 1817, 1818, 1819 and 1820*, Ladvocat, Paris, 1822

Boyle, Charles John, *Faraway; or Sketches of Scenery and Society in Mauritius*, Chapman and Hall, London, 1867

Chevalier, Louis, *Madagascar – populations et ressources*, Presses Universitaires de France, Paris, 1952

DuBois, W.E.B., *Black Reconstruction in America, 1860–1880*, New York, 1935 (republished The World Publishing Co., New York, 1964)

DuBois, W.E.B., *The World and Africa*, International Publishers, New York, 1946

Emin Pasha (Eduard Schnitzer), *Emin Pasha in Central Africa*: Being a Collection of his Letters and Journals edited and annotated by Prof. G.Schweinfurth, Prof. F.Ratzel, Dr R.W.Felkin and Dr G.Hartlaub, trans. Mrs R.W.Felkin, George Philip & Son, London, 1888

Gordon, Sir Arthur, *Mauritius: Records of private and public life 1871–1874*, vol. I, R. & R.Clark, Edinburgh, 1894

Kang Youwei, *The One-World Philosophy of Kang Yu-wei*, trans. Laurence G.Thompson, Allen and Unwin, London, 1958

Liang Qichao, 'Lun bu bian fa zhi hai' ('On the Harm of Not Reforming'), in *Selected Works of Liang Qichao*, ed. Li Huaxing and Wu Jiaxun, People's Publishing House, Shanghai, 1984, pp. 4–11

Padmore, George, *Africa and World Peace*, Secker & Warburg, London, 1937 (second edition Frank Cass, London, 1972)

Padmore, George, *Pan-Africanist Congress* (reprint of report of the Fifth Pan-Africanist Congress, Manchester, 1945), 1947 (second edition Hammersmith Bookshop, London, 1963)

Padmore, George, *Pan-Africanism or Communism?*, Dobson Books, London, 1956

Shijie Zhishi (*World Knowledge*), Life Bookshop, Shanghai, 1935

Transvaal Command Papers, 1904–7, in Royal Commonwealth Society, London

World Knowledge see *Shijie Zhishi*

SECONDARY SOURCES

Ai Zhouchang, 'Jindai Huagong zai Nan-Fei' ('Chinese Labourers in South Africa in Recent Times'), in *Lishi Yanjiu* (*Historical Research*), no. 6, Peking, 1981

Ai Zhouchang, 'Jindai Zhong-Fei guanxi' ('Sino–African Relations in Recent Times'), in *West Asia and Africa*, no. 1, Peking, 1984

Andriamirado, Sennen, *Le Défi du Congo-Océan ou l'epopée d'un chemin de fer*, Le Groupe Jeune Afrique département Edition Conseil, Paris, 1984

Armstrong, James C., 'The Chinese at the Cape in the Dutch East India Company Period, 1652–1795', unpublished paper, Nairobi, 1979

Boxer, C.R., *Fidalgos in the Far East*, Martinus Nijhoff, The Hague, 1948

Boxer, C.R., *The Portuguese Seaborne Empire, 1415–1825*, Hutchinson, London, 1969

Boxer, C.R., 'The Rise and Fall of Nicholas Iquan', in *Tien Hsia* (monthly), Hong Kong, April–May 1941

Clemens, John, *Discovering Macau: A Visitor's Guide*, Macmillan, Hong Kong, 1972

Davidson, Basil, *Discovering Africa's Past*, Longmans, London, 1978

Drake, Fred W., *China charts the world: Hsü Chi-yü (Xu Jiyu) and his geography of 1848*, Harvard University Press, Cambridge, Mass., 1975

Elvin, Mark, *The Pattern of the Chinese Past*, Eyre Methuen, London, 1973

Fage, J.D., *A History of Africa*, Hutchinson, London, 1978

Fitzgerald, C.P., *The Southern Expansion of the Chinese People*, Barrie and Jenkins, London, 1972

Grottanelli, Vinigi L., *Pescatori dell'Oceano Indiano*, Cremonese, Rome, 1955

Hsiao Tzu-yi, *Fei-chou Hua-ch'iao ching-chi* (*The Economy of the Overseas Chinese in Africa*), Overseas Book Company, Taipei, 1955

Lessa, Almerindo, 'Anthropobiologie et anthroposociologie de Macao', thesis, University of Toulouse, May 1970

Ly Tio Fane Pineo, Dr Huguette, *La Diaspora chinoise dans l'océan indien occidental*, Association des Chercheurs de L'Océan Indien and Institut d'Histoire des Pays d'Outre-Mer, Aix en Provence, 1982

Mihalyi, Louis J., 'Characteristics and Problems of Labour in the Usambara Highlands of East Africa during the German Period, 1885–1914', in *East Africa Journal*, v, Nairobi, May 1970

Montalto de Jesus, C.A., *Historic Macao*, Kelly and Walsh, Hong Kong, 1902 (3rd edition, Oxford University Press, 1984)

Ng, Georgy, 'L'immigration chinoise à Maurice', in *Le Cernéen*, Port Louis, Mauritius, 10 September 1973

Réalités malgaches, article 'Les Chinois à Madagascar', 30 April 1982

Richardson, Peter, *Chinese Mine Labour in the Transvaal*, Macmillan, London, 1982

Richardson, Peter, 'The Recruiting of Chinese Indentured Labour for the South African Goldmines, 1903–1908', in *Journal of African History*, XVIII, I (1977), Cambridge University Press, pp. 85–108

Sautter, Giles, 'Notes sur la construction du chemin de fer Congo-Océan (1921–1934)', in *Cahier d'études africaines*, Paris, 1967, pp. 254–6

Slawecki, Leon M.S., *French Policy towards the Chinese in Madagascar*, Shoe String Press, Inc., Hamden, Connecticut, 1971

'The Chinese in South Africa', in *South African Panorama*, Department of Information, Pretoria, October 1980

Teixeira, Fr. M. SJ, 'A Missão da Coreia', in *Macau e a Sua Diocesa*, XVI, Macao, Tipografia Marsul, 1982

Teixeira, Fr. M. SJ (ed.), *Boletim Ecclesiástico da Diocesa de Macau*, November–December 1979

Teixeira, Fr. M. SJ, 'Os Cafres em Macau', article of 24 June 1982 given to the author

Teixeira, Fr. M. SJ, *Os Militares em Macau*, Imprensa Nacional, Macau, 1976

Tsang Mang Kin, Joseph, 'The Chinese Influx', paper, Port Louis, Mauritius

Wilson, Monica and Thompson, Leonard, *The Oxford History of South Africa*, Clarendon Press, Oxford, 1969

Contemporary relations (Chapters 3–5)

PRIMARY SOURCES

Specialist journals

including: *Africa*, London; *Africa Confidential*, London; *Africa Contemporary Record*, London; *Africa Economic Digest*, London; *Africa Now*, London; *African Revolution*,

Algiers; *Afrique Express*, Brussels; *China Quarterly*, London; *China Yearbook*, Taipei; *East Africa Journal*, Nairobi; *Evergreen, A Magazine of Chinese Youth and Students*, Peking, mid-1960s; *Ikwezi*, London; *Jeune Afrique*, Paris; *Mozambique Revolution*, Dar es Salaam, organ of the Front for the Liberation of Mozambique (FRELIMO); *Peking Review* (*Beijing Review* since 1979); *Réalités malgaches*, Madagascar; *Revolution Africa Latin America Asia*, Lausanne; *Sechaba*, organ of the African National Congress (ANC), London; *Survey of the China Mainland Press*, Hong Kong; *West Africa*, London; *World Knowledge* (*Shijie Zhishi*), Peking; *Xinhua* (New China News Agency) *Bulletin*, Peking; *Zimbabwe News*, organ of the Zimbabwe African National Union (ZANU).

Selected documents
Bulletin of the Chinese Association for African Studies, no. 7, May 1982
Cabral, Amilcar, *Unity and Struggle*, Heinemann, London, 1980
'Chinese Aid to Madagascar', paper issued by Ministry of Economic Planning, Madagascar, 12 October 1978
'Communism and Africa', anonymous booklet of December 1965, attributed to Foreign & Commonwealth Office, London
Dioum, Aminata, unpublished response to article in *Jeune Afrique* by Marie-Ange Donzé, 'Les Chinois sont-ils racistes?' (in the author's possession)
Hevi, Emmanuel John, *An African Student in China*, Pall Mall Press, London, 1963
Itote, Waruhiu (General China), *'Mau Mau' General*, East African Publishing House, Nairobi, 1967
Kenyan government memorandum on Chinese technical cooperation, 1981 (given to the author by the Kenyan Ministry of Culture and Social Services)
Mao Zedong, *Selected Works*, vols 1 and 2 (1967), 3 and 4 (1975), 5 (1977), Foreign Languages Press, Peking
Nyerere, Julius, *Freedom and Development: Uhuru na Maendeleo*, Oxford University Press, Dar es Salaam, 1973
Nyerere, Julius, *Freedom and Socialism – Uhuru na Ujamaa*, Oxford University Press, Dar es Salaam, 1968
Padmore, George, *Pan-Africanism or Communism?*, Dobson Books, London, 1956
Pan-Africanist Congress (PAC), report of National Executive Committee Meeting, Moshi, 19–22 September 1967, in Marx Memorial Library, London
Rainbow of Friendship see *Youyide Caihong*
'Sino–African Technical Cooperation', Taiwan government brochures, 1970 and 1971
Société Togolaise d'Etudes de Développement, report on Chinese rice project on the River Sio, June 1981 (supplied to the author by USAID, Abidjan)
Tung Chi-ping (Dong Jiping) and Evans, Humphrey, *The Thought Revolution*, Leslie Frewin, London, 1967
'Work Bulletin of the Chinese People's Liberation Army (Gongzuo Tongxun)', released by the State Department through the Library of Congress, 5 August 1963, in Cheng, Chester J. (ed.), *The Politics of the Chinese Red Army*, Stanford: Hoover Institution on War, Revolution and Peace, 1966

Youlou, Abbé Fulbert, *J'Accuse La Chine*, La Table Ronde, Paris, 1966
Youyide Caihong (*Rainbow of Friendship*), collected poems of the Chinese workers on the Tan–Zam railway, People's Literature Publishing House, Peking, 1975
Zhang Yi, *When the Light Dawned* (*Poxiao Shifen*), Taipei, 1985

SECONDARY SOURCES

Adie, W. A. C., 'Chou En-lai on Safari', in *China Under Mao – Politics Takes Command*, ed. Roderick MacFarquhar, MIT Press, Cambridge, Mass., 1966
African Survey see Institute of West Asian and African Studies
Ali, Ali Abdalla, *Sudan–China Trade and Aid Relations*, Economic and Social Research Council, National Council for Research, Khartoum, bulletin no. 29, November 1975
Arnold, Guy, *Aid in Africa*, Kogan Page, London, Nichols Publishing Co., New York, 1979
Attwood, William, *The Reds and the Blacks*, Hutchinson, London, 1967
Bailey, Martin, *Freedom Railway*, Rex Collings, London, 1976
Bartke, Wolfgang, *China's Economic Aid*, Institute of Asian Affairs, Hamburg, C. Hurst & Co., London, 1975
Benson, Mary, *The African Patriots*, Faber, London, 1963
Bermingham, Jack and Clausen, Edwin, *Sino–African Relations 1949–1976*, Munger Africana Library, California Institute of Technology, Pasadena, 1981
Cooley, John K., *East Wind over Africa*, Walker & Co., New York, 1965
Cronjé, Suzanne, *The World and Nigeria – The Diplomatic History of the Biafran War 1967–1970*, Sidgwick & Jackson, London, 1972
Davidson, Basil, Slovo, Joe, and Wilkinson, Anthony R., *Southern Africa: the New Politics of Revolution*, Pelican Books, London, 1976
Davidson, Basil, *The People's Cause*, Longmans, London, 1981
Fomicheva, Margarita Vasilyevna and Krasil'nikov, Aleksandr Sergeyevich, *China and Africa – The subversive activity of the Maoists in Africa* (*Kitai i Afrika*), Mysl' (Thought) Publishing House, Moscow, 1976
Gibson, Richard, *African Liberation Movements*, Oxford University Press, 1972
Gilkes, Patrick, 'Sale of Arms to Africa', in *Annuaire de l'Afrique et du Moyen-Orient – Les armées et la défense*, Jeune Afrique, Paris, 1980
Hall, Richard S. and Peyman, H., *The Great Uhuru Railway: China's Showpiece in Africa*, Gollancz, London, 1976
Halliday, Fred and Molyneux, Maxine, *The Ethiopian Revolution*, Verso Editions and NLB, London, 1981
Hevi, Emmanuel John, *The Dragon's Embrace: the Chinese Communists and Africa*, Pall Mall Press, London, 1967
Hu You'e, 'Trends in African Political and Economic Development in the 1980s', in *West Asia and Africa*, no. 4, Peking, 1984
Hutchison, Alan, *China's African Revolution*, Hutchinson, London, 1975
Institute of West Asian and African Studies, Peking, *Feizhou Gaikuang* (*African Survey*), World Knowledge Publishing House, Peking, 1981

Ismael, Tareq Y., 'The People's Republic of China and Africa', in *Journal of Modern African Studies*, 9, 4, Cambridge University Press, December 1971, pp. 507–29

Larkin, Bruce D., *China and Africa, 1949–1970*, University of California Press, Berkeley, 1971

Legvold, Robert, 'Soviet and Chinese Influence in Black Africa', in *Soviet and Chinese Influence in the Third World*, ed. Alvin Z.Rubinstein, Praeger Publishers, New York, 1975

Legum, Colin, 'Africa and China: Symbolism and Substance', in *Policies Toward China: Views from Six Continents*, ed. A.M.Halpern, McGraw-Hill, New York, 1965

Legum, Colin and Hodges, Tony, *After Angola – The War over Southern Africa*, Rex Collings, London, 1976

Maitan, Livio, 'La Chine modèle de développement', in *Développement*, Société Internationale pour la Développement, no. 2, Rome, 1979

Marcum, John, *The Angolan Revolution*, vol. 1, *The Anatomy of an Explosion (1950–1962)*, MIT Press, Cambridge, Mass., and London, 1969; vol. 2, *Exile Politics and Guerrilla Warfare (1962–1976)*, MIT Press, Cambridge, Mass., and London, 1978

Martin, David and Johnson, Phyllis, *The Struggle for Zimbabwe*, Zimbabwe Publishing House, Harare, 1981

Mertens, Pierre and Smets, Paul-François, *L'Afrique de Pékin*, Brussels, 1966

Le Moniteur africain, Dakar, article, 'Les "Deux Chines" et l'Afrique', no. 505, 3 June 1971

Neuhauser, Charles, *China and the Afro–Asian People's Solidarity Organization, 1957–1967*, Harvard East Asian Monographs, Cambridge, Mass., 1970

Ogunsanwo, Alaba, *China's Policy in Africa, 1958–71*, Cambridge University Press, 1974

Problèmes politiques et sociaux, article, 'La Chine vue du Tiers-Monde', no. 408, Documentation française, Paris, 13 February 1981

Rabenoro, Césaire, 'Les Relations exterieures de Madagascar de 1960 à 1972', thesis, Aix en Provence, November 1981

Richer, Philippe, 'L'aide chinoise est-elle différente?', in *Actuel Développement*, no. 17, January–February 1977, pp. 31–5

Sampson, Anthony, *The Treason Cage*, Heinemann, London, 1958

Schatten, Fritz, *Communism in Africa*, Allen and Unwin, London, 1966

Shichor, Yitzhak, *The Middle East and China's Foreign Policy, 1949–1977*, Cambridge University Press, 1979

Shu Gang, 'Inquiry into the Course of the African National Democratic Revolution', paper produced by the Institute of West Asian and African Studies, Peking, 1981

Slawecki, Leon M.S., *French Policy towards the Chinese in Madagascar*, Shoe String Press, Inc., Hamden, Connecticut, 1971

Smith, William Edgett, *Nyerere of Tanzania*, Gollancz, London, 1973

Stevens, Christopher, *The Soviet Union and Black Africa*, Macmillan, London, 1976

Taylor, Charles, *Reporter in Red China*, Gollancz, London, 1967

Thompson, W.Scott, *Ghana's Foreign Policy 1957–1966*, Princeton University Press, 1969

Van Ness, Peter, *Revolution and China's Foreign Policy*, University of California Press, Berkeley, 1970

Wei Liang-tsai, *Peking versus Taipei in Africa, 1960–1978*, The Asia and World Institute, Taipei, 1982

Weinstein, Warren and Henriksen, Thomas (eds), *Soviet and Chinese Aid to African Nations*, Praeger Publishers, New York, 1980

Wilson, Dick, 'A Paler Shade of Yellow', in *New Society*, London, 11 October 1984

Yahuda, Michael, *China's Role in World Affairs*, Croom Helm, London, 1978

Young Fung-tai, *The Guerrilla Warfare Supported by the Chinese Communists in Southern Africa*, World Anti-Communist League, Taipei, 1973

Yu, George T., *China and Tanzania: A Study in Cooperative Interaction*, Center for Chinese Studies, University of California, Berkeley, 1970

Yu, George T., *China's African Policy – a Study of Tanzania*, Praeger Publishers, New York, 1975

Yu, George T., 'The Maoist Model – Appeal, Relevance and Applicability', in *The Logic of 'Maoism' – Critiques and Explication*, Praeger Publishers, New York, 1974

Notes

Introduction

p. xiv *into Japanese hands.* Slawecki, p. 2.

Chapter 1: Chinese Columbus

p. 1 *on its coming.* Episode cited in the *Ming Dynasty Statutes* of 1511, in a history published by Zheng Xiao in 1552, and other works. See Chen Gongyuan, and Duyvendak, 'True Dates' and *China's Discovery*, p. 33.

p. 1 *Chinese and African peoples.* 'The Giraffe and Sino–African Friendship', article by Lin Mingyang in *People's Daily*, Peking, 16/1/83.

p. 3 *dust with his hand'.* Verse of Mu'allaqat of Tarafah, sixth-century poet of Hirah in Mesopotamia, quoted in Richard Pankhurst, *An Introduction to the Economic History of Ethiopia*, Sidgwick & Jackson, London, 1981, p. 37.

p. 3 *and Adulis.'* Kosmas Indikopleustes, trans. McCrindle, xi, 337.

p. 4 *to China in 762.* The foregoing account follows the reconstruction given in Shen Fuwei, 'Du Huan's Journey'. I am very dubious about Shen's idea that 'Molin' is a Chinese attempt to express 'the Land of Mahram', Mahram being the sea-god of the Axumites. But Shen's location of Molin in the region of Eritrea seems to me to accord better with Du's ethnic and topographical data than the previous claims made for e.g. Malindi and Meroë. For possible Persian influences on the Upper Nile see Fage, p. 64. A late-ninth-century Arab author, Yaqūbi, says of the Baqlīn kingdom in the Eritrean Sahel that the religion of its people 'resembled that of the Magians and Dualists'. See Trimingham, *Islam in Ethiopia*, Frank Cass & Co. Ltd, London, 1965, pp. 49 ff.

p. 5 *shine like pearls.'* Quoted in Wheatley, 'Analecta'.

p. 6 *on the Tanzanian coast.* Quoted Davidson, *Old Africa Rediscovered*, p. 132 (1959 edition).

p. 8 *are foreign ships.'* Li Chao (ninth century), quoted Elvin, p. 137.

p. 9 *and proceed from there'.* Zhou Qufei, ch. 2, under *Gulin* (Kulam-Malay). See Su Jiqing edn of Wang Dayuan.

p. 11 *voracious dilettante'.* Wheatley, 'Analecta'.

p. 13 *below their waists.'* Duan Chengshi.

p. 13 *but not the Buddha'.* Zhao Rugua.

223

p. 14 *for supremacy'*. Ibid.

p. 14 *bride-to-be.* Chen Yuanjing, quoted Wheatley, 'Analecta'.

p. 16 *pure and upright'*. Duan Chengshi.

p. 16 *weep bitterly.'* Zhao Rugua.

p. 17 *called Kunlun slaves.'* Song History, ch. 490.

p. 18 *to the Arab countries.* Zhou Qufei, Zhao Rugua.

p. 18 *rich people in Canton'*. Zhu Yu, ch. 2.

p. 19 *fall ill and die.'* Ibid.

p. 19 *do not run away'*. Ibid.

p. 19 *utter it themselves.'* Ibid.

p. 19 *for their kinsfolk.'* Zhao Rugua.

p. 19 *some birds.* Zhu Yu, loc. cit.

p. 19 *of Zhongli.* Zhao Rugua.

p. 21 *the western Indian Ocean.* This account of Zheng He's voyages is based on the chronology established in 1938 by the Dutch scholar J.J.L. Duyvendak, and subsequently followed by all Western scholars including Needham (1971) and Wheatley (1975), and most Chinese ones. Shen Fuwei, 'Zheng He's Treasure Fleet', has recently put forward a radical new theory maintaining that Zheng He's fleet reached East Africa earlier than has previously been supposed and visited more places than have previously been identified. I have some reservations about this particular theory of Shen's. (1) It does not seem to me to tally with the inscriptions put up by Zheng He and his captains in southeast China in 1431–2, listing the places visited on their first six voyages. (2) It is weakened by Shen's tendency to make over-enthusiastic phonetic equations between places mentioned in the Ming dynasty records and East African coastal towns, e.g. between *Bila* and the port of Mozambique, and between *Muluwang* and the Somali town of *Merca*. Further research may demonstrate that Shen is at least partly right. But in view of these doubts I have thought it better to stick to the traditional reconstruction.

p. 22 *eunuch chamberlains'*. Ma Huan quoted by Chen Gongyuan; Swanson, p. 38.

p. 24 *a myriad myriad years.'* Inscription appended by Shen Du to his painting of the giraffe from Bengal. See Duyvendak, 'True Dates'; China's Discovery, pp. 33–4.

p. 24 *hinders good government.'* Quoted Duyvendak, China's Discovery, p. 33.

p. 24 *Our shortcomings.'* Shuyu Zhouzilu, chs 9, 11. Quoted Duyvendak, China's Discovery, p. 33.

p. 25 *('Black Kids').* Hei Er in Chinese. This was probably an attempt at translating the Arabic *Zang*, 'the Blacks'. See Wheatley, 'Analecta'. Other interpretations have ranged from pygmies (Chang Kuei-sheng) to Eil on the coast of Somalia (Shen Fuwei, 'Zheng He's Treasure Fleet').

p. 27 *their likeness.'* Lines by Jin Youzi, quoted Duyvendak, 'True Dates'.

p. 29 *kowtowing kings.* For the foregoing details see Luo Moudeng.

p. 30 *like harmless seagulls'*. Zhang Xie, *Dong Xi Yang Kao*, 1618, quoted Davidson, *Black Mother*, p. 180.

p. 32 *lost in this place'*. *Voyages de Pyrard de Laval en 1602*, quoted A. and G. Grandidier, p. 299.

p. 33 *name of Shanga came from'*. Information collected by Elizabeth Wangari Rugoiyo and incorporated in the *Report on Shanga Excavation*, 1980, by Mark Horton of Cambridge University.

p. 34 *nestle their fledglings.'* Quoted e.g. by Mathew and by Davidson, *Black Mother*, p. 173. A version of the first couplet is given by Freeman-Grenville, 'Chinese Porcelain in Tanganyika', in *Tanganyika Notes and Records*, December 1955.

p. 35 *as magic?* I am indebted for this suggestion to Mr J. de V. Allen of Mombasa and Dr Mark Horton.

p. 35 *up and down that coast'*. See accounts of de Barros in Theal, vol. I, p. 4, and Faria e Sousa in Theal, vol. VI, p. 170.

p. 35 *south to east. . . .'* Camões, *Lusiads*, V, 77, quoted Needham, IV, 3, p. 507.

p. 36 *'very fine linen cloth'*. Letter of July 1499 written from Calicut by the Florentine merchant Girolamo Sernigi, quoted Needham, IV, 3, p. 508. For Needham the reference to a 'sword on the end of a spear' – the *ji*, or Chinese gisarme – is conclusive proof that the Chinese are meant.

p. 36 *Jesuits of Mozambique*. Letter of Dom Luiz de Meneses, Viceroy of Mozambique, to Antonio Cardim Troes, Lieutenant General, 21 January 1719. Theal, vol. V, pp. 45–52.

Chapter 2: The Advent of the Celestial

p. 37 *What brings you here?'* Quoted Boxer, *Portuguese Seaborne Empire*, p. 37; Davidson, *Discovering Africa's Past*, p. 96.

p. 38 *earliest Chinese cooks*. Chinese cooks were reported in Lisbon by a Florentine traveller about 1580. Quoted Boxer, *Fidalgos*, p. 225.

p. 39 *slaves and servaunts'*. Quoted Teixeira, 'Os Cafres em Macau'.

p. 39 *there last year.'* Letter of Jan Pieterszoon Coen, Dutch Governor of Batavia, 1623; quoted Boxer, *Fidalgos*, p. 85, Teixeira, 'Os Cafres em Macau'.

p. 40 *Black Daredevils. Wu gui fang fan*. Information supplied by the Management Committee for Cultural Relics, Quanzhou, Fujian province, 5/8/82.

p. 41 *'industrious Chinese'*. Van Riebeeck's journal, 21 April 1652. See Wilson and Thompson, p. 66; Armstrong; Ly Tio Fane, pp. 201, 204.

p. 41 *the thirteenth century*. Domestic slaves began to be freed in increasing numbers from the eighth century onwards. See Elvin, pp. 74, 172.

p. 43 *win them over.'* Quoted Ly Tio Fane, p. 309. This author's translation.

p. 44 *dangerous they are.'* Letters of B. H. de Froberville, 4 September and 17 October 1829.

p. 45 *ironclad steamers?'* Emin Pasha, p. 417.

p. 46 *could develop Africa.* See e.g. views expressed by Sir Richard Burton on a visit to the Gold Coast in 1882 (Byron Farwell, *Burton*, Longmans, London, 1963, p. 356). W.H.Milton, Senior Administrator of the British South Africa Company, thought Chinese coal and gold miners the 'only solution' for Rhodesia. Letter, 14 April 1900, Zimbabwe National Archives.

p. 46 *coffee and tobacco plantations.* Letter in Tanzanian National Archives, Dar es Salaam. For the upshot see Mihalyi.

p. 47 *a white man's country.' Daily Telegraph*, 12/2/04.

p. 47 *to the Transvaal. The Times*, London, 17/2/04.

p. 47 *the dark past'.* For the remarks of Rider Haggard and Churchill, see *Daily Chronicle*, 13/6/03, reporting a meeting of the Imperial South African Association.

p. 47 *advent of the Celestial'.* See *Bulawayo Chronicle*, 29/8/03.

p. 47 *first time in his life'.* Phrase used by Mr Fairbridge of the Salisbury Chamber of Mines. See *Rhodesia Herald*, 16/3/01.

p. 48 *Clayton process'. Financial Times*, 20/5/04.

p. 49 *'quite good' living quarters. Ibid.*, 6/9/04.

p. 49 *'ample' hospital accommodation.* Letter from Lord Milner, Governor-General of South Africa, to Alfred Lyttelton, Colonial Secretary, 17/12/04. Transvaal Command Paper 2401, 1905.

p. 49 *they may fancy'. Financial Times*, 6/9/04, report on the Simmer and Jack mine.

p. 49 *the most important language.'* Quoted Brian Gardner, *The African Dream*, Cassell, London, 1970, p. 235.

p. 50 *landslide which followed.* Letter of Gilbert Parker, MP to Drummond Chaplin, 20/1/06. Zimbabwe National Archives.

p. 50 *Asquith and Lloyd George.* Richardson, *Chinese Mine Labour*, p. 5. See also Buell, *The Native Problem in Africa*, Macmillan, New York, 1928, vol. I, pp. 22–3.

p. 50 *within the memory of man'.* Selborne to Earl of Elgin, Colonial Secretary, enclosing letter forwarded by Botha, 21/5/06. Transvaal Command Paper 2819, 1906.

p. 52 *would join the natives.'* Deputation of the 'Het Volk' Party, addressing Selborne, 5/5/06. The spokesman was F.T.Meethling of Krugersdorp. Transvaal Command Paper 2819, 1906.

p. 52 *re-engaging for further service.* Letter, Milner to Lyttelton, 23/7/04, Transvaal Command Paper 2104, 1904; comment of the chairman of the Johannesburg Chamber of Mines, quoted *Financial Times*, 16/9/04.

p. 52 *throughout the country'.* Letter, Hely-Hutchinson to Drummond Chaplin, 27/12/03. Zimbabwe National Archives.

p. 53 *dam below the compound'.* Incident reported on the Van Ryn mining estate, 14/5/05. Transvaal Command Paper 2819, 1906.

p. 53 *even on the smallest scale.' The Globe*, 14/5/03.

p. 53 *villages on the Rand.' Daily Chronicle*, 11/10/04.

p. 53 *the Continent'. The Globe*, loc. cit.

p. 53 *of this description?' The Friend*, 12–14/1/04.

p. 54 *'a death for every sleeper'*. The original phrase was 'Un Noir par traverse'. It was first used with reference to the Matadi-Léopoldville railway built by the Belgians. See Sautter.

p. 54 *'insolent inertia'*. Sautter, *op. cit.*

p. 54 *to the training personnel'*. *Ibid.*

p. 55 *stable African civilization'*. See George Louis Beer (Chief of Colonial Division of US Delegation), *African Questions at the Paris Peace Conference*, Macmillan, New York, 1923, p. 186.

p. 55 *Chinaman's shop'*. Charles John Boyle, p. 22.

p. 56 *on the Chinese.'* Debates of Council, Mauritius, 20 July 1886. For full text see Ly Tio Fane, pp. 312–14.

p. 57 *Sino–African treaty.* See article by Li Changxing in *People's Daily*, Peking, 30/12/82.

p. 58 *other coloured people'*. Petition of Leung Quinn to the Chinese ambassador, London, 14/10/07. Quoted Ly Tio Fane, p. 345.

p. 58 *the lottery of life. . . .'* Quoted in Barry Kosmin, 'Ethnic and Commercial Relations in Southern Rhodesia, 1898–1943', thesis, 1974, in Zimbabwe National Archives.

p. 59 *We can't do this.'* Letter of F.J.R.Peel, 22/12/24. Quoted in Kosmin, *op. cit.*

p. 59 *their patience. . . .'* Chevalier, p. 102.

p. 59 *'not gamblers'*. *The Star*, Johannesburg, 4/11/37. For foregoing details see Ray E.Phillips, *The Bantu in the City*, Lovedale Press, 1938, pp. 217–20.

p. 60 *with the Indians.'* Gordon, letter to Lord Kimberley, 27/7/1881.

p. 61 *speak almost none.* Interview, Fay Chung, Chinese resident, Harare, Zimbabwe, 3/5/82.

p. 61 *take directly from Europeans.* Information supplied by Father Trevor Huddleston, Mauritius, 3/10/81.

p. 62 *'South Africa for the Chinese'*. Speech of John X.Merriman to a meeting of the Afrikaner Bond. *South Africa News*, 10/1/06. See Transvaal Command Paper 2819, 1906.

p. 63 *more confidence in himself'*. Letter, Governor of Tamatave province to Governor-General, 7/11/30. Quoted Slawecki, p. 145.

p. 63 *to and from Europe.* E.g. Wang Tao, Kang Youwei, Liang Qichao and Sun Yat-sen. See Ai Zhouchang, 'Sino–African Relations'.

p. 64 *jewels and silk.'* DuBois, *Black Reconstruction in America*, p. 728.

p. 64 *wage slavery and contempt.'* Address to All-Africa People's Conference, Accra, December 1958. Quoted in Ali Mazrui, *On Heroes and Uhuru-Worship*, Longmans, London, 1967, p. 220.

p. 65 *which included the Chinese.* See Padmore, *Pan-Africanism or Communism?*, p. 95.

p. 65 *Do they make guns?'* Quoted Richard Greenfield, *Ethiopia: A New Political History*, Pall Mall Press, London, 1965, p. 125.

p. 65 *than Ethiopia was.* *Ibid.*, p. 155.

p. 66 *peace at any price.'* *World Knowledge*, II, 4, 1 May 1935.

p. 66 *'immensely prolonged'*. *Ibid.*

p. 66 *peoples of Africa.'* Ibid.

p. 66 *addiction to putschism'*. Padmore, *Pan-Africanism or Communism?*, p. 297.

p. 66 *not one ton of wheat.'* Padmore, *Africa and World Peace*, p. 153 n. 2.

p. 66 *their black brothers'*. Ibid., p. 150.

p. 68 *Spanish rule in Morocco.* Reported remark of Mao in 1971, cited in the *Collo-que internationale d'études historiques, Abd-el Krim et la république du Rif*, Mas-péro, Paris, 1976, p. 401. See Basil Davidson, *The People's Cause*, Longmans, London, 1981, p. 157.

p. 68 *the Eighth Route Army.'* Mao Zedong, 'Refutation of the Theory of National Subjugation', in *On Protracted War*, May 1938. Vol. II, *Selected Works*, Foreign Languages Press, Peking, 1967, p. 127.

p. 68 *of world affairs.'* Ibid.

Chapter 3: The Chinese as Missionary

p. 69 *no one will insult us again.'* Speech in Peking, 1/10/49. Quoted e.g. by Han Suyin, *The Morning Deluge*, Jonathan Cape, London, 1972, p. 542.

p. 71 *cultural renaissance of 1919].'* *Work Bulletin* no. 17, 25/4/61.

p. 71 *in this generation.'* Ibid.

p. 71 *has had more experience than we'*. Ye Jianying in March 1961. Quoted Larkin, p. 150.

p. 73 *dignified human being.* Benson, p. 200; Sampson, p. 162.

p. 73 *with the Peking Hotel.* Sampson, p. 145. See also Benson, p. 218.

p. 73 *try to convey them.'* Statement of M. F. Aroma, Vice Secretary General of the Ugandan National Congress Youth Movement, visiting China with a four-member youth delegation. New China News Agency (NCNA), 8/9/60, *Survey of the China Mainland Press* (SCMP) 2338.

p. 74 *blood of your blood.'* *New World Review*, New York, April 1959. See also NCNA, 23/2/59, SCMP 1962.

p. 74 *diplomatic relations with Peking.* I.e. the Sudan (4/2/59), Guinea (4/10/59), Ghana (5/7/60), Mali (25/10/60), Somalia (14/12/60), Tanganyika (9/12/61), Uganda (18/10/62) and Kenya (14/12/63). Most of the Arab states of the Mediterranean littoral took the initiative slightly earlier. See *African Survey*, appendix 2, pp. 360–2; Fomicheva and Krasil'nikov, p. 260.

p. 75 *in a strange land'*. NCNA, 5/6/65, SCMP 3475; see Yu, *China's African Policy*, pp. 16–17.

p. 75 *had been broken off'*. Speech in Peking, 17 February 1965. See Yu, *op. cit.*, p. 27.

p. 75 *we have arrived . . . .'* Speech in Mogadishu, NCNA, 3/2/64, SCMP 3156.

p. 75 *General Gordon.* Adie, 'Chou En-lai on Safari'; see also *Peking Review* no. 5, 31/1/64. Zhou also commented on the shared tribulations of China and Ethiopia in the 1930s. *Peking Review* no. 6, 7/2/64.

p. 75 *throughout the African continent.'* Speech in Mogadishu, NCNA, 3/2/64, SCMP 3156.

p. 76 *to which the rebels belonged.* Notably those in Conakry, Guinea, and Dar es Salaam, Tanzania.

p. 77 *were being prepared.* Interview, Mario de Andrade, Angolan man of letters and former secretary-general of the MPLA, Paris, 24/11/83.

p. 77 *Chinese uniform.* Chinese uniforms apparently clothed some of the Algerian insurgents (Cooley, p. 156). They were said to have been worn by some of the MPLA guerrillas (Marcum, vol. II, p. 212), but the claims derive from Rhodesian and South African sources and may be suspect.

p. 79 *field commanders.* E.g. in addition to Machel, Wilton Mkwayi (ANC), José Chiwale (UNITA), Josiah Tongogara (ZANU) and 'Nino' Vieira (PAIGC).

p. 79 *political leaders as well.* E.g. in addition to Cabral, Viriato da Cruz (MPLA) and Pierre Mulele from Congo-Léopoldville (see pp. 98–9).

p. 79 *Sandhurst or Aldershot'.* Interview, Sipho Magwaza, former PAC guerrilla, 30/12/83.

p. 79 *trip to India.* Interview, Israel Maduma, former ZAPU guerrilla, 26/5/83.

p. 80 *from his native land.'* Van der Post, *A Story Like the Wind*, Hogarth Press, London, 1972, p. 172.

p. 80 *can learn how to make them.'* See 'Crude Weapons that Helped Defeat a Mighty Army', article in *Revolution Africa Latin America Asia*, vol. I, no. 7, November 1963. The magazine was edited by Jacques Vergès, a radical lawyer of mixed French and Vietnamese parentage from the island of Réunion. In 1987 Vergès attracted world-wide attention through his role as the defence lawyer in the trial of the Nazi war criminal Klaus Barbie.

p. 81 *because I was a Zulu'.* Interview with Sipho Magwaza.

p. 82 *the situation at home.'* George Rutanhire of ZANU, quoted Martin and Johnson, p. 82.

p. 82 *in the Cameroons.'* Schatten, p. 207.

p. 82 *in his weakest spot.* Interview, Rakhetla Psehlana, PAC, London, 14/12/83.

p. 83 *in our land.'* Cabral, p. 80.

p. 83 *African initiative.* Interview, Sipho Magwaza.

p. 83 *which the instructors had adapted.* Interview, Mario de Andrade.

p. 83 *other countries in other parts of the world.* E.g. the Soviet Union, East Germany, Czechoslovakia, Romania, Yugoslavia, Cuba, North Korea and Algeria.

p. 83 *'Fowler's Modern English Usage'.* Interview, Rakhetla Psehlana.

p. 83 *emasculated paper tiger'.* *Zimbabwe News*, April 1974.

p. 83 *crushed to pulp'.* Letter from J. Kivombo, *Zimbabwe News*, 3/3/68.

p. 83 *silks and satins'.* *Zimbabwe News*, September–October 1978.

p. 84 *as light as a feather.'* *Mozambique Revolution*, March–April 1969.

p. 84 *Chinese Nationalist side.* Cited by Robert Mugabe, 1976, to warn of the likely prospect of traitors in the ZANU ranks. See Martin and Johnson, p. 213.

p. 84 *a sensational team.'* Recollection of Josiah Tongogara, *Zimbabwe News*, September–October 1978.

p. 84 *or a piece of thread'.* See *Mozambique Revolution*, September 1965; *Zimbabwe News*, September–October 1978.

p. 85 *like a fish'*. See *Mozambique Revolution*, September 1965; Cabral, p. 77; report of the PAC Executive Committee Meeting, Moshi, Tanzania, 19/9/67–22/9/67 (in Marx Memorial Library, London); *Zimbabwe News*, January–February 1978.

p. 85 *went their way*. Martin and Johnson, pp. 331–2. Ethnic considerations were also of course important, viz. the identification of ZANU with the majority Shona tribe.

p. 85 *solely by opportunism*. The Zimbabwe Ministry of Foreign Affairs maintained in May 1982 that Marxism–Leninism–Mao Zedong Thought was still, 'in a more subdued way', their government's ideology. Interview, 14/5/82.

p. 85 *that the revolution will be successful.*' Interview, Farayi Munyuki, editor, *The Herald*, Harare, 9/5/82.

p. 86 *strategic rear area'*. See *China Quarterly* no. 62, June 1975, p. 377.

p. 86 *under Portuguese rule*. Quoted in *People's Daily*, Peking, 13/1/83.

p. 86 *of their war*. Interview, Zimbabwean Foreign Ministry, 12/5/82. See also tributes paid by Mugabe in *Zimbabwe News*, November–December 1978, and *People's Daily*, 11/1/83. At a banquet for Premier Zhao Ziyang on 9/1/83 Mugabe said of China that 'no country had helped ZANU more'.

p. 86 *water is to fish'*. See *Mozambique Revolution*, July–September 1971.

p. 86 *'staying power'*. *Africa Contemporary Record* (ACR), 1968–9, p. 294.

p. 86 *pointed to Africa'*. The British-born Commissioner of Police for Lesotho. See ACR 1971–2, p. B315.

p. 87 *Mau Mau.*' *Daily Telegraph*, 29/1/73.

p. 87 *to sell his own goods.*' *Work Bulletin* no. 17, 25/4/61.

p. 89 *'Point Two' to follow*. Interview, Abdul Rahman Mohamed Babu, former Tanzanian cabinet minister, London, 9/8/83. See Ogunsanwo, p. 141.

p. 89 *the Peking Hotel*. Information supplied by James Oporia-Ekwaro, former Ugandan ambassador to China, London, 3/3/83.

p. 89 *'Tanzania is his home.*' Hall and Peyman, p. 78.

p. 89 *lived in Malaya*. Detail reported by Cooley, p. 230.

p. 90 *like a map of Africa*. Interview, Polycarpe Mwamba-Kalembwe, Zairean who studied medicine in China 1976–80, Paris, 21/8/85.

p. 91 *good Christians*. Interview, Babu, 3/8/83. See Hall and Peyman, p. 149.

p. 92 *shaming political offenders*. Zhang Yi, pp. 162, 165.

p. 92 *'trusting, reborn men'*. Sessions of this kind were recorded in the film *Mozambique – A Treatment for Traitors* shown on UK television, Channel 4, 23/7/84.

p. 93 *village as a whole*. Interview, Rashidi Kawawa, then Minister without Portfolio, Tanzania, former Prime Minister of Tanganyika and Second Vice President, Tanzania, Dar es Salaam, 1/12/81.

p. 93 *'Leadership Code'*. Zambia in 1973 and Zimbabwe in 1984.

p. 93 *more, more, more!*' Thompson, p. 177.

p. 94 *short shrift*. E.g. Zuberi Mtemvu, who attempted to outflank Nyerere on the left in the early sixties, went to China effectively at his own invitation and got a notably cool reception. Interview, Babu, 3/8/83.

p. 94 *was too ambitious*. Interview, Yaw Turkson, former Ghanaian diplomat, Oxford, 21/6/83.

p. 94 *handling by themselves.* Interview, Babu, Foreign Minister of Zanzibar in 1964, London, 9/8/83.

p. 94 *of universal evolution'.* NCNA, 23/1/64.

p. 94 *for African countries.* See Zhou remarks at press conference in Algiers, 26/12/63, quoted *Peking Review* no. 1, 3/1/64; also Adie, 'Chou En-lai on Safari'.

p. 95 *for many decades to come.* For an idea of the timescale, see *Work Bulletin* no. 17, 25/4/61. At the stage the Chinese then considered Africa to have reached, 'we had not yet begun the period of the Northern Expedition [of Nationalists and Communists against the warlords in 1926–7] and that of the War of Resistance against Japan, and we were still far from the events of 1949 in China'.

p. 95 *with uniforms and arms.* E.g. in Guinea and Mali.

p. 95 *irrespective of their origins.'* East African Standard, Nairobi, 7/6/65.

p. 96 *into the African continent.'* Memorandum of T. Neil, 9/2/62. Kenya National Archives.

p. 96 *as a Chinese province.* Slawecki, p. 180.

p. 96 *within a few years'.* Quoted Wei, p. 147.

p. 96 *we cannot understand.'* Speech by James Gichuru, Kenyan Minister of Finance, *East African Standard,* 12/6/65.

p. 97 *his British friends.* Interview, Mancham, 4/7/83. See Mancham, *Paradise Raped,* Methuen, London, 1983, pp. 54–5.

p. 97 *ought to be overthrown.* Interview, Chinese Foreign Ministry, 21/7/82.

p. 97 *in Kisumu instead.'* Memorandum of an official in the Kenyan Ministry of Commerce and Industry regarding a Chinese trade delegation, 22/12/64. Kenya National Archives.

p. 98 *in Europe weren't.* Interview, Institute of International Studies, Peking, 29/6/82.

p. 98 *did not know much about Africa.* E.g. he seemed hazy about the size of the Kenyan population, the location of Zanzibar and the name of the Algerian president. Ross Terrill, *Mao: A Biography,* Harper & Row, New York, 1980, p. 61n.

p. 98 *we can have all of Africa.'* Tung Chi-ping, p. 223.

p. 99 *for the Congolese campaign.* For China's connection with the Tutsi in Burundi and its sister state, Rwanda, see Weinstein, 'Chinese Aid and Policy in Central Africa', in Weinstein and Henriksen; also Hevi, *Dragon's Embrace,* pp. 105–10, and Wei, pp. 168–79. The Tutsi were at odds with Belgium, the former colonial power, and the Chinese consequently backed them as the main anti-European force in the region rather than the majority Hutu tribe.

p. 101 *One per head.* Wei, pp. 96–7.

p. 101 *'freaks and monsters'.* East African Standard, as early as 24/4/65.

p. 102 *'are our Green Guards.'* Interviews, Babu, 9/8/83, and other Tanzanians.

p. 102 *'Stalin's Failure in China'.* Title of book by Conrad Brandt, Harvard University Press, 1958.

p. 103 *'I told you not to come.'* Interview, Yaw Turkson, former Ghanaian diplomat, Oxford, 21/6/83.

p. 103 *the local New China News Agency journalists.* The governments were those of Kenya, Ethiopia, Ghana, Senegal, Dahomey, Burundi and the Central African Republic. Egypt, in the Arab north, took similar action.

p. 103 *of Chinese publications.* In Nigeria, Kenya, Zambia, Malawi, Somalia and Senegal. Even Tanzania was obliged to prohibit the wearing of Mao's badges (Hutchison, p. 145).

p. 104 *that Africa may have.'* Quoted Hall and Peyman, p. 74.

p. 104 *white regimes in the south. Africa Confidential* (AC), 4/9/70 and 25/8/72. See also Hall and Peyman, p. 198.

Chapter 4: Idealism versus Statecraft

p. 105 *to African ideals.'* Quoted Attwood, p. 323.

p. 105 *represented smaller nations.'* Salim Salim, Tanzanian representative at the United Nations, later Prime Minister of Tanzania, 15/11/71. Quoted Yu, 'The Maoist Model'.

p. 106 *Da Peisheng.* These were not members of ethnic minorities like the Uighurs and Kazakhs, but Chinese Moslems (Hui).

p. 106 *fundamentally similar to theirs.* The efforts made by the Chinese to present themselves as benevolent patrons of Islam are reminiscent of those made by Napoleon on his arrival in Egypt in 1798.

p. 106 *one and the same.* Interview, Israel Maduma, London, 26/5/83.

p. 107 *'second South Vietnam'.* Phrase used in *People's Daily,* 17/1/66. See also *Peking Review* no. 22, 29/5/64, no. 27, 3/7/64, no. 34, 21/8/64.

p. 107 *loosen their grip on others.* See *Peking Review* no. 36, 3/9/65.

p. 108 *tiger by the back'.* See *Peking Review* no. 2, 10/1/64; no. 20, 15/5/64.

p. 108 *butchers' knives'.* NCNA 18/2/61, SCMP 2443; *People's Daily,* Peking, 28/11/64.

p. 108 *utterly fearless.'* For a text of the play, complete with photographs, see *Evergreen,* special number, August 1965.

p. 108 *took American funds.* E.g. the PAC and FRELIMO. Interview, Rakhetla Psehlana. See Gibson, p. 14. The founder of FRELIMO, Eduardo Mondlane, had an American wife.

p. 108 *apparent desire to aid them.* E.g. Guinea (Attwood, pp. 44–5, 126) and Tanzania (Smith, pp. 139, 145–6).

p. 109 *'odious act'.* Cooley, p. 205. The conference was organized in Warsaw by the World Peace Council.

p. 109 *harmonized a little'.* AC, 25/9/64.

p. 109 *rare signs of exasperation.* Interview, Yaw Turkson, Oxford, 21/6/83. For Nkrumah's Vietnam diplomacy see Thompson, pp. 409–13.

p. 110 *Chinese Moslem.* Cooley, p. 197.

p. 110 *with American support.* For the foregoing details see *Africa Now* no. 36, April 1984.

p. 110 *in January 1966.* ACR 1977–8, p. A77.

p. 110 *seize the archives.* Claim made by John Stockwell, former CIA employee, in his *In Search of Enemies – How the CIA Lost Angola*, Futura Publications, London, 1979, p. 209 n.

p. 111 *not isolated in Africa.* Quoted in *African Revolution*, Algiers, vol. I, no. 2, June 1963.

p. 112 *what we have suffered.'* Yang Hsi-k'un (H.K. Yang), Taiwan Ministry of Foreign Affairs, 13/8/60, quoted Wei, p. 290.

p. 112 *'leader of leaders'.* For the foregoing details see Wei, pp. 122 n. 52, 348.

p. 112 *to our African friends'.* *People's Daily*, 8/2/60; NCNA, 9/2/60, SCMP 2195.

p. 113 *Chiang Kai-shek's staff.* Anecdote reported by a former Tanzanian ambassador to Peking. The country in question was Zaïre, and the incident took place in early 1973.

p. 114 *so many of them.'* Quoted Smith, p. 167.

p. 114 *to each other.* Comments of a former assistant to President Nyerere.

p. 115 *the circular chamber'.* *Christian Science Monitor*, 27/10/71.

p. 116 *investment and technical skills.* Marcum, vol. I, pp. 278–9.

p. 116 *to nuclear weapons grade.* For the foregoing details see ACR 1980–81, pp. B811, B849, 1981–2, p. B742; *New York Times*, 28/6/81; *International Herald Tribune*, 30/6/81; *Far Eastern Economic Review*, 3/3/83.

p. 116 *the Chinese motherland.* Point made by the Institute of International Studies, Peking, interview, 20/7/82.

p. 116 *not be so bright.* Ibid.

p. 117 *made the most of the occasion.* Soviet sources claim that Zhou Enlai and his colleagues 'didn't even try to rebuff' the criticism of Moscow which some participants voiced. See Fomicheva and Krasil'nikov, p. 81.

p. 118 *their leader before.* Foregoing details supplied by Israel Maduma, interview, 19/6/83.

p. 119 *conference in Tanzania.* Interview, Mario de Andrade.

p. 119 *which really mattered.* Interview, Babu, London, 9/8/83, and other Tanzanians.

p. 119 *to eat in peace.'* Quoted Hevi, *Dragon's Embrace*, p. 77; Attwood, pp. 296–7.

p. 120 *stand by a fallen friend.* For African reactions see Smith, p. 161, Ogunsanwo, pp. 130, 148.

p. 120 *nor you really black.'* Interview, Sipho Magwaza.

p. 120 *the Russians were white.* See Neuhauser, p. 41, Ogunsanwo, pp. 121, 166.

p. 121 *who belong to the whole world.'* Cabral, p. 80.

p. 121 *their new countries should take.* See reactions of Lilian Ngoyi of the ANC, quoted Sampson, pp. 145–6, and Benson, p. 219; and of a Somali quoted in Pieter Lessing, *Africa's Red Harvest*, Michael Joseph, London, 1962, p. 42.

p. 121 *regardless of their ideology'.* Padmore, *Pan-Africanism or Communism?*, p. 342.

p. 121 *'too much like the British'.* Quoted Attwood, p. 242. See also Walter Sisulu of the ANC quoted Sampson, p. 163.

p. 121 *may change their minds'.* See Ogunsanwo, p. 145.

p. 122 *to their country.* Interview, Institute of International Studies, Peking, 20/7/82.

p. 122 *at the Chinese coast. Ibid.*

p. 122 *encircle their country.* See bulletin circulated to officers of the Kunming military region, 2/4/73, quoted in Shichor, p. 163.

p. 122 *wherever they stretch.' Peking Review* no. 39, 29/9/78.

p. 123 *for the Biafran cause.* NCNA 22/9/68, quoted Cronjé, pp. 219, 276. See also Ogunsanwo, p. 235.

p. 123 *careful of your friends.'* Interview, former Somali diplomat in China, Mogadishu, 12/1/82.

p. 123 *a matter for Africans.* Interview, Chinese Foreign Ministry, 21/7/82.

p. 123 *you backed the wrong man.'* Quoted Hall and Peyman, p. 193.

p. 125 *the other Portuguese colonies.* Through General Spinola's statement of 27/7/74, quoted ACR 1974–5, p. C38; see also Marcum, vol. II, p. 244. The advance guard of the Chinese team had already arrived in June, but the main body of the instructors only appeared in early August – *after* Spinola's statement.

p. 126 *stores of Chinese rice.* See Marcum, vol. II, p. 274; Claude Gabriel, *Angola: le tournant africain?*, Editions La Brèche, Paris, 1978, p. 194.

p. 126 *their old ties with the* MPLA. In June 1975 Lucio Lára, secretary-general of the MPLA, was received in Peking. Marcum, vol. II, p. 265.

p. 127 *130 Chinese officers.* For the foregoing details see Zhang Yi, pp. 345–8. Zhang Yi was a former Chinese diplomat in Zaïre who defected while on transit through Switzerland in May 1982 and ultimately settled in Taiwan. See also *Africa Economic Digest* (AED), 3/10/80.

p. 129 *not an 'arms merchant'.* Boast of Mao to President Nimeiry of the Sudan, quoted by Nimeiry 1/6/72. See Hutchison, p. 173 n. 9. By the late 1970s, however, Peking had begun to charge for arms supplies in keeping with its overall drive to earn foreign exchange.

p. 129 *you must make up your own minds.'* Interview, Zimbabwe Ministry of Foreign Affairs, 12/5/82.

p. 130 *Zaïre and Mozambique.* Interviews, Chinese Foreign Ministry, 21/7/82, and Institute of International Studies, Peking, 29/6/82. A very similar warning of Soviet designs on the Cape of Good Hope was given in March 1977 by Vice Premier Li Xiannian to a British delegation led by the editor in chief of *The Times.* See *China Quarterly* no. 70, June 1977, p. 461.

p. 130 *French and Belgians had?* See David Bonavia in *The Times,* 4/6/78.

p. 130 *Aims in Africa Coincide.* Fox Butterfield, *New York Times,* 27/6/78.

p. 130 *on to the scene.* Interviews, NCNA, Harare, 12/5/82; Chinese Foreign Ministry, 21/7/82.

p. 130 *dwindled to a trickle.* Interview, Farayi Munyuki, 9/5/82. The Zimbabwe Foreign Ministry prefer to say that the level of help was 'especially high' in 1974–5. Interview, 14/5/82. See AC, 25/8/78, 30/10/78, 20/6/79.

p. 130 *for a negotiated peace.* Interview, Farayi Munyuki. For lack of Chinese enthusiasm for the prolongation of the war see ACR 1979–80, p. A117, AC 17/3/78 and 22/8/79.

p. 131 *make Soviet encroachment more difficult.* Foregoing observations made by the NCNA, Harare, 12/5/82.

p. 131 *to a multiracial government*. Interview, Chinese Foreign Ministry, 21/7/82.

p. 131 *South Africa's nuclear programme*. See e.g. ACR 1978–9, p. A20.

p. 132 *to Soviet arms supplies*. For the foregoing details see Martin and Johnson, pp. 160, 164.

p. 135 *impact of Mao's ideas*. Interview, Chinese Embassy, Harare, 26/4/82.

p. 136 *ceased to subscribe*. Zhang Yi, p. 211.

p. 136 *loss of her great husband'*. Interview, Zimbabwe Ministry of Foreign Affairs, 14/5/82.

p. 136 *in front of the television cameras*. *Ibid*.

p. 137 *no longer one of the club'*. Tanzanian official, 17/10/81.

p. 137 *put their own house in order?'* Comment reported by a British diplomat in Peking, 6/7/82. By the late 1980s, however, even governments as doctrinally committed as those of Tanzania, Mozambique and Congo-Brazzaville had felt obliged to 'readjust' their policies quite considerably.

p. 138 *a less controversial choice*. Interview, official of the Zimbabwe Ministry of Foreign Affairs, 12/5/82.

p. 139 *he sighed*. Interview, journalist, *Sunjata* magazine, Bamako, Mali, 13/3/82.

p. 139 *a few bases round the coast*. Interview, Institute of International Studies, Peking, 29/6/82.

p. 139 *latest enemy, Vietnam*. Part of the object of Zhao Ziyang's African tour (see pp. 140–1) was to secure African votes for the seating of the Chinese-backed coalition of Prince Sihanouk and the Khmer Rouge as the legitimate government of Cambodia at the March 1983 Non-Aligned Conference in New Delhi.

p. 140 *seems to be in charge.'* Interview, Zimbabwe Ministry of Foreign Affairs, 14/5/82.

p. 140 *no mistakes in relation to Africa.'* Interview, Chinese Foreign Ministry, 21/7/82.

p. 141 *in the old ZANU camps*. Interview, Farayi Munyuki.

p. 141 *delivered to Zambia*. AED, 21/2/87.

p. 141 *'We are the Third World.'* On 22/2/74. See Yahuda, p. 266 n. 1.

p. 142 *tabernacle of justice'*. Quoted *Peking Review* no. 27, 4/7/75.

p. 142 *of Third World interests*. Interview, Israel Maduma, 26/5/83.

p. 142 *every part of the globe*. Apprehension voiced by 'a Rwandan military officer of some prominence'. See Weinstein, 'Chinese Aid and Policy in Central Africa' in Weinstein and Henriksen.

Chapter 5: The Poor Help the Poor

p. 144 *contribution to humanity.'* Mao, 'In Commemoration of Dr Sun Yat-sen', talk of 12 November 1956, *Selected Works*, vol. 5. See also *Peking Review* no. 34, 21/8/64.

p. 144 *'that they are Chinese'*. Quoted Tibor Mende, *China and her Shadow*, Thames and Hudson, London, 1961, p. 211. See also ACR 1970–1, p. A58.

p. 145 *were helping the poor.* See *Peking Review* no. 18, 1/5/64, Zhou's report on his African tour.

p. 145 *on which Chinese aid would be based.* See *Peking Review* no. 4, 24/1/64, no. 5, 31/1/64.

p. 146 *to go through a needle's eye.* Nan Hanchen, quoted in *Peking Review* no. 10, 5/3/65.

p. 146 *diverted to Africa.* Interview, Chinese Foreign Ministry, 21/7/82.

p. 146 *US $2 billion.* Exchange rate as of mid-1986. Dollars referred to throughout this chapter are US dollars.

p. 146 *$13 billion.* Figures supplied by the Overseas Development Administration, London, August 1987.

p. 146 *to 1 billion ($300 million).* Interview, Chinese Foreign Ministry, 21/7/82.

p. 147 *150,000 Chinese technicians.* Interview, Research Institute of International Economic Cooperation, Peking, 12/7/82.

p. 150 *more than 500 aid projects.* Interview, Chinese Foreign Ministry, 21/7/82.

p. 152 *a British diplomat.* In Lusaka. Hall and Peyman, p. 51.

p. 152 *blazed a trail in the wilderness'.* NCNA, 27/12/61. See Bailey, p. 57, and Hall and Peyman, p. 39.

p. 152 *obscure colonial episode.* To judge from the records of the Frankfurt construction firm Philipp Holzmann and other surviving documents, the Germans explored the possibility of using Chinese labour for their East African railways but never in fact went ahead. Gao was apparently confused by the importation of Chinese (from Singapore) to grow coffee and tobacco in the Usambara mountains in the 1890s. I have consequently not included the German East Africa railways in the map illustrating the use of Chinese labour in colonial Africa on p. 42.

p. 153 *unbroken band of rail.* Interview, Institute of International Studies, Peking, 20/7/82.

p. 153 *to take the railway on.* See Hall and Peyman, pp. 72–3. Babu, then a member of the Tanzanian cabinet, who went to Peking to prepare the way for Nyerere's visit in January 1965, says that he suggested the railway to the Chinese leaders as a topic Nyerere might like to discuss. Interview, London, 3/8/83.

p. 154 *25,000 Chinese technicians.* Interview, Research Institute of International Economic Cooperation, 12/7/82.

p. 154 *end of the Second World War.* It has since been overtaken by the Baikal–Amur railway (BAM), completed by the Soviet Union in Siberia in 1984.

p. 155 *two rival schemes.* Interview, Chinese engineers on Tan–Zam railway, Dar es Salaam, 26/11/81.

p. 155 *to African economies.* Arnold, pp. 109–10. Arnold's is a conservative estimate. The Chinese Foreign Ministry, interview 21/7/82, maintained that the Russians gave four times as much military as economic aid. Joseph P. Smaldone, 'Military Aid', in Weinstein and Henriksen pp. 76–116, records $886m of Soviet economic aid commitments to Africa (including North Africa) in 1968–77, as against arms deliveries worth $4,400m in 1967–76.

p. 156 *than the Russians were willing to provide.* By 1973 China had given economic aid to thirty African countries, the Soviet Union only to twenty. Of the twenty countries aided by both powers, twelve got more aid from China than the Soviet Union. Total Chinese aid amounted to $1.642bn., total Soviet aid to $1.229bn. See Bartke, pp. 20, 23. Figures include aid given to the North African states of Morocco and Algeria.

p. 156 *something impossible to accomplish.' Peking Review* no. 14, 1978.

p. 157 *leader's entourage.* For the foregoing details see Zhang Yi, pp. 158–9, 189–92.

p. 157 *'eat, wear and use'.* Interview, Chinese embassy, Bamako, Mali, 12/3/82.

p. 160 *steadily growing demand.* Interview, Dr François Wanji, Centre de Médicine Chinoise, Douala, Cameroon, 9/4/82. Other African practitioners active in 1981–2 were Dr E. Eben of the Laquintinie Hospital, Douala, and Dr Abdallah of the V. I. Lenin Hospital, Zanzibar. In April 1980 five Malian acupuncturists received their diplomas (*L'Essor*, Bamako, Mali, 8/5/80).

p. 160 *send him back to us immediately.'* Hall and Peyman, p. 73.

p. 160 *er bu ma').* Interview, Guangdong province doctors returned from Equatorial Guinea, Canton, 12/8/82.

p. 162 *impression of superiority.* See 'Sudan–China Trade and Aid Relations', paper by Ali Abdalla Ali, Economic and Social Research Council, National Council for Research, bulletin no. 29, Khartoum, November 1975.

p. 162 *long-term penal sentences.* Interview, Ugandan student, Peking, 14/7/82. See Zhang Yi, pp. 349–50.

p. 162 *or impossible'. Daily News,* Dar es Salaam, 21/2/75.

p. 163 *to meeting at home.* Interview, NCNA, Dakar, 23/3/82.

p. 163 *the ones who don't'.* Interview, Guangdong province engineer returned from building farm tools factory in Kinshasa, Zaïre, Canton, 9/8/82.

p. 164 *the Chinese sighed.* Comments of Chinese medical team, V. I. Lenin Hospital, Zanzibar, 29/10/81.

p. 164 *textbooks to teach them from.* Interview, Guangdong province doctors returned from Equatorial Guinea, Canton, 12/8/82.

p. 164 *to do the work themselves.* Interview, NCNA, Dakar, 23/3/82.

p. 164 *'You want a road.'* Interview, Somali Highway Authority, Mogadishu, 30/1/82.

p. 165 *several Chinese were deported.* AC, 3/4/70.

p. 168 *every corner of the city.' World Knowledge* no. 10, May 1982. The tendency to justify projects to the Chinese public in this way has become even more marked under the post-Mao leadership.

p. 168 *cremate your body.'* Quoted *The Internationalist,* London, March 1972, p. 13.

p. 168 *sustained on the job.* Interview, Research Institute of International Economic Cooperation, Peking, 12/7/82.

p. 168 *ever trod before.* Interview, doctor returned from Equatorial Guinea, Quanzhou, Fujian province, 5/8/82.

p. 169 *from whom all Chinese should learn.* See Mao, 'In Memory of Norman Bethune', *Selected Works,* vol. 2, pp. 337–8.

p. 169 *already done a great deal.* Episode reported by a former assistant to President Nyerere.

p. 170 *lamented the Chinese.* Interview, Chinese engineers on Tan–Zam railway.

p. 170 *the Chinese had built for them?* Interview, Mwamkai Ramadhani, former technical trainee in Canton, Dar es Salaam, 26/11/81.

p. 171 *'express their opinion'.* Interview, Chinese medical team, V.I.Lenin Hospital, Zanzibar, 29/10/81.

p. 171 *'now that the Chinese are leaving.'* Comment reported by official of the European Development Fund, Bamako, 13/3/82.

p. 172 *went on strike.* Interview, Babacar Fall, Associated Press, Dakar, 3/3/82.

p. 173 *as long as that.* Interview, interpreter returned from Magbass sugar project in Sierra Leone, Xiamen (Amoy), Fujian province, 1/8/82.

p. 173 *stay there permanently.'* Article by Felix Kairza, *Daily News*, Dar es Salaam, 22/1/79.

p. 173 *'we can go home'.* Interview, Chinese aid team, Mbarali State Farm, Tanzania, 13/11/81.

p. 174 *three times a day to drink tea?* Interview, Mohamed Elbou, Mauritanian employee of the *Voice of America*, Abidjan, Ivory Coast, 25/2/82.

p. 174 *the Chinese grimly.* Interview, Chinese embassy, Mauritius, 30/9/81.

p. 175 *to help us.' Madagascar Matin*, 5/5/82.

p. 175 *no more than $200 million.* Estimate of British diplomat, Peking, 6/7/82. See *Far Eastern Economic Review*, 3/2/83.

p. 176 *'look after African countries'.* Interviews, Research Institute of International Trade, Peking, 13/7/82 and 22/7/82.

p. 177 *of our lives'.* Interview, H.Stanley, Mafia Coconuts Ltd, Dar es Salaam, 15/10/81.

p. 178 *or their '4960' tea.* Interview, Mohamed Lamine Doumbia, journalist, *Sunjata* magazine, Bamako, 13/3/82.

p. 178 *consisted of Chinese exports.* Figures supplied by Research Institute of International Trade, interview, Peking, 13/7/82.

p. 180 *for so many years.* Interview, Tanzanian Ministry of Finance, Dar es Salaam, 7/11/81.

p. 180 *refrained from taking sides.* Episode reported by Mario de Andrade, former Minister of Information, Guiné-Bissau, London, 16/10/84.

p. 180 *20,000 tons of grain.* See *The Times*, London, 16/3/85.

p. 181 *confined himself to four.* See *People's Daily*, 15/1/83, *Beijing Review* no. 24, 11/6/84; no. 11, 18/3/85.

p. 182 *incompetent managers.* Reported by a former British financial adviser to the government of Zambia.

p. 182 *first time in years.* AED, 3/8/85. TAZARA's performance has continued to be profitable, and the line has recently gained a renewed importance as the one railway able to carry Zambian and Zimbabwean exports that does not either pass through South Africa or suffer from the disruption caused by South African-supported guerrilla activity.

p. 183 *on the Yellow River.* For the foregoing details, see *Beijing Review* no. 21, 27/5/85; no. 17, 28/4/86.

p. 183 *Sports Aid.* Information supplied by Mr Tang Tien-chung of Godalming, who was approached by Sports Aid for assistance with the translation.

p. 183 *Chinese Live Aid. Beijing Review* no. 31, 4/8/86.

p. 184 *at a minimum level.* In a 'White Paper on Aid' released on 21/10/87, the UK charity Oxfam reported that the British government had contributed in 1986 less than half the target figure of 0.7% of GNP set by the United Nations for the industrialized countries to make available in overseas aid. The United States and Japanese governments had contributed even smaller proportions of their respective countries' GNPs.

p. 184 *room for improvement.'* Letter to *Beijing Review* no. 33, 13/8/84.

p. 185 *but doing more.'* Mme Chen Muhua, quoted AC, 17/11/82.

Chapter 6: Bridging the Chasm

p. 187 *in earlier dynasties.* The *Guangdong Tongzhi* (*Guangdong Encyclopaedia*) of 1822 notes (ch. 330) that 'the black devil slaves employed by the barbarians are the same as the so-called "Kunlun slaves" of the Tang period. The *Ming History* calls them "black devils", and they live in the various islands overseas . . .'.

p. 187 *the French colonial government.* See Virginia Thompson and Richard Adloff, *The Malagasy Republic*, Stanford University Press, 1965, p. 272.

p. 188 *use Portuguese instead.* Detail supplied by a British diplomat formerly employed in Hong Kong.

p. 188 *she was reckoned to be.* See Dick Wilson, 'A Paler Shade of Yellow'.

p. 188 *wanted to look like them.* Some of the restaurants in London's Chinatown are said to this day to be unwilling to employ waitresses from Hong Kong whose complexion is particularly dark.

p. 189 *'blacks with black households'.* See article 'Black People' in *Liulangzhe* (*The Vagrant*) no. 3, Hong Kong, 1981.

p. 189 *by themselves.'* Drake, p. 154.

p. 189 *Xu's book.* See Donald Treadgold, *The West in Russia and China*, Cambridge University Press, 1973, vol. II, p. 103.

p. 190 *don't look like Africans to me.'* See Taylor, p. 54.

p. 191 *'Mugabe's Chinese secretary'.* Interview, Fay Chung, Harare, 3/5/82. See Martin and Johnson, pp. 179–80.

p. 193 *dared to eat them.* Zhang Yi, pp. 138–9.

p. 193 *'They know we don't do that.'* Interview, interpreter returned from Magbass sugar project in Sierra Leone, Xiamen (Amoy), Fujian province, 1/8/82. Similar point made by Guangdong province doctors returned from Equatorial Guinea.

p. 195 *since they came here.'* Quoted Hall and Peyman, p. 144.

p. 197 *fertilizing the land'.* For the foregoing details see Hevi, *African Student*, pp. 47–50, 97.

p. 197 *'The boys went mad. . . .'* Comment of a former Tanzanian ambassador in Peking.

p. 198 *'Hallo, uncle black man'.* 'Shushu hei ren, ni hao!' Interview, former Somali student in Peking, Mogadishu, 12/1/82.

p. 198 *doesn't think I'm black!'* Anecdote reported by Chinese student in London, 8/10/85.

p. 198 *exactly as we thought.'* Hevi, *op. cit.*, p. 123.

p. 199 *twenty-two Zanzibaris.* For the foregoing details see Hevi, *op. cit.*, pp. 162–4, 195; Kojo Amoo-Gottfried in *Race*, London, vol. v, no. 4, April 1964, pp. 72–4.

p. 200 *halfway to Peking airport.* Incident reported by a British student who lived in Peking in 1973–4.

p. 200 *they would be shot.* Interview, Languages Institute, Peking, 14/6/79.

p. 201 *a Chinese girl in his room.* See article 'African Blues in China', *Newsweek*, 6/9/82.

p. 201 *carriers of* AIDS. Reported on the six o'clock news, BBC 1, London, 8/1/87.

p. 201 *a serious eye injury. Beijing Review* no. 31, 3/8/79; AC, 1/7/81.

p. 202 *on African visitors.* Interview, Khalid Tahir, former Somali student in Nanking, London, 9/8/83.

p. 202 *'What is this so-called friendship?'* For the foregoing details see *The Times*, London, 2/6/86, 3/6/86 and 7/6/86; *Far Eastern Economic Review*, 5/6/86, 19/6/86 and 26/6/86; *Sunday Morning Post*, Hong Kong, 15/6/86.

p. 204 *free of racial prejudice.* Comment of a Chinese student, London, 13/12/84.

p. 205 *(about $3,000).* Incident reported by Ugandan student in Peking, interview, 10/7/82.

p. 205 *of China's image abroad.* Information supplied by a West German diplomat, Peking, 17/6/82.

p. 205 *their brains as 'porridge'.* Interview, Ugandan student, Peking, 14/7/82.

p. 205 *usually the best in the class'.* NCNA, 15/12/82.

p. 205 *as learnt geometry. Ibid.*

p. 205 *and 'discipline'. Beijing Review* no. 31, 3/8/79.

p. 206 *school discipline and Chinese law'. Ibid.*

p. 206 *undermined their friendship for China.* For foregoing details see *Beijing Review* no. 43, 24/10/83.

p. 209 *and enlarge our friendship.' Peking Review* no. 51, 20/12/74.

p. 211 *the Caribbean rock group Boney M. Newsweek*, 8/9/86.

p. 211 *'intellectual aid'.* For foregoing details see *China Daily*, 5/11/86.

Index

9–11, 25; early accounts of Africa, 3, 11–16, of Africans, 4–5, 13–19, 26; and African slaves, 17–19, 39–40; tribute system, 20, 23, 27; navigation, 8–9, 11, 21–2; early voyages to Africa, 9, 11, 12, 20, 21–36; eunuchs, 21–3, 31; labourers in Africa, 38, 41–55, 62, 150, 152, viewed as showing the way to Africans, 46–7, clashes with Africans, 52–3, 54, impact on Africans, 54, on modern contracting projects, 179–80; traders, 3, 5, 8, 9, 11, 12, 16, 21, 22, 43, 212, settlement in western Indian Ocean and Africa, 55–63, 70–1, 96, 110, 177, 187, and Chinese labourers, 56, readiness to mingle with Africans, 58–9, attitudes to Africans, 55, 58, 190, compared with attitudes of Indian traders, 59–60, and growth of Chinese national consciousness, 62–3, and trading corporations of modern China, 179, 183; modern intellectual awakening, 63, outlook of intellectuals contrasted with that of their black contemporaries, 64–5; resistance to Europeans, xiii, 37, 43–4, 49–50, 54, 62–3, 65, 90, to Japanese, 68, 69, 80, 169; missionary impulse, 69–70, 74, 83, 87–8, 92, 94, 105, 106, 122, 133, 144, compared with that of European missionaries, 91; challenge to Europeans in Africa, xiv, xv, xviii, 76, 87, 91, 96, 98, 104, 140–1, 150, 153–4, 158, 160, 162, 176, 186, 191, 196, 211; hospitality to African visitors, 72–4, 79, 90, 108, 125, 196, 197; embassies in Africa, 48–9, 76, 89, 90, 96–7, 100, 101, 104, 110, 123, 132, 173, 191–4, 206; and African guerrilla movements, 76–87, 105, 118, 120, 123, 125–6, 130, 132, 134, 140–1,

arms supplies, 77, 87, 125–6, 130, 132, 141, and Soviet arms supplies, 126, 132, money, 77, military training, 77–87, 118, 125, 141; and African governments, 87–104, 135–8, 140–2; and African intellectuals, 94, 133, 136, 142; and dissidents, 94, 97–100, 113, 133; publications in Africa, 94, 136–7; military training for dissidents, 98–100; intelligence service, 98; duels in Africa, 105–34, 138, 141; with the United States, 106–11, 114, 117, 119, 122, 140, 141, 165, 199; with Taiwan, 111–16, 119, 139, 155; with the Soviet Union, xiv, 116–34, 141, 155–8, 175, 180, 199; *rapprochement* with the West, 122, 130, 135, 138, 204; nationalism criticized by Africans, 134, 157; military aid to African governments, 156, arms supplies, 127, 129, 141, military training, 92, 127, 141; post-Mao liberalization, 134–5, 171, 182, modernization, 134–5, 143, 175, 178; economic aid to Africa, xviii, 91, 113, 144–75, 180–5, 191, 204, linked to aid to minorities in China, 144, compared with Western aid to Africa, 145–6, 158–9, 162, 171, with Taiwanese aid, 155, with Soviet aid, 145, 155–7, appreciated by Africans, 158–9, 180, viewed by Chinese as heroic endeavour, 145, 166, 170, as sacrifice, 168, 'sold' to the Chinese public, 166, 168, shortcomings of, 162–5, 170, burden on China, 169, 171–2, 174, and Chinese disillusionment, 170–2, and post-Mao retrenchment, 174–5, revived, 181–5; technicians involved in aid programme, 147, 154–6, 158, 163–8, 171, 179, 184, 191, 195–6, 206, compared with Western

aid personnel, 160, 162, 173, with Soviet personnel, 160, 173, linguistic efforts, 160, 163, 191, rules of conduct, 160, 205, willingness to 'muck in', 160, culture shock experienced by, 192–4, unsociable, 160–1, 191–6, disillusionment of, 172–4, sent to learn from Africa, 207; agronomists, 150, 158, 193; doctors, 5, 144, 147, 157, 164, 172–4, 191, 194, appreciated by Africans, 159–60, 180, medicines, 5, 159, 169, medical seminars, 182; cooks, 38, 57, 180, 193; trade with Africa, 2, 22, 175–81, 183–5, exports, 6, 8, 12, 23, 27, 33–4, 176–80, imports, 5, 26–7, 175, 178, 180, re-exporting, 178, contract engineering, 178–80, 184, 211, joint ventures, 179–81, and African reactions, 176, 178, 180–1, 183, trading ambitions compared with those of Japan, 183–4; informal relations with Africans, 186–206, compared with those of Westerners with Africans, 186, 195, 206; attitudes to black people, 16, 18, 40, 60, 66, 120, 188–9, 198, 203, 206, 210, to Africa, Africans, 4, 18–19, 189–91, 193, 196, 198, 200–1, 206, influenced by Western attitudes, 189, 196, compared with Western attitudes, 184, 203, 206; and African students, 196–206; and African diplomats, 89, 204–5; and African women, 32, 53, 59–60, 172, 187, 190, 194, 195; women, 32, 60, 173, 194, and African students, 200–3; students, 183, 197, 198, and African students, 200–3, 205; efforts to improve informal relations, 205–6, 211; Africanists, 207; appreciation of African culture, 207–8; similarities to Africans, 209–10; adaptability, 58–60,